The Global Wordsworth

TRANSITS

LITERATURE, THOUGHT & CULTURE 1650–1850

Transits is a series of scholarly monographs and edited volumes publishing beautiful and surprising work. Without ideological bias the series seeks transformative readings of the literary, artistic, cultural, and historical interconnections between Britain, Europe, the Far East, Oceania, and the Americas during the years 1650 and 1850, and as their implications extend down to the present time. In addition to literature, art and history, such "global" perspectives might entail considerations of time, space, nature, economics, politics, environment, gender, sex, race, bodies, and material culture, and might necessitate the development of new modes of critical imagination. At the same time, the series welcomes considerations of the local and the national, for original new work on particular writers and readers in particular places in time continues to be foundational to the discipline.

Since 2011, sixty-five Transits titles have been published or are in production.

Recent Titles in the Series

Fire on the Water: Sailors, Slaves, and Insurrection in Early American Literature, 1789–1886
Lenora Warren

Community and Solitude: New Essays on Johnson's Circle
Anthony W. Lee Ed.

The Global Wordsworth: Romanticism Out of Place
Katherine Bergren

Cultivating Peace: The Virgilian Georgic in English, 1650–1750
Melissa Schoenberger

Intelligent Souls? Feminist Orientalism in Eighteenth-Century English Literature
Samara Anne Cahill

The Printed Reader: Gender, Quixotism, and Textual Bodies in Eighteenth-Century Britain
Amelia Dale

For a full list of Transits titles go to https://www.bucknell.edu/script/upress/series.asp?id=33

TRANSITS

The Global Wordsworth

Romanticism Out of Place

KATHERINE BERGREN

LEWISBURG
BUCKNELL UNIVERSITY PRESS

Library of Congress Cataloging-in-Publication Data

Names: Bergren, Katherine, author.
Title: The global Wordsworth : Romanticism out of place / by Katherine Bergren.
Other titles: After Wordsworth
Description: Lewisburg, PA : Bucknell University Press, [2019] | Series: Transits : literature, thought & culture | Revision of author's thesis (doctoral)—University of California, Los Angeles, 2013, titled After Wordsworth : global revisions of the English poet. | Includes bibliographical references and index.
Identifiers: LCCN 2019012618 | ISBN 9781684480135 (cloth : alk. paper) | ISBN 9781684480128 (paperback : alk. paper) | ISBN 9781684480142 (epub) | ISBN 9781684480166 (web pdf)
Subjects: LCSH: Wordsworth, William, 1770–1850—Influence. | Romanticism—Influence.
Classification: LCC PR5888 .B46 2019 | DDC 821/.7—dc23
LC record available at https://lccn.loc.gov/2019012618

A British Cataloging-in-Publication record for this book is available from the British Library.

♾ The paper used in this publication meets the requirements of the American National Standard for Information Sciences—Permanence of Paper for Printed Library Materials, ANSI Z39.48-1992.

www.bucknell.edu/UniversityPress

Manufactured in the United States of America

To Jim Bergren and Nancy Vander Pyl

CONTENTS

ABBREVIATIONS

A	Lydia Maria Child, *An Appeal in Favor of That Class of Americans Called Africans* (Amherst: University of Massachusetts Press, 1996)
Ab	Michelle Cliff, *Abeng* (New York: Plume, 1995)
AF	Jamaica Kincaid, *Among Flowers: A Walk in the Himalaya* (Washington, D.C.: National Geographic, 2005)
D	J. M. Coetzee, *Disgrace* (New York: Penguin, 1999)
DA	Laura Mullen, *Dark Archive* (Berkeley: University of California Press, 2011)
CPW	Matthew Arnold, *The Complete Prose Works of Matthew Arnold*, 11 vols., ed. R. H. Super (Ann Arbor: University of Michigan Press, 1960–1977)
E	William Wordsworth, *The Poetical Works of William Wordsworth*, ed. E. de Selincourt, vol. 5, *The Excursion* (Oxford: Clarendon Press, 1949)
HH	Claude McKay, *Home to Harlem* (Boston: Northeastern University Press, 1987)
L	Jamaica Kincaid, *Lucy* (New York: Farrar, Straus and Giroux, 1990)
MGB	Jamaica Kincaid, *My Garden (Book):* (New York: Farrar, Straus and Giroux, 1999)
MS	V. S. Naipaul, *Miguel Street* (New York: Vintage, 2002)
P	William Wordsworth, *The Prelude, 1799, 1805, 1850*, ed. Jonathan Wordsworth, M. H. Abrams, and Stephen Gill (New York: Norton, 1979)
PrW	William Wordsworth, *The Prose Works of William Wordsworth*, 3 vols., ed. W. J. B. Owen and Jane Worthington Smyser (Oxford: Clarendon Press, 1974)
PW	William Wordsworth, *The Poetical Works of William Wordsworth*, 5 vols., ed. E. de Selincourt (Oxford: Clarendon Press, 1940–1949)

SI	Andrea Levy, *Small Island* (New York: Picador, 2004)
WW	J. M. Coetzee, *White Writing: On the Culture of Letters in South Africa* (New Haven, Conn.: Yale University Press, 1988)

The Global Wordsworth

INTRODUCTION

READERS OF JAMAICA KINCAID'S SEMIAUTOBIOGRAPHICAL novel *Lucy* (1990) would be forgiven for concluding that Kincaid hates William Wordsworth. Within the novel's first thirty pages, the titular character has memorized, regurgitated, and rejected Wordsworth's poem about daffodils. For Lucy, daffodils exist only to conjure up her education in the British West Indies, where the flower had little meaning outside of its appearance in an English poem. But while Lucy dreams, with violent nonchalance, of mowing down a field of daffodils with a scythe, Kincaid's own vision is different. When asked about this primal scene in her novel, she replies, "I hope it makes people read the poem." Kincaid's explanation is simple: "You can't begin to understand me until you read certain things."[1] Indeed, Lucy's plight—reciting a poem about flowers she's never seen—is more poignant if a reader remembers that "I wandered lonely as a cloud" concludes with a memory of daffodils that "flash upon that inward eye."[2] Having never seen a daffodil, Lucy can have no such memory, no such flash. This scene is common in fiction and memoirs from former colonies of the British Empire, and it usually hits two beats: memorizing the poem and knowing nothing about the flower.

> Lorna Goodison: I don't like "The Daffodils" because in my whole life as a child I always recited "a host of golden daffodils," and I had never seen one.
>
> V. S. Naipaul: Wordsworth's notorious poem about the daffodil. A pretty little flower, no doubt; but we had never seen it. Could the poem have any meaning for us?
>
> Michelle Cliff: Probably there were a million children who could recite "Daffodils," and a million who had never actually seen the flower, only the drawing, and so did not know why the poet had been stunned.

> Stuart Hall: When I first got to England in 1951, I looked out and there were Wordsworth's daffodils. Of course, what else would you expect to find? That's what I knew about. That is what trees and flowers meant. I didn't know the names of the flowers I'd just left behind in Jamaica.
>
> Shirley Lim: "You British," I said, in the calloused manner of youth sneering at the mistakes of the past, "made us look for daffodils, so we never saw the *bunga raya* (hibiscus) growing everywhere in Malaysia."[3]

This is just a sample of colonial daffodil scenes, chosen because they happen to name the tension between the poem's omnipresence and the flower's absence, a tension that is intrinsic to the experience of encountering Wordsworth in a climate where daffodils don't grow. I will return to the daffodil problem in chapter 1, but I want to suggest here that this emphasis on the daffodils' absence does more than reflect the botanical makeup of the West Indies; it also presents a latent analysis of the poem's own concerns. "I wandered lonely as a cloud" is, after all, a poem in which the daffodils' physical absence is a turning point that incites the speaker's imagination and revelatory joy. By seizing on this absence, colonial readers are simultaneously objecting to the poem's subject and directing their readers' attention back to it. What happens, they seem to ask, if it is not a poet on a couch who daydreams about daffodils? What happens if the second half of the poem comes first, if the speaker first dreams about absent or unknown daffodils and only later sees them dancing in the breeze? Kincaid believes that we must first read Wordsworth in order to understand her own writing. This book is about what happens if we reverse the order of Kincaid's recommendation. It proposes that we conceive of writers like Kincaid not as mere receivers of Wordsworth but as his makers: it proposes we read them in order to understand him.

The international circulation of Wordsworth's poems is an odd fit for a poet who is often seen as one of the most local, even parochial, of Romantic poets—a true "Laker," patron saint of nature writing and the individual's connection to place. In 1815, Francis Jeffrey made fun of Wordsworth for "dashing his Hippocrene with too large an infusion of lake water"; Lord Byron exhorted Wordsworth and Robert Southey in the dedication to *Don Juan* to "change your lake for Ocean."[4] This line of thought has been both durable and central to Wordsworth's lingering status as the quintessentially Romantic poet. Writing in 1971, M. H. Abrams defined Romanticism by suggesting that the era's poets (minus Byron) enacted a break with their eighteenth-century predecessors, reformulating the relationship between human and creator as the bond between human consciousness and the natural world. Wordsworth is the alpha and omega of this argument; chapters on his poetry begin and end *Natural Supernaturalism*, and Abrams argues that

Wordsworth "was *the* great and exemplary poet of the age, and his Prospectus [to *The Recluse*] stands as the manifesto of a central Romantic enterprise against which we can conveniently measure the consonance and divergences in the writings of his contemporaries."[5] Scholars of feminism, New Historicism, and empire have broadened the field beyond this understanding of Romanticism, but it has not died out. If students who enroll in my classes on Romantic-era writers know something about British Romanticism, they usually offer up its association with "nature."[6] And strains of Abrams's argument find expression in certain trajectories of Wordsworth scholarship. The importance of Wordsworth's poetry to the Green Romanticism of the 1990s, for instance, tended to affirm his association with a traditional conception of Romanticism founded on its canonical poets' treatment of man and nature (particularly local nature).[7] Wordsworth's relative absence from the global turn in Romantic studies strikes me as similarly significant; as Romanticism has expanded to analyze contexts beyond England, Wordsworth has been more a counterexample than an illustration of the era's global entanglements.[8] This book acknowledges Wordsworth's ability to act as a synecdoche for a particular kind of Romanticism, but my aim is not to reinforce it. Rather, my guiding question is, What can we see more clearly about Wordsworth's poetry—and the Romanticism it has been taken to represent—when we return his poetry's global travels to the picture?

READING BACKWARD

The Global Wordsworth primarily strives to hear the conversations between Wordsworth and three writers from around the world: Lydia Maria Child in the antebellum United States, J. M. Coetzee in post-Apartheid South Africa, and Kincaid in her contemporary Vermont garden. These conversations are, strictly speaking, impossible. Coetzee and Kincaid were born about a century after Wordsworth died, and though Child was a contemporary, she was not a correspondent of Wordsworth's. Nevertheless, I have endeavored to read Wordsworth within the distant literary and geohistorical contexts into which he was hailed by writers around the world. And I have found that reading Wordsworth out of the context of his immediate period—reading him *after* reading Kincaid—opens up new ways of reading him historically, of apprehending the complex negotiations Wordsworth makes in his most locally rooted writing with the world systems of imperialism, colonial expansion, and global capitalism. In its approach, less strictly chronological and more prone to looping, expanding, and contracting, *The Global Wordsworth* is indebted to Jerome Christensen's *Romanticism at the End of History*, which seizes on Romantic anachronism as evidence of how the past cannot "seal itself off as period or epoch or episode with no or necessary consequences for our time." Similarly, it draws upon Alan Liu's *Local Transcendence*, a collection sensitive to how historical events can be imbued with a significance that transcends their local, temporal rootedness.[9]

This book's looping methodology has implications for how we understand theories of reception and influence, some of which are characterized by what Wai Chee Dimock calls "numerical bias," or the tendency to attribute too much meaning to the temporal proximity and chronological ordering of events.[10] Influence studies, for example, often mandate a hierarchy of writers—usually one author grappling with a dominant predecessor (Wordsworth trying his hand at the English epic in the shadow of Milton, for example). In this model, time has its thumb on the interpretive scale: given their chronology, Milton will always be the influencer and Wordsworth the influenced. Yet there are many theories of reception and influence that display a surprisingly flexible attitude toward the march of time: as Robert Kiely writes, "Temporal boundaries, like geographical borders, have always been crossed in two directions."[11] T. S. Eliot's "Tradition and the Individual Talent" (1920) holds that "the past should be altered by the present as much as the present is directed by the past" because "what happens when a new work of art is created is something that happens simultaneously to all the works of art which preceded it. The existing monuments form an ideal order among themselves, which is modified by the introduction of the new (the really new) work of art among them."[12] One of the modes that Harold Bloom describes in *The Anxiety of Influence* (1973), the *apophrades*, refers to a style achieved by certain "strong" poets "that captures and oddly retains priority over their precursors, so that the tyranny of time almost is overturned, and one can believe, for startled moments, that they are being *imitated by their ancestors*."[13] Hans Robert Jauss's assertion in *Toward an Aesthetic of Reception* (1982) that a literary text cannot "offer the same view to each reader in each period" concludes by loosening a text's place in the past so that the text becomes more like "an orchestration that strikes ever new resonances among its readers and that frees the text from the material of the words and brings it to a contemporary existence."[14] Each of these statements thwarts the exigencies of chronology, gesturing at a phenomenon that Bloom, for one, sees as "absurd"—the appearance that later texts are influencing earlier ones, that earlier texts can be "freed" to enjoy contemporary existences different from the lives they lived in the past.

For Eliot, the idea was not absurd largely because he saw it as a reaction occurring in the reader's mind. As he instructs, "You cannot value [the new artist] alone; you must set him, for contrast and comparison, among the dead." And once you've done this, set the new among the dead, the "*whole* existing order must be, if ever so slightly, altered; and so the relations, proportions, values of each work of art toward the whole are readjusted."[15] Jean Rhys's *Wide Sargasso Sea* (1966) did not change a word of what Charlotte Brontë wrote in *Jane Eyre* (1847), but it changed *Jane Eyre*, and the relationship between the two novels has become a classic example of how "the past should be altered by the present as much as the present is directed by the past." For *Wide Sargasso Sea* does not merely display Brontë's influence on Rhys. Instead, by turning Bertha Mason into the protagonist Antoinette Cosway and reconstructing Brontë's scenes from her perspective, Rhys's novel compels us to read Antoinette, in all her complexity, back into *Jane Eyre*. In Rhys's hands, Antoinette makes clear something fundamentally true about Brontë's novel—namely, the doubling of Jane's character in the repudiated figure of Bertha. It is certainly possible to notice this doubling without Rhys's help; the textual evidence is in *Jane Eyre*. Yet the reading of Bertha as Jane's double didn't become common until well after the publication of *Wide Sargasso Sea*, largely through the influence of Sandra M. Gilbert and Susan Gubar's *The Madwoman in the Attic* in 1979.[16] *Wide Sargasso Sea* draws a straight line from Brontë to Rhys, from influencer to influenced, yet it also bends that line toward Brontë: the novel's depiction of Antoinette Cosway insists upon its own ability to change how readers interpret *Jane Eyre*.

In the life that her novel gives to one of Brontë's characters, Rhys performs a type of reception that I call repurposing: she plants another text in her novel, bringing it to life in a place far from its own, and records its growth. Briefly, repurposing may be distinguished from related modes of reception, like influence and appropriation, that are equally pertinent to Wordsworth yet beyond the scope of this study. Wordsworth's influence on other writers around the world is, of course, extensive. The *Dutt Family Album* (1870), for example, written by an Indian family of poets, features poems whose Wordsworthian themes (the beauty of a native landscape, the disappearance of a certain "visionary gleam") are accompanied by echoes of Wordsworth's verse (a reference to an "inward eye," plucked from "I wandered lonely as a cloud"; a speaker who mourns that "the glory of the scene hath fled . . . oh, where?" like Wordsworth's speaker in the "Immortality" ode).[17] Also adjacent to repurposing is appropriation—writers who invent a Wordsworth who can speak for their concerns. During Wordsworth's own life, Barron Field, a friend of Charles and Mary Lamb who tried (and failed) to become a member of Wordsworth's circle, interpolated the final section of "The Old Cumberland Beggar" in his essay "On the Aborigines of New Holland and Van Diemen's Land" (1825).[18] A judge in Australia, Field argued that Aborigines, unlike most other racial groups, in his view, "have never yet shown a disposition to lead any other life than that of the hunter and fisher, or to acknowledge any other government than that of the strongest, and any other law than that of nature."[19] Nevertheless, he felt that settlers in New Holland ought to renew their civilizing efforts, even though the endgame of settler colonialism was likely to be the "decay or extermination of the simple race of Australia." And if this be the case,

> Yet deem this man not useless,
> But let him pass,—a blessing on his head!
> And, while in that society, to which
> The tide of things has led him, he appears
> To breathe and live but for himself alone,
> Unblam'd, Uninjur'd, let him bear about
> The good, which the benignant law of heaven
> Has hung around him, and while life is his,
> Still let him prompt the lib'ral colonist
> To tender offices and pensive thoughts.[20]

In these lines, Wordsworth's reference to the beggar's "vast solitude" is replaced by Field's reference to "society"; "unlettered villagers" become "lib'ral colonists." Field goes on from here. "The Old Cumberland Beggar" is not an unproblematic poem; its suggestion that the beggar is valuable because he gives people the opportunity to feel generous is, as David Simpson says, a challenge to critics seeking to evaluate Wordsworth's capacity "as a minimally decent human being."[21] It is not altogether surprising that Field should think of this poem, in which the subject resides so firmly beyond the pale of civil society, in concluding his essay on the relations of Australian settlers to Aboriginals.[22] But by substituting Wordsworth's words with his own, Field devotes the poem to a specific purpose and assigns it a new context; he effectively writes a new poem. The relationship between Wordsworth's poem and Field's is thus one of replacement and mutual exclusivity rather than negotiation or dialogue. Cumberland and Australia remain a world apart; the villagers of one and the colonists of the other cannot coexist. It is thus the attempt to engage Wordsworth in an impossible dialogue that distinguishes repurposing from other modes of reception. The fact that this dialogue occurs across time and space means that repurposing can connect Wordsworth's local sphere to other faraway local spheres and reveal their reciprocal implication and inextricable interdependence. Writers who repurpose Wordsworth are revivifying him, rendering him dynamic by recording and inventing his existences outside of nineteenth-century England. Like Pierre Menard's *Quixote* or Kenneth Goldsmith's *Day* poems, precisely the same as their originals yet entirely different, Wordsworth's writings become capable of saying new things when they carry their representations of England into distant contexts.

READING GLOBALLY

As may already be clear, the *global* in this study's title refers not to a vast, undifferentiated "out there" against which the boundaries of Wordsworth's localism may be glimpsed but to specific places at specific times—Boston in 1833, Cape Town in the years just after Apartheid—that are local spheres in their own right, connected to Wordsworth's local sphere by multiple intersecting pathways. This approach is one of several key insights from world literature studies that I borrow in order to argue for the importance of Wordsworth to global Romantic studies. For at first glance, the global afterlives of "I wandered lonely as a cloud" might seem only to reinforce the boundaries of Wordsworth's Lake District setting. In Britain, daffodils are not a particularly localized phenomenon; they can bloom in London and Edinburgh alike. For colonial students, the flowers are always absent, a reminder that students cannot share the local experiences of the writers they read in school. At best, daffodils are an import, as in Kiran Desai's *The Inheritance of Loss* (2006), where an Indian woman returns from visits to England with suitcases full of "Marmite, Oxo bouillon cubes, Knorr soup packets, After Eights, daffodil bulbs, and newer supplies of Boots cucumber lotion and Marks and Spencer underwear—the essence, quintessence, of Englishness as she understood it."[23] In this litany of commodities, daffodils stand out as the only object without a brand name, but perhaps a brand is implied: Wordsworth's daffodils, Lake District daffodils. Wordsworth's speaker may spy "ten thousand" daffodils at a glance, but here the flowers help constitute the rare "quintessence" of Englishness—only as much as can fit in a suitcase.

In cases like this one, the relationship between metropole and colony conforms to a familiar model. Colonial readers are inundated with poems about daffodils, and they "write back," as Bill Ashcroft, Gareth Griffiths, and Helen Tiffin have described, "restructuring European 'realities' in post-colonial terms, not simply by reversing the hierarchical order, but by interrogating the philosophical assumptions on which that order was based."[24] Such interrogations are explicit in the excerpts I quoted previously. Why must we learn this poem? What meaning is it supposed to have for us? For readers outside England who ask such questions, the English text, "functioning as a surrogate Englishman in his highest and most perfect state, becomes a mask for exploitation," writes Gauri Viswanathan.[25] The potential pleasures of the text cover up its curricular purpose, which is to teach students about English literature, history, geography, and botany—and, more implicitly, to teach them to value these subjects over others. This is Olive Senior's point in her poem "Colonial Girls School": "Declensions in Latin / and the language of Shakespeare," "Steppes of Russia, / Wheatfields of Canada"—these subjects "told us nothing about ourselves / There was nothing about us at all."[26] Two complaints in this final line exemplify the kind of "exploitation" that Viswanathan describes: the subjects Senior and her peers studied in school not only contained "nothing about us at all" but also suggested that "there *was* nothing about us at all," or at least nothing worth studying. England is all plenitude, the colony all paucity.

Or so it appears. A common critique of *The Empire Writes Back* holds that its reliance on a center-periphery model simplistically locks metropole and colony in a Manichaean battle, thus "relat[ing] all contestations of modernity in the non-Western world to what is perceived as the primal trauma of colonization."[27] (Transatlantic scholarship has often seen the United States and Britain locked in a similarly binary relationship in spite of the field's foundations in monographs like Paul Gilroy's *The Black Atlantic* [1993], which focuses on the complex and multiple networks connecting Africa, Europe, the Caribbean, and the United States.[28]) In the formulation of *The Empire Writes Back*, colonial and postcolonial writers necessarily aim their revisions of works from the English canon "back" at the center; their agency is limited to that of a respondent. But what about readers beyond England who insist that Wordsworth's experience is "as germane to the Jamaican Blue Mountains as it was to English Cumbria"?[29] Is this sentiment merely evidence of false consciousness? Or what of those who write not *back* but *out* along a new arc? Michelle Cliff's *Abeng* (1984), set in preindependence Jamaica, describes the plight of Mr. Powell, a teacher frustrated by the mismanagement of the local schools. When he cannot convince the governor's office to send him new primers for his students, he goes off book: "There was a lot of class time to be filled" (*Ab*, 89). In order to provide his students with new content, he pairs British poets with writers of the Harlem Renaissance: "Langston Hughes collided with Lord Tennyson. Countee Cullen with John Keats. Jean Toomer with Samuel Taylor Coleridge. He read McKay alongside Wordsworth." The first eight lines of McKay's sonnet "If we must die," written in Harlem during the antiblack riots of 1919, immediately follow.[30]

Paul Youngquist's recent manifesto on "black Romanticism" asks a pointed question of Wordsworth, who memorably defined a poet as "a man speaking to men": "What sort of 'man' inhabits Romanticism"? Youngquist proposes that "black Romanticism recovers the historical force of black lives" to challenge the conception of man as a "norm of humanity" against which other people "get measured, devalued and dismissed."[31] His arsenal of tactics centers, logically, on the historical era we generally associate with Romanticism: roughly the mid-eighteenth through the mid-nineteenth centuries. But someone like Cliff, writing in the late twentieth century, belongs in that arsenal as well. Her pairings—Cullen and Keats, McKay and Wordsworth—dutifully nod at the issue of literary influence: one thinks of Cullen's "To John Keats, Poet, at Springtime" and Wordsworth's influence on McKay's sonnets, which McKay was, for the most part, pleased to have acknowledged.[32] But

Cliff's choice of poem here indicates that she is not primarily invested in tracing the legacy of nineteenth-century British poetry or connecting black poets to the white poets who influenced them. The specific inclusion of McKay's "If we must die"—and not, for instance, his "Old England," a poem that expresses longing for "homeland England" in Jamaican English—ensures that the pairing does more than draw an arrow from influencer to influenced, from Britain to Jamaica. To pair McKay and Wordsworth and quote this particular sonnet—a poem about racial violence against black Americans in the years after the Great War—is to send Wordsworth out on the same journey that McKay himself traveled from Jamaica to the United States. This trajectory, which plants Wordsworth in *Abeng*'s 1950s Jamaica only to ship him off, back in time, to McKay's interwar United States, is more complicated (and interesting) than the journey implied by "writing back." Instead of merely responding to the British canon, *Abeng* writes this canon into new existences. And so reading McKay alongside Wordsworth provides the opportunity to read Wordsworth alongside McKay—to read Wordsworth's sonnets to Milton or Toussaint L'Ouverture in light of McKay's sonnet on the Red Summer of 1919, to read nineteenth-century British poets in light of the Harlem Renaissance.

In analyzing scenes like this one, *The Global Wordsworth*'s subject is not precisely literary influence or reception, cultural memory or translation, mimicry or "writing back." Rather, this study investigates how such repurposings inspire interpretations of Wordsworth's poetry that have previously been unclear or invisible. The many voyages that Wordsworth has taken in the pages of Anglophone literature compel us as critics to perform what Vilashini Cooppan calls "globalized reading," a strategy that places canonical texts and their noncanonical retellings in dialog rather than opposition. Reading Wordsworth in this way means understanding his texts as both "locally inflected and translocally mobile," situated in both their own historical context and the context of their circulation across time and space.[33] The afterlives of Wordsworth's daffodils make clear that there is not one universal "world" to which Wordsworth and Kincaid belong equally; a gap always separates the two. But the discrete worlds inhabited by Wordsworth and his readers are nevertheless variously connected. This book centers not on the gap separating writers like Wordsworth and Kincaid but on the specific material and historical constitution of their connections. These connections affect how we as critics read Wordsworth and how we conceptualize Romanticism.

Indeed, earlier studies of Wordsworth's reception, like Stephen Gill's *Wordsworth and the Victorians* and Joel Pace and Matthew Scott's *Wordsworth in American Literary Culture*, did just that by detailing the making of Wordsworth in Victorian England and nineteenth-century America, respectively, thus contextualizing (and subtly defamiliarizing) the figure that Wordsworth has become in literary studies.[34] Yet since then, there has not been an extended effort to read Wordsworth alongside writers from around the world who put his poetry to use, an approach whose relevance stems not just from the fact that Wordsworth's poetry traveled widely—which is true of many Romantic-era writers—but also from the tension that exists between those travels and Wordsworth's continued association with localism and the English countryside.[35] What emerges when we read Wordsworth alongside his diverse afterlives is a poet whose representations of local, natural landscapes came to invoke a broader global context as he aged—not in order to expand the boundaries of the local or juxtapose its sphere with that of the world but rather in order to detail the entanglement of the two. Scholars of Romanticism have, over the past quarter century, developed a canon of writers who were influenced by—and helped forge—the era's rapidly changing global networks: novelists of empire, poets of anti-imperialism, writers of Eastern tales, authors of travelogues, abolitionist activists. What does it mean for global Romanticism if we add Wordsworth to that roster? If the era's economic and imperial networks are seen as the province of Wordsworth—that most local and parochial of Romantic poets, especially in his later years—the depth and saturation of those global networks becomes clearer.

My approach to Romanticism considers how globalization inflected both Wordsworth's texts (specifically, their representations of locality) and Wordsworth's texts in motion—how they circulated through space. By *globalization*, I mean the worldwide spread of technological innovations that speed the movement of people, commodities, and information across long distances, making the world more interconnected and effectively compressing time and space. For some, globalization is a postmodern phenomenon, a twentieth-century rupture produced by mass migration and electronic media.[36] Others, whom Fredric Jameson refers to as the "nothing new" faction, are more indebted to Immanuel Wallerstein's sense of globalization as a world system extending back centuries, which thus includes the "long histories of imperialism, colonization, decolonization, and postcolonialism."[37] A dominant national literature that travels these interconnected global networks cannot remain very insular. Rather, as Dimock writes, such a literature mimics the routes it travels and is "better seen as a crisscrossing set of pathways, open-ended and ever multiplying, weaving in and out of other geographies, other languages and cultures."[38] In this vision, cultural forms do not flow merely in one direction from dominant to dominated, influencer to influenced, past to present, England to the West Indies. The relationship is reciprocal at the same time as it is highly unequal.[39] Moreover, such cultural productions do more than describe or react to the extension of transnational networks and pathways. In Pheng Cheah's recent formulation, literature has the power to be normative as well as descriptive: literature can forge its own worlds. (It can even change the world.) In this light, texts written outside England that repurpose Wordsworth's poetry are only at a basic level demonstrating the spatial extension of his influence. Such texts are more importantly exerting a "normative force," fashioning new worlds in which Wordsworth rubs shoulders with writers of the Harlem Renaissance.[40]

If, in its early years, ecocriticism focused on writers like Wordsworth and Thoreau in order to analyze the dynamic relationship between solitary "man" and local "nature," studies of globalization have substantially altered the terms of engagement. The recent surfeit of work on the Anthropocene—the proposed geologic era defined by the influence of human activity on the earth—conceives of globalization as "a process of *environmental* interconnection, as much as or even more than a commercial or communicative one."[41] This environmental interconnection is also the focus of ecocritics like Ursula K. Heise and Lawrence Buell, whose interest in ecology is founded on cosmopolitan rather than local engagement.[42] Romantic ecocritics have kept apace: *interconnection* is a key term for Timothy Morton and Ashton Nichols, for instance, who focus not on the solitary man in nature but on "the vast, sprawling mesh of interconnection," or on the "complex web of interrelated interdependence."[43] Although Wordsworth remains for many a figure of the ecocritical old guard, his later writings in particular highlight what is shared between recent ecocriticism and globalization studies—namely, a sense of the intimate entwinement and complex interpenetration of human and nonhuman, local and global.

Many of the studies I have just mentioned do not adhere to a strictly linear sense of time. Dimock's transnational approach to American literature leads her to analyze literature in "deep time" and detail the limitations of historicism and the kinds of interpretative moves it fosters with its bias toward events linked by chronological proximity. Eric Hayot's manifesto on world literature suggests radical revisions to periodization in literary studies, envisioning literary history as a pie that is cut not into the familiar slices we expect, with Romanticism nestled evenly between the eighteenth century and the Victorian era, but rather into pieces shaped like "gerrymandered Congressional districts."[44] Scholars of the Anthropocene have perhaps been most adamant that analyzing literature within a world system means eschewing a linear temporal logic. Their insistence is at first surprising: the Anthropocene, as a proposed geologic era, would seem to fit neatly into the regimented scheme of existing geologic eras, each inscribed in slow and legible succession into the earth's strata. Yet even sedimentary rocks can thwart the predictable progression of time: strata sometimes feature what geologists call "unconformities," which are visible gaps in the geologic record. Riffing on this technical definition, Tobias Menely and Jesse Oak Taylor seize upon "the unconformity of the Anthropocene, in which divergent and seemingly incompatible histories rub up against each other, highlighting the potential for the future to remake the past."[45] Globalized reading (like Anthropocene reading) excavates narrative forms that double back upon themselves, paths that unspool in four dimensions to entangle Romantic-era Britain, pre-independence Jamaica, and interwar United States within the bounds of one story.

GLOBAL SENSE OF PLACE IN ROMANTIC STUDIES

I mentioned two points of contact between the figure of Wordsworth and the processes of globalization: how globalization imprinted Wordsworth's depictions of local place and the global circulation of Wordsworth's texts.[46] This circulation may be worldwide, but it is patchy: since the early twentieth century, for instance, Wordsworth has been frequently studied by scholars in Japan and less frequently in other East Asian countries.[47] And Wordsworth never became a celebrity on the Continent, as Byron did. Adding to that unevenness, my focus here is on the Anglophone world and not on Wordsworth in translation, thanks in part to my disciplinary training in English as well as what Jonathan Arac terms "anglo-globalism"—the way in which "English in culture, like the dollar in economics, serves as the medium through which knowledge may be translated from the local to the global."[48] That said, the wide circulation of Wordsworth's texts is probably less surprising than my point about the global entanglements in Wordsworth's representation of local place. Since at least the publication of Jerome J. McGann's *Romantic Ideology* in 1983, Wordsworth has been associated with escapism and political avoidance. As summed up by Marjorie Levinson, "Wordsworth is most distinctively Wordsworth, most Romantic, and most successful in those poems where the conflicts embedded in his materials, motives, and methods are most expertly displaced and where, as a result, the poetry looks most removed from anything so banal as a polemic or position."[49] This argument about Wordsworth's displacement of his historical and political context has seemed equally true of his relationship to a broader global context. In part, this reputation is as much an issue of neglect as displacement: compared to writers like Thomas De Quincey or Anna Barbauld, Wordsworth wrote little about people and places beyond England. When he did, the results were ambivalent. With regards to the antislavery movement, scholars have recognized in Wordsworth's early poetry the appropriation and concealment of abolitionist discourse and, in his later writing, its outright dismissal.[50] With regards to imperialism, scholars have seen in *The Prelude* a flight from otherness and complicity with the ideological project of empire.[51] It would be difficult to disagree with these insights: Wordsworth was simply neither anti-imperialist nor a committed abolitionist. Nevertheless, Wordsworth's worldliness is not a contradiction in terms. This book argues for a new arc to Wordsworth's career: from the 1805 *Prelude* to the 1835 *Guide to the Lakes*, he increasingly envisions the local and the global as imbricated rather than opposed, developing what cultural geographer Doreen Massey describes as a global sense of place—an understanding of a particular locale that takes into account how it manifests its interconnectedness with other places, even other places in other times.[52]

Massey's locus classicus is Kilburn High Road in northwest London circa 1990, its IRA graffiti, its sari shop, its airplanes overhead en route to Heathrow much clearer evidence of a global network than any features of Wordsworth's Lake District. Indeed, for many readers outside England, Wordsworth's approach to landscapes is incommensurable with their own. This is Coetzee's point when he accuses Wordsworth of "not considering that plains, as well as mountains and oceans" resulted from the geologic shifts that Wordsworth associates with sublimity.[53] Malaysian American poet Shirley Lim recalls an ill-fated hike modeled after Wordsworth's: "Reading about glacial detritus and glacial-formed lakes and then about Wordsworth's and Coleridge's inspiring walks in the Lake Country, I tried hiking through patches of laterite wasteland, suffering numerous *lallang* cuts on my bare legs."[54] Yet such responses, which emphasize the chasm between Wordsworth's relationship to the natural environment and those of his global readers, are not universal. Other readers of Wordsworth beyond England feel kinship not with the particular local features of the landscape he describes but with his way of looking at those features. Writing about her education in Singapore, postcolonial scholar Shirley Chew hazards that "much later . . . we realized that Chinese landscape painting (not to mention Chinese literature) had given us analogies for Wordsworth's ideas and instilled habits of perception which we exercised on his poetry."[55] Palestinian writer Jean Said Makdisi suggests that contra the irrelevance of daffodils in the West Indies, "the study of Romantic poets extolling the beauties of the English countryside, which I had never seen, taught me to look at the yellow sands of Egypt, at the imposing cedar and pine-covered mountains of Lebanon, at the shimmering silver leaves of the olive trees, at the deep blue of Mediterranean fading into the lighter shade at the horizon."[56] In this scenario, the circulation of Romantic poetry connects English and Lebanese landscapes not on the basis of shared physical features but rather through a way of looking that can be deployed in twentieth-century Beirut and Romantic-era Britain. The yellow sand that Makdisi sees differently thanks to English poetry constructs the Lebanese landscape less as an isolated and discrete locale and more as what Ursula Heise calls "a deterritorialized environmental vision" that heralds "the emergence of new forms of culture that are no longer anchored in place."[57]

The Global Wordsworth takes responses like Makdisi's as inspiration to reexamine Wordsworth, seizing on the entanglements that bind his depictions of English locales to his apprehension of an immanent global sphere. It is common to divide Wordsworth's career into two distinct phases, his "great decade," 1797 to 1807, and everything after. But there is a larger arc that connects these two phases and, moreover, insists upon the relevance of his later works: Wordsworth became more concerned with representing the global context of his locales as he aged.[58] I begin charting this process in Wordsworth's earlier works with his representations of the relationship between England and the Continent in the Lucy poems and *The Prelude*. Yet this book's heart is with the later Wordsworth of *The Excursion* and the *Guide to the Lakes*, where his paeans to nearby landscapes suggest a significant overlap between the local and global spheres by populating those familiar English landscapes with people, ships, waters, and plants from abroad.[59]

Through three central case studies, this book strives to hear conversations between Wordsworth and writers who repurposed him around the world. Like Manu Samriti Chander, I wish to hasten the day when scholars "feel relatively uncomfortable" teaching and writing about Wordsworth without reference to writers like Coetzee, Child, and Kincaid.[60] These case studies, which pair specific Wordsworth texts with their global afterlives, are organized according to the chronological arc of Wordsworth's career: chapter 2 begins with Coetzee and canonical poems from Wordsworth's "great decade," chapter 3 picks up in 1814 with the then popular epic *The Excursion* and its appearance in Lydia Maria Child's antislavery writing, and chapter 4 focuses on Kincaid and Wordsworth's prose *Guide to the Lakes*, the final version of which was published in 1835. This organization highlights the arc of Wordsworth's career. In the poems I analyze written before 1807, England's "global" context is merely continental. *The Prelude* constructs Cambridge in relationship to the Alps; "I travelled among unknown men," composed in Germany, contrasts England with lands beyond the sea. But by the time Wordsworth finished his last version of the *Guide to the Lakes*, the global sphere has become more expansive and England's relationship to it more complex: Wordsworth not only describes the Lake District using the discourse of imperialism but also records how its features have been materially affected by the practices of British colonialism.

Chapter 1 stands somewhat apart from the focus and methodology of the subsequent chapters by analyzing the foundational interaction between Wordsworth's localism and his global dissemination—or, to be more precise, between his local embedding in the Lake District and his embedding in other locales. Its subject is Wordsworth's daffodils, simultaneously the most potent sign of the gap between Wordsworth and his readers and evidence of the surprising and hardy shoots Wordsworth's poetry grows in different soil. The chapter first consults an archive of matriculation exams administered in British colonies, exams that included composition questions designed to draw upon colonial students' local knowledge—for example, students were instructed to write a "brief biography of a Baboon or of a Jackal" or a description of the "most pleasant holiday resort in South Africa."[61] Such prompts, which appear on the same exam as questions about canonical British literature, structurally opposed local knowledge and knowledge of Wordsworth, emphasizing the gap between him and his non-English readers. But for writers like Andrea Levy, Cliff, and Kincaid, this gap was less an epistemological black hole than a provoking blank to be negotiated and filled in. The chapter models the process analyzing this negotiation, reading Wordsworth's poetry and its global afterlives not in chronology but in conversation.

Chapter 2 begins by acknowledging that Coetzee may have included Wordsworth in *Disgrace* (1999) simply to demonstrate the irrelevance of Wordsworth and the European landscape tradition he represents in the "new" post-Apartheid South Africa. (This is a common view of *Disgrace*, which critics have taken to be more seriously concerned with Byron than with Wordsworth.) Indeed, while Coetzee's protagonist, David Lurie, is a university professor, he is not in a position to vouch for Wordsworth's importance—in the novel's first half, he alternates between delivering uninspiring lectures on Romantic poetry and sleeping with one of his students. Yet I argue that when teaching book 6 of *The Prelude*, "Cambridge and the Alps," Lurie subtly evokes that book's two topics: the wonder of Alpine tourism, which does not excite his students, and Wordsworth's educational disappointments at Cambridge, a topic surprisingly germane to Lurie's students, themselves bored by a mediocre teacher. By imbricating the two realms of book 6 in this way, Lurie's lesson casts *The Prelude* in a different light; for while Wordsworth characterizes Cambridge and the Alps as antithetical, the settings are bound by a shared rhetorical pattern where disappointment and diffidence yield to poetic revelation and election, first at Cambridge and then, more memorably, in the Alps. The second half of *Disgrace* abandons its university setting to follow Lurie to his daughter Lucy's farm on South Africa's Eastern Cape. As Lucy's name suggests, the references to Wordsworth in this half of the novel center on his Lucy poems, and the echoes between the two Lucy's are numerous: the name, most obviously, but also Lucy Lurie's refusal to tell the story of her own assault and her repeated assertion that she is, like Wordsworth's Lucy, "a dead person." Brief forays into South African history—the history of "mother tongue" education and the development of the *plaasroman*, or South African farm novel—reveal that Lucy Lurie's troubled relationship to the South African landscape is overdetermined by her heritage, gender, and sexuality. In turn, this relationship has ramifications for Wordsworth's "I travelled among unknown men," the only Lucy poem to name England as its setting. The chapter concludes by arguing that this lyric uses the figure of Lucy to blur the boundaries of the nation it seeks to isolate and single out for praise.

Chapter 3 sees this blurring become deliberate, for by 1814, when Wordsworth published *The Excursion*, his depictions of the local sphere had become significantly more entangled with globalization's effects. Today, few people read *The Excursion*, let alone admire it. But when Child, an American abolitionist, quoted *The Excursion* in the epigraphs to her *Appeal in Favor of That Class of Americans Called Africans*, she was quoting the best-loved poem of a staunchly English poet. In deploying Wordsworth's epic in her antislavery tract, she seized upon the poem's political capital—capital that other American readers, awed by the poem's Englishness and vague morality, did not recognize. But there is, on the surface, a problem with her use of Wordsworth: *The Excursion* is adamant about the destruction wreaked by industrialization, while Child touted industrialization as the United States' path out of chattel slavery. Chapter 3 argues, however, that Child was not merely appropriating Wordsworth for her own cause. Her inclusion of his poetry in the *National Anti-Slavery Standard* makes clear that she saw her activism on behalf of enslaved people as akin to Wordsworth's defense of factory laborers. The political capital that *The Excursion* came to hold outside England raises the question of how the poem itself depicts the relationship between England and the rest of the world. The multiple speakers of *The Excursion* spend book 8 lauding an old-fashioned vision of England—isolated and protected Albion—and describing how her landscapes have changed thanks to the influx of global trade and the growth of British imperialism. Yet together, the speakers insist that it would be difficult to organize these competing visions of England in a tidy matrix of before and after or pro and con: Albion fostered as much illiteracy as honor in its subjects; there is beauty in the smoke that hangs over fast-growing towns of exploited factory workers. The enmeshment of local landscapes with the global forces that alter them is, for Wordsworth, not straightforwardly a boon to be embraced or a fate to be fought. While Child uses Wordsworth to support an argument for political and moral progress, Wordsworth—writing about an excursion with no destination—can envision no such linear future.

Some of this ambivalence toward globalization fades in Wordsworth's *Guide to the Lakes*, where the form of the nonfiction guide gives Wordsworth the opportunity to complain forthrightly about the changes wrought on Lake District landscapes by Britain's botanic imperialism. Chapter 4 returns to Kincaid, this time focusing on the essays collected in *My Garden (Book):* (1999), to argue that Kincaid and Wordsworth similarly apprehend the appeal and dangers of gardening—the human manipulation and shaping of nonhuman landscapes. For both writers, the material rootedness of gardens signifies local belonging at the same time as most gardens contain nonnative plants, seeds, bulbs, and soils. Kincaid's essays bear witness to the long afterlife of colonial botanic exploration, which shaped not just the biodiversity of the West Indies but also her home garden in Vermont. Writing after decades of British botanic excursions, Wordsworth's *Guide to the Lakes* sees material evidence of British colonialism in tracts of larch trees that provide needed lumber while evoking West Indian plantations and construes Lake District tourism in imperial terms, with English midlanders becoming "settlers" in the North. Yet for both writers, there is an almost embarrassing gratification in growing exotic plants that hail from afar—in knowing that "they owe their existence to our hands," as Wordsworth puts it.[62] The chapter concludes by analyzing Kincaid's *Among Flowers* (2005), a memoir of a plant-hunting trip in the Himalayas, in which her transposition of United States Department of Agriculture (USDA) hardiness zones to areas beyond the United States suggests a different way of mapping the globe, where climatic similarities become capable of binding Vermont to Nepal.

Wordsworth lived for eighty years. His collected poetry runs to five volumes and his prose to three. His impact has been temporally and geographically extensive, covering nearly two centuries and six continents. In comparison, the works I discuss here in detail are few, necessarily presenting a cross section rather than a comprehensive survey of Wordsworth and the authors who put him to new use. This cross section, representing many times and places, plots centuries of negotiation between Wordsworth's status as the English Romantic poet and his dissemination around the Anglophone world. Interpreting Wordsworth in light of the authors who responded to him reveals that he did not just become more conservative and parochial, as his cantankerous letters on the Kendal and Windermere Railways demonstrate. He also became more expansive in his later years, more concerned (to borrow David Simpson's term) with how Britain's imperial and capitalist endeavors would affect the people and landscapes of his local geography.[63] This trajectory, combined with the fact that texts like *The Excursion* and the *Guide to the Lakes* were immensely popular in their time, shifts our focus to a different Wordsworth—a poet who is not wholly defined by the poetry of his "great decade," a poet whose career is not merely an example of political apostasy or avoidance but is also crucial to our understanding of global Romanticism. In this reorientation, the field of global Romanticism becomes a product of not just scholars but also authors around the world who read and responded to Romantic writing—thus a product of not just the past few decades but rather the past two centuries—as long as Romantic poetry has been traveling the globe.

NOTES

1 Kathleen M. Balutansky, "On Gardening: An Interview with Jamaica Kincaid," *Callaloo* 25, no. 3 (2002): 799.

2 *PW*, 2:216.

3 Wolfgang Binder, "An Interview with Lorna Goodison," *Commonwealth* 13, no. 2 (1991): 50; V. S. Naipaul, *The Overcrowded Barracoon* (Harmondsworth: Penguin, 1984), 24; *Ab*, 85; Stuart Hall, "The Local and the Global: Globalization and Ethnicity," in *Dangerous Liaisons: Gender, Nation, and Postcolonial Perspectives*, ed. Anne McClintock et al. (Minneapolis: University of Minnesota Press, 1997), 176; Shirley Lim, "The Dispossessing Eye: Reading Wordsworth on the Equatorial Line," in *Discharging the Canon: Cross-Cultural Readings in Literature*, ed. Peter Hyland (Singapore: Singapore University Press, 1986), 128.

4 Francis Jeffrey, *Contributions to the Edinburgh Review by Francis Jeffrey* (London: Longman, Brown, Green, and Longmans, 1855), 600; George Gordon Byron, *The Major Works*, ed. Jerome J. McGann (Oxford: Oxford University Press, 2000), 374.

5 M. H. Abrams, *Natural Supernaturalism: Tradition and Revolution in Romantic Literature* (New York: W. W. Norton, 1971), 13–14, emphasis mine.

6 Abrams edited the first seven editions of the *Norton Anthology of English Literature* and thus had a long-standing influence on undergraduate education in English. M. H. Abrams and Stephen Greenblatt, eds., *The Norton Anthology of English Literature*, 7th ed. (New York: W. W. Norton, 2000).

7 Jonathan Bate, credited with bringing the then nascent field of ecocriticism to the study of Romanticism, argued for "the intuitive link . . . between the poetry of Wordsworth and the 'natural beauty' of the English Lake District." See his *Romantic Ecology: Wordsworth and the Environmental Tradition* (New York: Routledge, 2013), 10.

8 This unimportance is, as I say, relative and certainly not absolute. See, for instance, Evan Gottlieb's recent collection, which includes two chapters on Wordsworth: Gottlieb, ed., *Global Romanticism: Origins, Orientations, and Entanglements, 1760–1820* (Lewisburg, Pa.: Bucknell University Press, 2015), 81–94, 95–108.

9 As Alan Liu argues, the anecdotes utilized by historicist literary critics function as "microworlds each as intricately detailed, yet also as expansive in mythic possibility . . . as a Wordsworthian Lakeland, a Blakean ordered space, a Keatsian Grecian urn." More recent Romantic studies interested in temporal flexibility and disjunction include Eric Gidal's work on the poems of Ossian, which uses the model of the geologic unconformity to analyze the poems' mixtures of temporalities, and Emily Rohrbach's analysis on Romantic anticipation via a tense she describes as the "might will have been." See Liu, *Local Transcendence: Essays on Postmodern Historicism and the Database* (Chicago: University of Chicago Press, 2008), 128; Gidal, *Ossianic Unconformities: Bardic Poetry in the Industrial Age* (Charlottesville: University of Virginia Press, 2015); Rohrbach, *Modernity's Mist: British Romanticism and the Poetics of Anticipation* (New York: Fordham University Press, 2016), 2; and Jerome Christensen, *Romanticism at the End of History* (Baltimore: Johns Hopkins University Press, 2000), 3.

10 A short period of time separating a text's date of composition and the dates of other nearby events "is assumed to be adequate, to capture both cause and consequence: both the web of relations leading to the making of the text and the web of relations flowing from its presence in the world." Wai Chee Dimock, *Through Other Continents: American Literature across Deep Time* (Princeton, N.J.: Princeton University Press, 2006), 124.

11 Robert Kiely, *Reverse Tradition: Postmodern Fictions and the Nineteenth Century Novel* (Cambridge, Mass.: Harvard University Press, 1993), 5.

12 T. S. Eliot, *Selected Essays* (New York: Harcourt, Brace, 1950), 5.

13 Harold Bloom, *The Anxiety of Influence* (New York: Oxford University Press, 1973), 141, emphasis in the original.

14 Hans Robert Jauss, *Toward an Aesthetic of Reception* (Minneapolis: University of Minnesota Press, 1982), 21. Other phenomenologists have been less engaged by the differences among

readers and how these differences can create multiple "horizons of expectation," to use Jauss's terminology. Wolfgang Iser recognizes that readers have different interpretations but traces such differences back to the literary text rather than the subject positions of readers, reasoning, "The fact that completely different readers can be differently affected by the 'reality' of a particular text is ample evidence of the degree to which literary texts transform reading into a creative process that is far above mere perception of what is written" See Jauss, 19; Iser, *The Implied Reader: Patterns in Communication in Prose Fiction from Bunyan to Beckett* (Baltimore: Johns Hopkins University Press, 1974), 279.

15 Eliot, *Selected Essays*, 5.

16 Their chapter on *Jane Eyre* opens with an epigraph from Jean Rhys's novel *Good Morning, Midnight*, suggesting a familiarity with Rhys's oeuvre. And while the reading of Bertha as Jane's double seems almost intuitive now, Sandra M. Gilbert and Susan Gubar's defensive language reveals that they thought themselves to be making a surprising point: "The parallels between Jane and Bertha may at first seem somewhat strained"; "Is [Bertha] not, then, as many critics have suggested, a monitory image rather than a double for Jane?" Gilbert and Gubar, *The Madwoman in the Attic*, 2nd ed. (New Haven, Conn.: Yale University Press, 2000), 360–361.

17 Mary Ellis Gibson, ed., *Anglophone Poetry in Colonial India, 1780–1913: A Critical Anthology* (Athens: Ohio University Press, 2011), 232, 233.

18 Lillian F. Shankman, "Review of *Barron Field's 'Memoirs of Wordsworth,'*" *Wordsworth Circle* 9, no. 3 (1978): 240.

19 Barron Field, ed., *Geographical Memoirs on New South Wales* (London: John Murray, 1825), 202–203.

20 Field, 228.

21 David Simpson, *Wordsworth, Commodification and Social Concern: The Poetics of Modernity* (Cambridge: Cambridge University Press, 2009), 63.

22 See Saree Makdisi, *Making England Western: Occidentalism, Race, and Imperial Culture* (Chicago: University of Chicago Press, 2013), 113–114.

23 Kiran Desai, *The Inheritance of Loss* (New York: Grove Press, 2006), 46–47.

24 Bill Ashcroft et al., *The Empire Writes Back: Theory and Practice in Post-colonial Literatures*, 2nd ed. (London: Routledge, 2003), 32.

25 Gauri Viswanathan, *Masks of Conquest: Literary Study and British Rule in India* (New York: Columbia University Press, 1989), 20.

26 Olive Senior, *Talking of Trees* (Kingston: Calabash, 1985), 26, emphasis mine.

27 Ankhi Mukherjee, *What Is a Classic? Postcolonial Rewriting and Invention of the Canon* (Stanford, Calif.: Stanford University Press, 2013), 116. Siobhan Carroll's recent monograph complicates this binary relationship between home and colony by focusing on "atopias," regions that were feasibly reachable but practically inaccessible or inhospitable and thus unassimilable into the imaginary of the nation. Carroll, *An Empire of Air and Water: Uncolonizable Space in the British Imagination, 1750–1850* (Philadelphia: University of Pennsylvania Press, 2015), 14.

28 Paul Gilroy, *The Black Atlantic: Modernity and Double-Consciousness* (Cambridge, Mass.: Harvard University Press, 1993).

29 This was Louis James's experience teaching Aldous Huxley's essay "Wordsworth in the Tropics" in Jamaica in the 1960s; his students were "indignant at Huxley's thesis" that Wordsworth would have found less to praise in nature if he had visited the tropics. Louis James, *Caribbean Literature in English* (London: Routledge, 1999), 169n14.

30 Claude McKay, *Complete Poems*, ed. William J. Maxwell (Urbana: University of Illinois Press, 2008), 177–178.

31 Paul Youngquist, "Black Romanticism: A Manifesto," *Studies in Romanticism* 56, no. 1 (2017): 5, 6.

32 Leah Reade Rosenberg, *Nationalism and the Formation of Caribbean Literature* (New York: Palgrave Macmillan, 2007), 225n23.

33 Vilashini Cooppan, "World Literature and Global Theory: Comparative Literature for the New Millennium," *symploke* 9, nos. 1–2 (2001): 32–33.

34 Stephen Gill, *Wordsworth and the Victorians* (Oxford: Oxford University Press, 1998); Joel Pace and Matthew Scott, eds., *Wordsworth in American Literary Culture* (New York: Palgrave Macmillan, 2005).

35 Cf. Simpson, *Wordsworth, Commodification and Social Concern*; Samuel Baker, *Written on the Water: British Romanticism and the Maritime Empire of Culture* (Charlottesville: University of Virginia Press, 2010), pt. 2; Roy Osamu Kamada, *Postcolonial Romanticisms: Landscape and the Possibilities of Inheritance* (New York: Peter Lang, 2010); Ian Reid, *Wordsworth and the Formation of English Studies* (Aldershot: Ashgate, 2004). David Simpson and Samuel Baker have intervened in the line of thought that sees Wordsworth's representations of natural landscapes as retreats from or displacements of more worldly concerns. Roy Osamu Kamada has analyzed postcolonial writers' recourse to the Romantic sublime landscape, primarily as fashioned by Wordsworth. Ian Reid's work on English studies uses Wordsworth to analyze the similarities in how the field developed in a geographically wide range of institutions.

36 See, for instance, Arjun Appadurai, *Modernity at Large: Cultural Dimensions of Globalization* (Minneapolis: University of Minnesota Press, 1996), 3. This is also the position, more or less, of Fredric Jameson, who associates globalization with a new "multinational stage of capitalism." Jameson, "Notes on Globalization as a Philosophical Issue," in *The Cultures of Globalization*, ed. Fredric Jameson and Masao Miyoshi (Durham, N.C.: Duke University Press, 1998), 54.

37 Immanuel Wallerstein, *The Modern World System I: Capitalist Agriculture and the Origins of the European World Economy in the Sixteenth Century* (Berkeley: University of California Press, 2011); Paul L. Jay, *Global Matters: The Transnational Turn in Literary Studies* (Ithaca, N.Y.: Cornell University Press, 2010), 3.

38 Dimock, *Through Other Continents*, 3.

39 This reciprocal exchange of cultural forms in situations largely defined by domination or coercion is captured most notably with Mary Louise Pratt's term *transculturation* and later in Srinivas Aravamudan's *tropicalization*. Mary Louise Pratt, *Imperial Eyes: Travel Writing and Transculturation*, 2nd ed. (London: Routledge, 2008); Srinivas Aravamudan, *Tropicopolitans: Colonialism and Agency, 1688–1804* (Durham, N.C.: Duke University Press, 1999).

40 Pheng Cheah, *What Is a World? On Postcolonial Literature as World Literature* (Durham, N.C.: Duke University Press, 2016), 5–6.

41 Samuel Baker, "Sailing Blind: Climate, Intention, and Local and Global Orientation in Wordsworth and Byron," in *Global Romanticism*, ed. Gottlieb, 97, emphasis mine.

42 Ursula K. Heise, *Sense of Place and Sense of Planet: The Environmental Imagination of the Global* (Oxford: Oxford University Press, 2008), 17–67; Lawrence Buell, "Ecoglobalist Affects: The Emergence of U.S. Environmental Imagination on a Planetary Scale," in *Shades of the Planet: American Literature as World Literature*, ed. Wai Chee Dimock and Lawrence Buell (Princeton, N.J.: Princeton University Press, 2007), 227–248.

43 Timothy Morton, *The Ecological Thought* (Cambridge, Mass.: Harvard University Press, 2012), 8; Ashton Nichols, *Beyond Romantic Ecocriticism: Toward Urbanatural Roosting* (New

York: Palgrave Macmillan, 2011), xii. More specifically focused on Wordsworth are Scott Hess, *William Wordsworth and the Ecology of Authorship: The Roots of Environmentalism in Nineteenth-Century Culture* (Charlottesville: University of Virginia Press, 2012); and Lisa Ottum and Seth T. Reno, eds., *Wordsworth and the Green Romantics: Affect and Ecology in the Nineteenth Century* (Durham: University of New Hampshire Press, 2016).

44 As Eric Hayot suggests, "What we call Victorian literature might look quite different from the perspective of a Victorianist than from that of an imaginary scholar of the 1850–1950 period." Hayot, *On Literary Worlds* (New York: Oxford University Press, 2012), 165, 154.

45 Tobias Menely and Jesse Oak Taylor, "Introduction," in *Anthropocene Reading: Literary History in Geologic Times*, ed. Tobias Menely and Jesse Oak Taylor (University Park: Pennsylvania State University Press, 2017), 17.

46 Scholars of eighteenth-century and Romantic literature who take a similarly long view of globalization include those assembled in Felicity Nussbaum, ed., *Global Eighteenth Century* (Baltimore: Johns Hopkins University Press, 2003); and Gottlieb, *Global Romanticism*.

47 See Russell Noyes et al., "Wordsworth in Japan," *Wordsworth Circle* 1 (1970): 5–13.

48 Jonathan Arac, "Anglo-Globalism?," *New Left Review* 16 (2002): 40.

49 Jerome J. McGann, *The Romantic Ideology: A Critical Investigation* (Chicago: University of Chicago Press, 1983), 81–94; Marjorie Levinson, *Wordsworth's Great Period Poems: Four Essays* (Cambridge: Cambridge University Press, 1986), 4. Many critics challenge this line of thought; writing around the same time as McGann and Levinson, James K. Chandler examined a Wordsworth whose political ideology was not one of avoidance but rather conservatism, even in his early years. Chandler, *Wordsworth's Second Nature: A Study of the Poetry and Politics* (Chicago: University of Chicago Press, 1984).

50 Helen Thomas, *Romanticism and Slave Narratives: Transatlantic Testimonies* (Cambridge: Cambridge University Press, 2000), 104–114; Debbie Lee, *Slavery and the Romantic Imagination* (Philadelphia: University of Pennsylvania Press, 2002), 194–221.

51 Alison Hickey, "Dark Characters, Native Ground: Wordsworth's Imagination of Imperialism," in *Romanticism, Race, and Imperial Culture, 1780–1834*, ed. Alan Richardson and Sonia Hofkosh (Bloomington: Indiana University Press, 1996), 283–307; Saree Makdisi, *Romantic Imperialism: Universal Empire and the Culture of Modernity* (Cambridge: Cambridge University Press, 1998), 23–44.

52 Doreen Massey, *Space, Place, and Gender* (Minneapolis: University of Minnesota Press, 1994), 154. Bruce Robbins's work on cosmopolitanism has similarly brought the local and the global into closer proximity by arguing that cosmopolitanism is most interesting "not in its full theoretical extension . . . but rather (paradoxically) in its local applications." These local/global amalgams have many cousins: David Damrosch's glocalism, most obviously, but also Ursula Heise's ecocosmopolitanism and Lawrence Buell's local cosmopolitan (an epithet he invents for Thoreau). See Robbins, "Comparative Cosmopolitanisms," in *Cosmopolitics: Thinking and Feeling Beyond the Nation*, ed. Pheng Cheah and Bruce Robbins (Minneapolis: University of Minnesota Press, 1998), 260; Damrosch, *How to Read World Literature* (Chichester: Wiley-Blackwell, 2008), 109; Heise, *Sense of Place*, 10; Buell, "Ecoglobalist Affects," 239.

53 *WW*, 52.

54 Lim, "Dispossessing Eye," 131.

55 Shirley Chew, "Wordsworth's *Prelude*: A Prospect in the Mind," in *Discharging the Canon*, ed. Hyland, 140.

56 Jean Said Makdisi, *Beirut Fragments: A War Memoir* (New York: Persea Books, 1990), 111–112.

57 As Heise points out, deterritorialization is an ambivalent experience and can be "accompanied by experiences of loss, deprivation, or disenchanchisement," especially when it is imposed from above. Heise, *Sense of Place*, 10.

58 This study thus joins a growing body of work that argues against the "two Wordsworths" model. Mary Burton contested this narrative in 1942, and it has more recently received further critique with the work of critics like Sally Bushell, James M. Garrett, Stephen Gill, and Tim Fulford. See Burton, *The One Wordsworth*, 2nd ed. (Hamden, Conn.: Archon, 1972); Bushell, *Re-reading the Excursion: Narrative, Response, and the Wordsworthian Dramatic Voice* (Aldershot: Ashgate, 2002); Garrett, *Wordsworth and the Writing of the Nation* (Aldershot: Ashgate, 2008); Gill, *Wordsworth's Revisitings* (New York: Oxford University Press, 2011); Fulford, *The Late Poetry of the Lake Poets: Romanticism Revised* (Cambridge: Cambridge University Press, 2013). See also William H. Galperin, *Revision and Authority in Wordsworth: The Interpretation of a Career* (Philadelphia: University of Pennsylvania Press, 1989); Peter J. Manning, *Reading Romantics: Text and Context* (New York: Oxford University Press, 1990).

59 Wordsworth's later works, particularly the *Guide to the Lakes* and his letters and poems on the Kendal and Windermere Railways, intensified his association with not only the Lake District but also the development of the modern conservation movement more generally. See Gill, *Wordsworth and the Victorians*, 235–260; Jacqueline M. Labbe, *Romantic Visualities: Landscape, Gender and Romanticism* (New York: St. Martin's Press, 1998), 113–148; Hess, *Ecology of Authorship*, 116–155.

60 Manu Samriti Chander, *Brown Romantics: Poetry and Nationalism in the Global Nineteenth Century* (Lewisburg, Pa.: Bucknell University Press, 2017), 112.

61 *Matriculation Examination Questions, English* (Cape Town: Juta, 1948), 6.

62 *PrW*, 2:218.

63 As Simpson explains, "To be concerned usually means not having an answer, not having finished with an issue, being in a state of suspended attention that may produce a resolution but has not done so yet." Simpson, *Wordsworth, Commodification and Social Concern*, 5.

1

THE GLOBAL ROUTES OF DAFFODILS

"A PRETTY LITTLE FLOWER, NO DOUBT," wrote V. S. Naipaul, "but we had never seen it."[1] Like all plants, daffodils grow in some places and not in others; some people have never seen it and others have. This fact is rendered somewhat less simple by the fate of William Wordsworth's poem about the flower, a poem that became one of the most frequently memorized poems in the Anglophone world.[2] It is difficult to know precisely what this poem meant to the vast number of students around the world who encountered it; most did not write about their experience either at the time they memorized it or at a later date.[3] The recollections from Naipaul and others quoted at the beginning of this book sound univocal, each presenting in its own words the same key points: I memorized the poem, but I had never seen the flower it described. Indeed, such a reaction seems unavoidable given colonial education's general aim: to teach students primarily about the history, botany, and literature of the imperial power. (As Olive Senior writes, such an education "told us nothing about ourselves.")[4] But this category of response, represented by Naipaul's brief ode to the flower, is not the whole story. Rather, the way that readers from around the world represented daffodils in their own writing is characterized by great diversity: only some seized on the flower's insistent absence, while others populated that absence with fantastical versions of a flower they had never seen. This chapter is about the fantastical daffodils and the ground from which they sprung.

In focusing on the dissemination and reception of Wordsworth's most famous and infamous poem, this chapter develops a methodology of analyzing the local embeddedness of Wordsworth's writing in two senses simultaneously: the specific places his writing represents and the specific places where others wrote it into new existences. The agents of dissemination that bind these two sets of locales, that move Wordsworth from one place to another, will vary from chapter to chapter: here they comprise educational documents like textbooks and exams, for example, while in chapter 3, the role is filled by American magazines and newspapers. So while the specific conclusions that this chapter draws about Wordsworth's appearance in nineteenth-century British school anthologies—or about the appearance of daffodils in Haiti or Jamaica—cannot be applied to other methods of dissemination or to the meaning of *The Prelude* in post-Apartheid South Africa, my aim in this chapter is broadly to model an approach to Wordsworth's afterlives that can speak about his many entangled local appearances in the same breath, as it were.

The institutional disseminations and individual repurposings of "I wandered lonely as a cloud" are, in many ways, histories at odds (*PW*, 2:216). The rote memorization of the poem by a vast number of students around the world sounded Wordsworth globally and tried to make him sound the same everywhere, a smooth monolith of Englishness and good taste. Yet different readers of "I wandered lonely as a cloud" of course experienced the poem in different ways, and those who were later inspired to write Wordsworth's daffodils into their own novels did so with vibrant unpredictability. The relationship between these two kinds of stories—a poem's rote and creative performances, its external and internal lives—animates this book's case studies. The scatterplot of Wordsworth's unevenly textured repurposings and the more hegemonic trajectories of his dissemination gain meaning through their interrelation. I first trace Wordsworth's dissemination through two archives: nineteenth-century anthologies printed in England for use in schools and twentieth-century matriculation exams administered in British colonies. In English school anthologies, Wordsworth was described as a poet capable of inculcating taste in his young readers, and this association with taste proved durable, clinging to Wordsworth as his poetry traveled beyond England. But it was beyond England that Wordsworth became "English." Colonial matriculation exams managed this implicitly, not by naming Wordsworth's Englishness, but by juxtaposing his poetry with local subject matter that varied from colony to colony. In its second half, the chapter turns to Wordsworth's Caribbean lives by examining three novels written in the wake of daffodils. Andrea Levy, Michelle Cliff, and Jamaica Kincaid alike showcase what Helen Tiffin has dubbed the "daffodil gap" in their uses of "I wandered lonely as a cloud."[5] Yet as I will argue, for Levy and Cliff, the existence of this gap is not the conclusion but rather the inauguration of their encounters with Wordsworth, for the "daffodil gap" is the foundation for scenes of poetic improvisation and production, scenes where Wordsworth's daffodils are perversely inspiring in their alienness. The chapter concludes by turning back to Wordsworth himself, reading "I wandered lonely as a cloud" in conversation with the poem's afterlife in Kincaid's *Lucy* (1990).

WORDSWORTH AT HOME AND ABROAD

From the time Wordsworth entered English secondary curricula, he was fashioned as a writer of "taste."[6] In English schoolbook anthologies (which only partly constitute the historical record of English studies' nineteenth-century development), he was frequently anthologized and associated with taste, but what these schoolbooks actually mean by *taste* is difficult to say; one book's paean to the ability to "think deeply and feel correctly" is as clear a definition as any (which is to say, not very clear). More to the point, such books were tools in the production of cultural capital in the two senses of the term that John Guillory develops in his examination of Thomas Gray's *Elegy Written in a Country Churchyard*: linguistic capital (achieving basic literacy) and vernacular literacy (knowing which English poets were "good").[7] I focus here on what Guillory calls vernacular literacy and what the school anthologies emphasize as the gap between good and bad taste. In their paratextual commentaries, school anthologies developed a basic but relatively consistent aesthetic theory: taste can be taught to young people, and poetry can help.

One of the earliest anthologies to include Wordsworth, *Classical Selections in Verse* (1808), lacked the preface, organization, and annotations that later supported the teaching of taste.[8] But in *The Moral and Intellectual School Book*, William Martin promised poems "calculated to exalt the feelings, strengthen the judgment, improve the taste, and purify the heart."[9] In *Poetry for School and Home*, Thomas Shorter suggested, "There is no reason why [children's] judgment and taste should not be early educated by a familiarity with some of the best pieces of our best poets."[10] Joseph Payne in *Studies in English Poetry* selected specimens "for the higher cultivation of youthful taste."[11] Even more eccentric anthologies followed a similar path. The editor of *Selections from the British Poets* focused specifically on poems about natural history but still aimed "to improve the taste and expand the mind."[12] Though these textbooks make good taste sound like an end in itself, some went further, with Payne explaining, for instance, "The more general diffusion . . . of good taste by means of early cultivation, would probably so elevate the public standard as to suppress entirely such offenses as are now frequently committed against it."[13] Some schoolbooks are, of course, outliers. Edward C. Lowe avoided "didactic extracts, the weariness of which in class recitations teachers and pupils alike bemoan," and aimed only to teach readers to love animals and England and domestic duties.[14] But mostly, schoolbooks held to a few truths. Taste was either good or bad. Young people were capable of cultivating good taste with the help of good poetry. Once good taste had been achieved, broader successes might follow; poetry might have a civilizing effect, elevating "the public standard" and teaching young people to respect it.

It is not surprising, however, that the schoolbooks differ on exactly which poems would best cultivate good taste and whether Wordsworth was up to the task. In Ian Michael's analysis of 114 textbooks published between 1802 and 1870, Wordsworth is second only to Shakespeare in popularity (Byron, Cowper, and Longfellow, who was surprisingly popular across the Atlantic, round out the top five).[15] While some schoolbooks, like Mrs. Gething's *Selections from Modern Authors* (1838), include no poems by Wordsworth, many sought to associate his poetry with good taste and defend him from naysayers.[16] *Readings in Poetry* (1843) complained, "Cold must be the heart that could blame a bard whose every line shows him to possess all the affections of an amiable man," while Martin regretted that "Wordsworth is not understood by the generality of readers; they have not learned his creed."[17] Martin went on to present the Wordsworth poems that anthologies today tend to reproduce, like the short poems from *Lyrical Ballads*, "Nutting," "Tintern Abbey," and the "Immortality" ode. In contrast, *Readings in Poetry*, published by the Society for Promoting Christian Knowledge (SPCK), had a more overtly disciplinary aim and selected from Wordsworth's corpus "Lament of Mary, Queen of Scots," "Obligations of Civil to Religious Liberty" from *Ecclesiastical Sonnets*, and "Fidelity" (a poem about a dog). The majority of schoolbooks, however, include a mixture of poems that became and stayed canonical and poems that quickly faded from view, such as "Inside of King's College Chapel," "The Kitten and the Falling Leaves," "The Force of Prayer," and "On the Extinction of the Venetian Republic."[18]

The desire to teach taste reveals a catch-22 that Gauri Viswanathan has discussed in the realm of Indian education: students must be morally prepared to read literature, but literature itself was seen as a means of producing moral readiness.[19] Similarly, these schoolbooks suppose that by reading good poems, students will learn good taste. And as one schoolbook editor insists, good taste helps us discriminate what literature is good, to rise above the "commonplace readers" who "level all distinctions; they read all productions alike; they attach the same degree of importance to every action, to all affections and passions, weak and strong, great and small."[20] That this diatribe appears in Joseph Hine's schoolbook *Selections from the Poems of William Wordsworth, Esq.* (1831) indicates how deeply entangled Wordsworth's poetry was with the project of teaching taste. Hine's attitude toward Wordsworth often borders on zealotry, as one might expect of a man who developed a schoolbook in which the only pedagogical tool was Wordsworth. In Hine's view, Wordsworth alone answered the question, "Where is the poet of our age . . . that sympathizes with all parts of God's creation so deeply, widely, and highly," who could thus bestow on students "feelings and tastes mobile, enviable, and virtuous"?[21]

If Wordsworth could teach good taste, as Hine and many other editors believed, good taste could in turn teach readers to admire Wordsworth. As Martin's

Moral and Intellectual Schoolbook explains, "Wordsworth is at last beginning to be popular, and he will continue to gain popularity as mankind begins to think deeply and feel correctly."[22] This sentiment would be unremarkable were it not for the stated aim of the schoolbook: "Exalt the feelings, strengthen the judgment, *improve the taste*, and purify the heart."[23] Here we arrive at Viswanathan's catch-22: the schoolbook deploys Wordsworth in order to improve the taste and feelings of its readers, and it will have succeeded at this task when Wordsworth is a popular poet. In books like these, where Wordsworth was both a tool in the pursuit of good taste and evidence of its triumph, he became more than the sum of his poems, a shorthand for educational achievement. In comparison, a poet like Byron, whose inclusion in a schoolbook required caveats about how "weak or inexperienced minds" might be led astray by his poetry, was popular but not imbued with a pedagogical or ideological purpose.[24] Any "contemplation and serious thinking" that a reader enjoyed after reading Byron happened in spite of Byron's reputation as a man mad, bad, and dangerous to know: his persona was at odds with the gains that anthology readers might nevertheless glean from his poetry. Described as "the High Priest of Nature," Wordsworth was a different story. Thanks to his particular lyric "I," which often has the effect of collapsing the distinction between poet and speaker, the line between him and his poetry could become faint, as when Hine asserted that the man Wordsworth had "an uncommon sympathy with all that conduces to the formation and preservation of purity and youth" and a moment later stated that his poems might be "highly desirable for ladies' seminaries, and female perusal," as they inspire no blushes "either on the cheek of the reader or on the cheek of others."[25] Texts like *The Moral and Intellectual School Book* were similarly eager to connect the person and the poetry in their biographical notes, mentioning his descent from a "respectable family" and his marriage to Mary Hutchinson alongside praise for his verse.[26] As a middle-class, stably married, male poet who published plenty of short and approachable poems about nature, Wordsworth presented schoolbooks with a consistent persona capable of conjoining the man to his poetry and the poetry to an educational purpose.

To reiterate, unlike other writers from the same era who enjoyed similarly wide dissemination, Wordsworth had little to overcome in terms of reputation: for all his troubles with money, he was solidly middle class; he wasn't a woman; he wasn't associated with sexual scandals or opium use; he wasn't persecuted or reviled for his radical views (just spied on). This is not to deprive Wordsworth's life of its scandals and losses; one thinks of Annette Vallon, the child more or less covered up, the unpublished radical letter to the bishop of Llandaff, the bad reviews, the young children lost, his sister Dorothy's illness. But with a few edits and omissions, Wordsworth's literary productions could be seen as being of a piece with his persona, capable of producing a monolithic figure who represented the developing norms of good taste.

If English schoolbooks presented Wordsworth as a poet of good taste, what did Wordsworth look like in the colonies of the British Empire? To a certain extent, he looked quite similar. Jhumpa Lahiri's *The Namesake* (2003) opens in 1968 with the birth of the protagonist's first child in Cambridge, Massachusetts. Far from her family in Calcutta, Ashima endures childbirth alone, thinking back to a former life where "English had been her subject" and she had helped schoolchildren in her parents' neighborhood "to memorize Tennyson and Wordsworth, to pronounce words like *sign* and *cough*, to understand the difference between Aristotelian and Shakespearean tragedy." When her parents introduce her to her future husband and his parents, however, English becomes a superficial accomplishment rather than "her subject." Through the eyes of her future in-laws, Ashima is revealed to be "five feet four inches, tall for a Bengali woman, ninety-nine pounds. Her complexion was on the dark side of fair, but she had been compared on more than one occasion to the actress Madhabi Mukherjee. Her nails were admirably long, her fingers, like her father's, artistically slim. They inquired after her studies and she was asked to recite a few stanzas from 'The Daffodils.'"[27] In this character sketch, the ability to recite Wordsworth is a trait comparable to physical attractiveness. Like her slim fingers or acceptable skin color, her poetry performance establishes Ashima as well bred and marriageable. Accordingly, the reference to Wordsworth is elliptical: he is neither named nor quoted, in contrast to the earlier description of Ashima's tutoring duties with its references to specific writers. The content of "The Daffodils" and the identity of its creator are unrelated to the function of the poem, which is merely to demonstrate the bride's cultural capital via her educational achievements.

But the institutional framing of Wordsworth in colonial curricula also reveals a different Wordsworth, a poet whose Englishness exams set into relief. Schoolbooks from former British colonies have not been preserved en masse as English textbooks have been at the British Library, but many examples of matriculation exams used in former British colonies have been saved, and these assessments provide evidence of how Wordsworth was taught. Not surprisingly, the exams reveal that students were expected to understand the content of his poetry at multiple levels—to parse the poem's grammar and syntax, to recapitulate its content, and to evaluate its merit. When "I wandered lonely as a cloud" appeared on the Allahabad University matriculation exam in 1908, the poem served a purely grammatical purpose, as students were asked to parse the phrase "could not but be gay" (see figure 1.1).[28]

Answering the question requires no understanding of the poem's meaning, merely the ability to interpret Wordsworth's syntax. The exam moves swiftly on from Wordsworth through longer questions about Henry Wadsworth Longfellow and Philip Gilbert Hamerton before adjourning for the third paper on Urdu.

This is the kind of transition—from the English paper to the Urdu paper—that casts light on the dimensions of Wordsworth's Englishness: point out what lesson the poet intends to teach, explain clearly and concisely the phrases underlined, translate this passage from Urdu into English. Appearing in this litany of demands, Wordsworth looks different. Or rather, it is Western readers of Wordsworth who shift, hailed by the exam's imperative mood into an unfamiliar subject position—that of a colonial student of English literature. Many matriculation exams, especially those from Indian and South African universities, pair their English papers with questions designed to appeal to their particular student body: there are papers on vernacular languages and composition questions that refer to local cities or animals. As the exams construct this colonial student and his or her setting, they simultaneously construct the Englishness of Wordsworth. As Homi K. Bhabha explains, Englishness in these cases is less an intrinsic feature than a belated effect produced by setting Wordsworth's flowers and birds in Allahabad or Durban, where their difference resonates.[29] In their juxtaposition of English and Urdu or, as we shall see, a stock dove and a snake, colonial matriculation exams delineate in miniature the experience of encountering Wordsworth in an educational setting beyond England and highlight the aspects of his poetry that fashion him as a particularly "English" poet.

The first chairs in English were not established at English universities until the end of the Romantic era (1828 for University College, London; 1835 for King's College, London), and these universities, along with Cambridge and Oxford, did not institute public examinations for matriculation until the 1850s.[30] It took longer still for English literature to appear on these examinations as a subject. As late as 1881, the matriculation exam for London University (now UCL) featured no literature, including instead a paper on English language that focused exclusively on grammar.[31] But by this time, English literature had already permeated matriculation exams for universities in British colonies as well as the Indian civil service exams, a development that led writers of civil service exam guides to hope a future was nigh in which "universities will possess a large body of professors and tutors competent to lecture on English."[32] The syllabus for the University of Madras matriculation exam in 1872, for example, includes poetry by Homer (via Pope), Southey, Byron, Scott, and Thomas Hood.[33] Similarly, a guide to the Indian civil service exam from 1866 asks, "Whom do you reckon the greatest English poet of the nineteenth century? Justify your preference by argument and quotation." The answer key immediately narrows the field to either Byron or Wordsworth and then asks, "Compare Chaucer, Spenser, Dryden, Pope, and

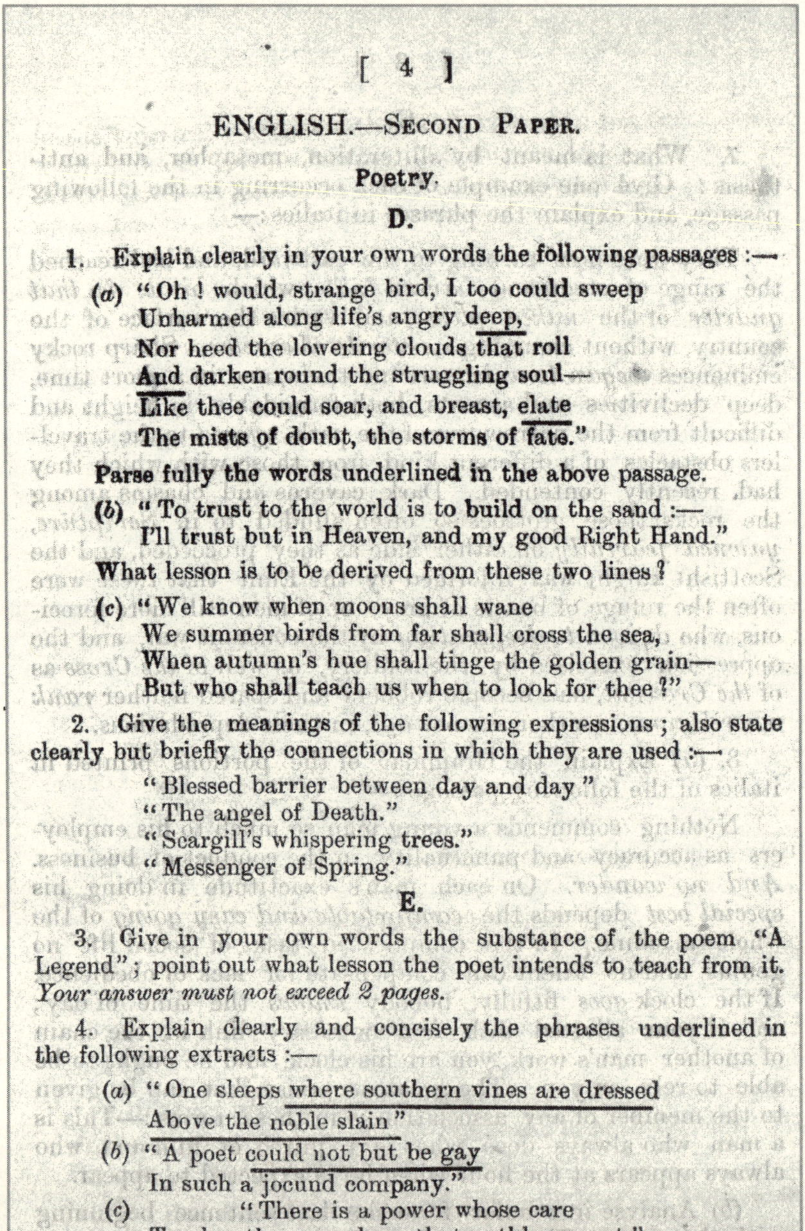

[4]

ENGLISH.—SECOND PAPER.

Poetry.

D.

1. Explain clearly in your own words the following passages :—

(*a*) " Oh ! would, strange bird, I too could sweep
Unharmed along life's angry deep,
Nor heed the lowering clouds that roll
And darken round the struggling soul—
Like thee could soar, and breast, elate
The mists of doubt, the storms of fate."

Parse fully the words underlined in the above passage.

(*b*) " To trust to the world is to build on the sand :—
I'll trust but in Heaven, and my good Right Hand."

What lesson is to be derived from these two lines ?

(*c*) " We know when moons shall wane
We summer birds from far shall cross the sea,
When autumn's hue shall tinge the golden grain—
But who shall teach us when to look for thee ?"

2. Give the meanings of the following expressions ; also state clearly but briefly the connections in which they are used :—

" Blessed barrier between day and day "
" The angel of Death."
" Scargill's whispering trees."
" Messenger of Spring."

E.

3. Give in your own words the substance of the poem "A Legend" ; point out what lesson the poet intends to teach from it. *Your answer must not exceed 2 pages.*

4. Explain clearly and concisely the phrases underlined in the following extracts :—

(*a*) " One sleeps where southern vines are dressed
Above the noble slain "

(*b*) " A poet could not but be gay
In such a jocund company."

(*c*) " There is a power whose care
Teaches thy way along that pathless coast."

FIGURE 1.1. "I wandered lonely as a cloud," Allahabad matriculation exam (1908), *The Allahabad University Matriculation Exam Papers from 1908 to 1909* (Allahabad: Ram Dayal Agarwala, 1911), 4. By permission of the British Library.

(*d*) "The frame thy wayward looks deride
Required a God to form."
(*e*) "His steeds to water at those springs
On chaliced flowers that lies."

F.

5. All thoughts of ill; all evil deeds,
That have their roots in Thoughts of ill;
Whatever hinders or impedes
The action of the nobler will:—
All these must first be trampled down
Beneath our feet, if we would gain
In the bright field of fair renown
The right of *eminent domain.*
We have not wings, we cannot soar;
But we have feet *to scale and climb*
By slow degrees, *by more and more,*
The cloudy summits of our time.

State, in your own words, the plain meaning of the above passage. Explain the grammatical construction of the words and phrases in italics.

6. Amongst the many advantages of experience, one of the most valuable is that we come to know the range of our own powers, and if we are wise we keep contentedly within them. This relieves us from the malady of eagerness: we know pretty accurately beforehand what our work will be when it is done, and therefore we are not in a hurry to see it accomplished. The coolness of old hands in all departments of labour is due in part to the cooling of the temperament by age; but it is due even more to the fulness of acquired experience, for we do not find middle-aged men so cool in situations where they feel themselves incompetent.

State, as briefly as possible, the plain meaning of the above passage. Analyse the first sentence.

URDU.—Third Paper.

(N.B.—*Write the answers to the different sections in separate answer books.*)

G.

1. Translate into English:—

ایک عورت کا اِکلوتا لڑکا جیوں ہی چلنے پھرنے لگا

FIGURE 1.1. (*continued*)

Wordsworth; first, in respect of the general spirit and manner of their poetry; and, secondly, in respect of their versification."[34] Yet most matriculation exams in South Africa and India were set by local universities and included vernacular languages—Sesotho in South Africa, for instance, or Urdu in India—in addition to English literature. In contrast, in the British West Indies, which lacked a university of its own until the University of the West Indies was established in 1948, the matriculation exams were set by universities in Britain.[35] A 1943 report on secondary education in Jamaica chaired by American educator I. L. Kandel reported that students there were expected to meet the standards set by the junior Oxford and Cambridge local examinations and the Cambridge school certificate and higher school certificate.[36] (The situation was much the same in the nineteenth century. The *Guide to the Cambridge Higher Local Examination* in 1899 includes in its prefatory material an alphabetical list of examination centers that jumps from "Crystal Palace, Exeter, Glasgow, Hull" to "Jamaica.")[37] As reformers realized, the language and subject matter of these British exams risked alienating West Indian students, and the Kandel report recommended that "the curriculum of all schools should be adapted to the cultural and economic needs of Jamaica, irrespective of the requirements of external examinations."[38]

Of course, the suitability of teaching British literature to colonial subjects had long been a debate, predating Thomas Babington Macaulay's "Minute on Education" in 1835 but spurred on by his assertion that few "could deny that a single shelf of a good European library was worth the whole native literature of India and Arabia."[39] Twentieth-century matriculation exams are not interested in making the case for English; that case was settled. Besides, what exam could make the case for the worth of a good European library? Exams are not designed to bring joy; in much the same way that education scholars in the United States currently criticize high-stakes testing for its effects on primary and secondary schooling, scholars of education in British colonies bemoaned how matriculation exams "tended to focus school achievement upon an examination syllabus."[40] What these exams do is show what the study of English can look like beyond England. To me, the English papers look maddening in their breadth, which spans the gap between the settings Wordsworth describes and the settings his colonial readers inhabit. Here are examples from two South African exams, both of which feature Wordsworth's poetry. In the first, an exam given in 1922 for the South African universities, students are asked to "give the substance of the following passage in about eighty words" (see figure 1.2).[41]

The first passage that follows is the opening stanza of "Resolution and Independence," an intriguing choice, since the poem is an especially local product with a rhyme scheme that only works in a Northern English accent. (On the facing page is a similar paraphrase exercise on "The World Is Too Much with Us.") But what

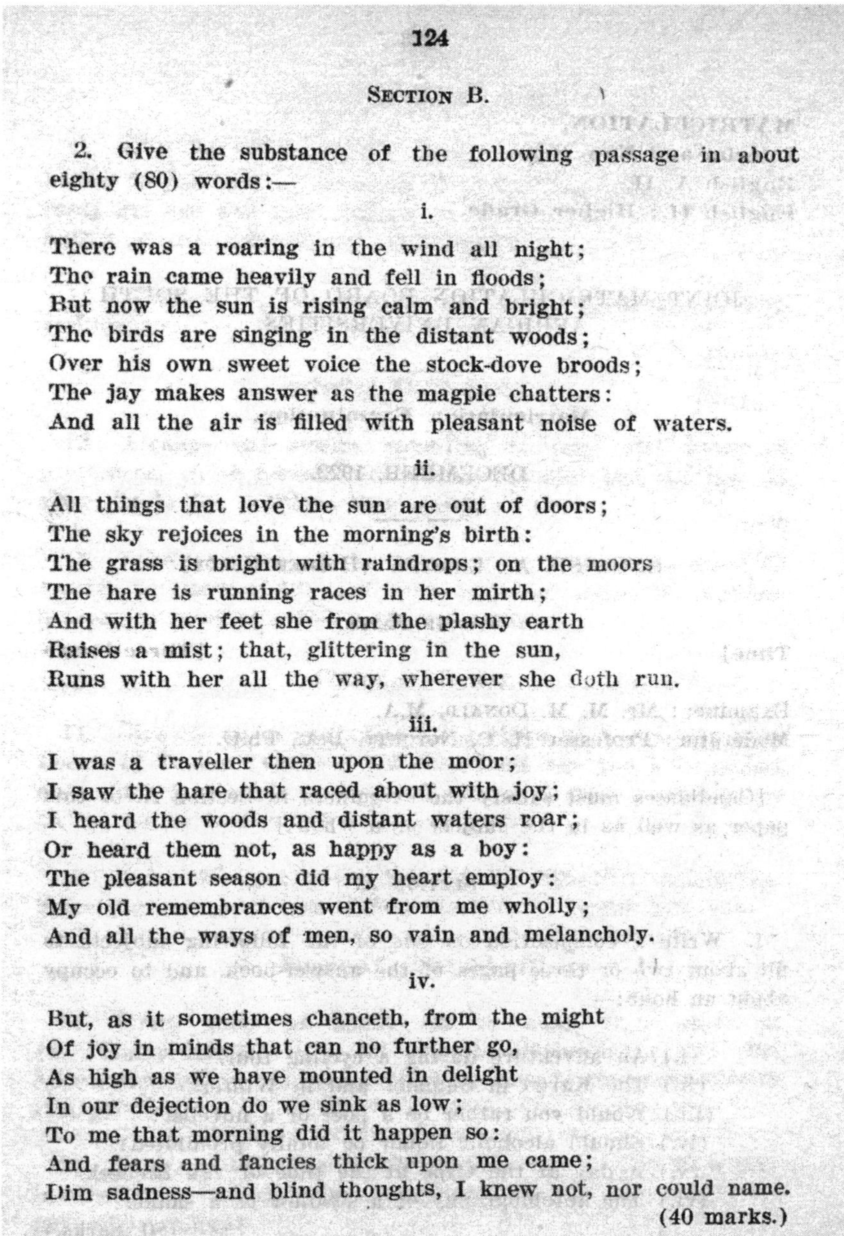

124

SECTION B.

2. Give the substance of the following passage in about eighty (80) words:—

i.

There was a roaring in the wind all night;
The rain came heavily and fell in floods;
But now the sun is rising calm and bright;
The birds are singing in the distant woods;
Over his own sweet voice the stock-dove broods;
The jay makes answer as the magpie chatters:
And all the air is filled with pleasant noise of waters.

ii.

All things that love the sun are out of doors;
The sky rejoices in the morning's birth:
The grass is bright with raindrops; on the moors
The hare is running races in her mirth;
And with her feet she from the plashy earth
Raises a mist; that, glittering in the sun,
Runs with her all the way, wherever she doth run.

iii.

I was a traveller then upon the moor;
I saw the hare that raced about with joy;
I heard the woods and distant waters roar;
Or heard them not, as happy as a boy:
The pleasant season did my heart employ:
My old remembrances went from me wholly;
And all the ways of men, so vain and melancholy.

iv.

But, as it sometimes chanceth, from the might
Of joy in minds that can no further go,
As high as we have mounted in delight
In our dejection do we sink as low;
To me that morning did it happen so:
And fears and fancies thick upon me came;
Dim sadness—and blind thoughts, I knew not, nor could name.

(40 marks.)

FIGURE 1.2. "Resolution and Independence," South African universities matriculation exam (1922), *Matriculation Examination Questions Set in the English Papers 1905–1922* (Cape Town: Juta), 124–125. By permission of the British Library.

if this paraphrasing occurs just after one has spent an hour writing a composition about the "karoo in summer and in winter" or the "autobiography of a swallow or a snake" (see figure 1.3)?

Between section A and section B, the exam does not merely shift from composition to reading comprehension; it can also move, depending on which topic the student chooses to address in section A, from South Africa to England, from the familiar to the remote, from one local sphere to another local sphere half a world away. Another exam from South Africa shifts gears similarly, posing reading comprehension questions about Wordsworth's sonnet "To Sleep," like "Quote a passage which stresses the monotony of lying awake" (see figure 1.4).[42]

Following the same pattern as the previous exam, this one prefaces its questions on Wordsworth's sonnet with a composition exercise, where students were instructed to write a letter on one of various subjects. (Perhaps option C, "Junior Clerk [male or female], about 17 years, required by Durban shipping company; good prospects; matriculation certificate. Write Box 85, *Natal Argus*.") After the sonnet appears a directive to write descriptions of two objects (teapot, garden roller, typewriter). In two pages, then, the South African student writing this exam may seek practical employment, parse a sonnet about insomnia, and describe commodities for "anyone who had not seen them" (has he or she seen a garden roller before?).

Those who enjoy literature generally recoil from exams like these, which place imaginative art in a context of high-stakes quantification in order to ask tedious questions of it. It feels deeply ironic to encounter a poet like William Blake in a poetry anthology published for the Oxford local examinations in 1913 (or on the GRE subject exam in literature, for that matter). Yet these South African exams provide the rare opportunity for readers from Britain or the United States to imagine encountering Wordsworth in a landscape dominated not by "the skylarks and the nightingales, the daffodils and roses of England," as Jean Said Makdisi describes, but rather by the karoo, snakes, and the seventeenth-century Dutch colonial administrator Jan van Riebeeck.[43]

DAFFODILS IN THE TROPICS

For the most part, my students have never heard of "I wandered lonely as a cloud." They certainly have not had to memorize it. They are not, as Jean Rhys writes, "tired of learning and reciting poems in praise of daffodils."[44] Yet like everyone who reads poetry, they respond at once to its intrinsic qualities (the words on the page), its institutional presentation (what the headnote on "Wordsworth" says), and the highly personal experiences it becomes associated with in their minds (a recent Skype conversation with a long-distance girlfriend). As Joan Shelley Rubin

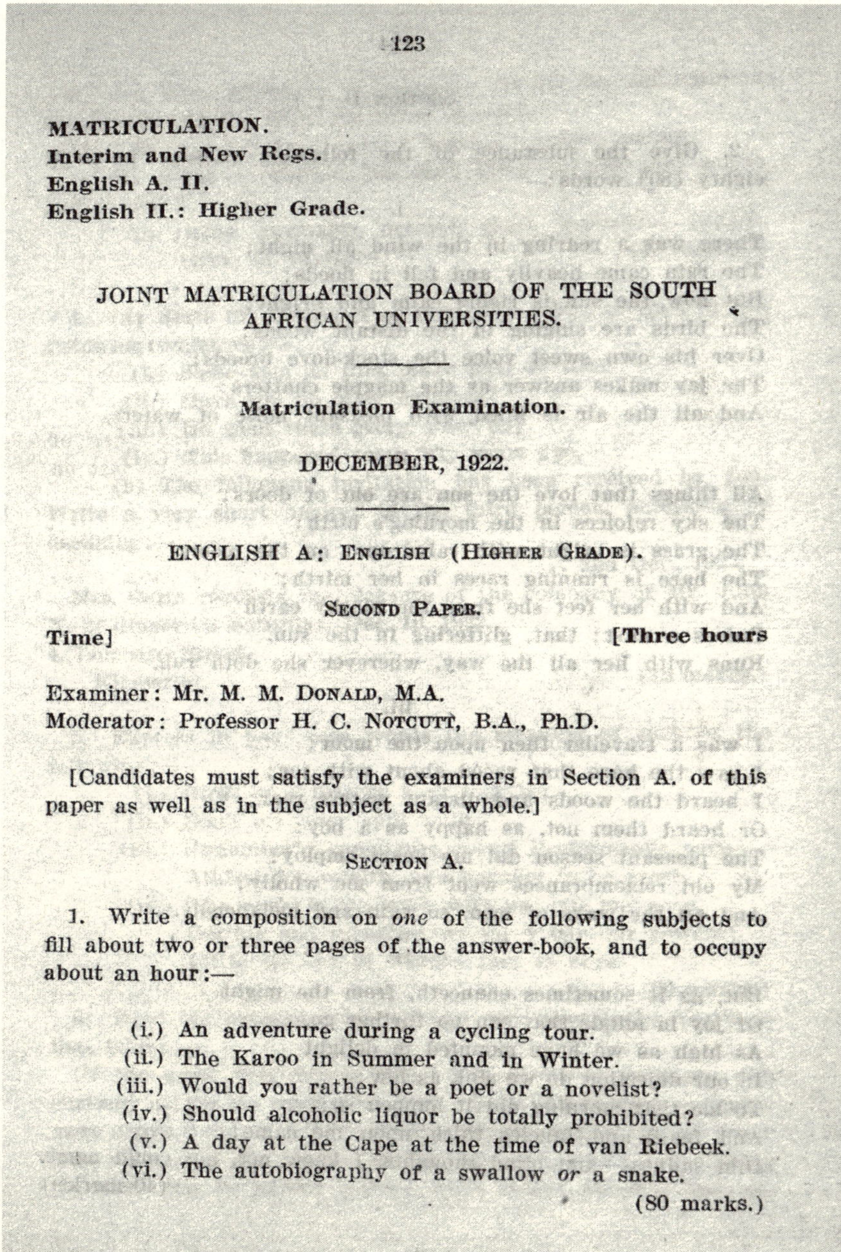

123

MATRICULATION.
Interim and New Regs.
English A. II.
English II.: Higher Grade.

JOINT MATRICULATION BOARD OF THE SOUTH AFRICAN UNIVERSITIES.

Matriculation Examination.

DECEMBER, 1922.

ENGLISH A: ENGLISH (HIGHER GRADE).

SECOND PAPER.

Time] **[Three hours**

Examiner: Mr. M. M. DONALD, M.A.
Moderator: Professor H. C. NOTCUTT, B.A., Ph.D.

[Candidates must satisfy the examiners in Section A. of this paper as well as in the subject as a whole.]

SECTION A.

1. Write a composition on *one* of the following subjects to fill about two or three pages of the answer-book, and to occupy about an hour:—

(i.) An adventure during a cycling tour.
(ii.) The Karoo in Summer and in Winter.
(iii.) Would you rather be a poet or a novelist?
(iv.) Should alcoholic liquor be totally prohibited?
(v.) A day at the Cape at the time of van Riebeek.
(vi.) The autobiography of a swallow *or* a snake.

(80 marks.)

FIGURE 1.3. Composition paper, South African universities matriculation exam (1922), *Matriculation Examination Questions Set in the English Papers 1905–1922* (Cape Town: Juta), 123. By permission of the British Library.

93

2. Write a letter on ONE of the following subjects, to fill not more than a page of your answer-book:—

(*a*) A boy in your district has the reputation of being a practical joker. You suspect he is responsible for some damage done in your garden. Write a letter to his parents.

(*b*) You have recently bought a wireless set which has been very unsatisfactory. Write a letter of complaint to the dealer from whom you bought it.

(*c*) "Junior Clerk (male or female), about 17 years, required by Durban shipping company; good prospects; matriculation certificate. Write Box 85, *Natal Argus*." [30]

3. Read the following poem carefully and then answer the questions upon it:—

A flock of sheep that leisurely pass by,
One after one; the sound of rain, and bees
Murmuring; the fall of rivers, winds, and seas,
Smooth fields, white sheets of water, and pure sky;
I have thought of all by turns and yet do lie
Sleepless! and soon the small birds' melodies
Must hear, first uttered from my orchard trees;
And the first cuckoo's melancholy cry.
Even thus last night, and two nights more, I lay
And could not win thee, Sleep! by any stealth:
So do not let me wear to-night away:
Without Thee what is all the morning's wealth?
Come, blessed barrier between day and day,
Dear mother of fresh thoughts and joyous health!

(*a*) How would you describe the four main divisions of the poem?

(*b*) Quote a passage which stresses the monotony of lying awake.

(*c*) Quote two metaphors which are applied to sleep.

(*d*) Make a list of all the word-pictures you can find in the poem.

(*e*) Give the poem a suitable title. [35]

4. Write clear, concise descriptions of TWO of the following objects, so that anyone who had not seen them would recognize them and know their use:—

a teapot, a sewing-machine, a garden-roller, a tennis-racquet, a typewriter. [24]

FIGURE 1.4. Composition paper and "To Sleep," South African universities matriculation exam (1940), *Matriculation Examination Questions English, February 1932–December 1941*, 4th ed. (Cape Town: Juta), 93. By permission of the British Library

points out in her study of poetry memorization, "The distinction between intrinsic and extraneous meaning is unavoidably fuzzy": the knowledge and experience we bring to a text affects the meaning we take away from it.[45] When I imagine myself not as someone for whom daffodils were a routine sight but as a student in South Africa in the 1920s, Wordsworth appears anew to me. The rain that "came heavily and fell in floods" at the beginning of "Resolution and Independence" forms a stark contrast to the desertlike climate of the karoo. Wordsworth writes about the "sweet voice" of the "stock-dove," a European bird, while South African students may write about snakes.[46] What happens when Wordsworth's poetry is planted in the minds of readers around the world and grows new shoots there? What do daffodils look like in the Caribbean? Wordsworth's "silly poem" is the only English poem that one character in Cliff's *Abeng* remembers from school, perhaps because one of her classmates colored the flower "deep red—like a hibiscus" (*Ab*, 129). Perhaps the "golden flowers" aren't daffodils at all but "buttercups," as in Lorna Goodison's "To Mr. William Wordsworth, Distributor of Stamps for Westmoreland," with "overseer thorns . . . planted among them."[47] Or maybe the daffodils are not deep hibiscus red but orange: in Edwidge Danticat's *Breath, Eyes, Memory* (1994), the narrator's aunt describes how in Haiti, "a strain of daffodils had grown that could withstand the heat, but they were the color of pumpkins and golden summer squash, as though they had acquired a bronze tinge from the skin of the natives who adopted them."[48] In Danticat's rendering, daffodils cannot make the jump from England to Haiti without being visibly changed. Moreover, her explanation is defiantly unscientific. The flowers' new color is not fed by soil and climate but rather inspired by the skin color of their gardeners, suggesting that daffodils' primary existence is social, not biological.[49] The surviving strain of flowers, distinct from the European species, has shed the trait most associated with daffodils—color—and yet the flowers remain recognizable as daffodils. Does the description of this pumpkin-orange strain change how we imagine the yellowness of daffodils? Does the appearance of the leech gatherer on a South African matriculation exam alter our perception of Wordsworth's relationship to England?

By encapsulating the distance between Durban and Cumbria, the difference between English and Urdu, these exams present in miniature what Tiffin, among others, has called the "daffodil gap": the chasm separating "the lived colonial or post-colonial experience and the imported/imposed world of the Anglo-written."[50] This gap is the subject of Kincaid, Goodison, Naipaul, Cliff, Stuart Hall, and Shirley Lim alike when they complain about the "pretty little flower." Yet the tidiness of the term *daffodil gap* is at odds with the highly local complexities of the "lived colonial or post-colonial experience" that it claims to describe. The authors I listed share a history with daffodils, but they lived in different places, inhabited distinct subject positions, and wrote diverse things. Reifying the gap between colonizer and colonized tends to mute these distinctions. As Mary Louise Pratt argues, "While subjugated peoples cannot readily control what the dominant culture visits upon them, they do determine to varying extents what they absorb into their own, how they use it, and *what they make it mean*."[51] Making daffodils the color of a deep-red hibiscus means something different than making daffodils the color of bronze skin. In scenes like these, daffodils are as much a productive provocation as evidence of a gap between the colonizer's culture and the lived experience of the colonized.

The existence of novels like Kincaid's *Lucy*, which present in fiction the autobiographical experience of memorizing Wordsworth, testifies to daffodils' provocative nature. But daffodils prompt not just fiction but also metafiction, novels that do not just repurpose Wordsworth but dramatize the *process* of repurposing Wordsworth—of writing and improvising poetry in his wake. Levy's *Small Island* (2004), for example, presents a familiar scene: one of the novel's protagonists, Hortense, memorizes Wordsworth's "I wandered lonely as a cloud" in her Jamaican school. But when Hortense teaches the poem to her grandmother, Miss Jewel, the novel shifts away from the routine scene of the colonial student in her British institutional setting to focus on Wordsworth's apparition in a distinctive cultural and familial setting. Like many students who have never seen the flower before, Miss Jewel wants a visual representation to accompany the poem, and her granddaughter obliges by drawing the flower in the dirt. Initially, Miss Jewel's relationship to the poem mimics that of her granddaughter. Like a student, Miss Jewel "learned every word," imitating the shape of Hortense's mouth and "recounting every perfect word with her chin high and her arms folded under her breasts."[52] But Miss Jewel quickly trades recitation for improvisation. At the beginning of this scene, the novel prints the first four lines of "I wandered lonely as a cloud." Soon it gives Miss Jewel's poem: "Ah walk under a cloud and den me float over de ill. An' me see Miss Hortense a look pon de daffodil dem." In this scene, Wordsworth's poem is more than an "emblem of good colonial education," for Hortense and her grandmother seize control of the daffodil: Hortense decides how it looks, and Miss Jewel improvises a relationship to it.[53] Outside the classroom, then, appears an efflorescence of daffodils and poems about daffodils: Wordsworth's lyric inspires a new poem, "Ah walk under a cloud"; his flower inspires a new flower, this one drawn rather than rooted in soil.

Miss Jewel's poem is meant to be at least a bit humorous—to satirize Wordsworth's poetic diction by rendering it in her Jamaican English. But Miss Jewel's version treads a finer line as well, leaving many of the original poem's key identifiers intact (daffodils, clouds) while becoming in the space of its two lines a lyric exploration of her highly mediated relationship to the flower. Wordsworth's speaker, as we shall see, spies daffodils twice in his poem: once by the lake and once in his mind. Within the bounds of her improvised poem, Miss Jewel never sees a daffodil: she sees Miss Hortense, and Miss Hortense sees the daffodils. And in her poem's larger context, Miss Jewel is doubly removed, for Hortense has never looked upon a real daffodil; she has only drawn one in the dirt. Before teaching Wordsworth's poem, Hortense reports that Miss Jewel "looked to me for all her knowledge of England" (*SI*, 36). In this scene, however, Miss Jewel is not terribly interested in England; she revises Wordsworth's poem so that it reflects her own distant relationship to his daffodils, conducted through the gaze of her granddaughter.

In *Small Island*, Levy repurposes Wordsworth by imagining characters who repurpose Wordsworth, simultaneously making and drawing attention to the art that can be fashioned out of the raw materials of his dissemination. Cliff performs a similar feat in *Abeng* with the character of Mr. Powell, the English teacher I mentioned in the introduction who teaches Wordsworth alongside Claude McKay. Like *Small Island*, *Abeng* begins its treatment of daffodils at a familiar point—the memorization of Wordsworth's poem in a Jamaican school. This school suffers from an excess of primers: the governor's office sends copies of the same schoolbook every year, each with "a pullout drawing of a daffodil" alongside Wordsworth's poem, and Mr. Powell cannot convince the office to supply different books (*Ab*, 85). On the one hand, this overabundance of primers leads to a dearth of content, "time left open by the repetitions of the manuals": the students have already read everything in the primer (*Ab*, 89). On the other hand, there is excess: after twenty-five years of receiving "the exact same manuals year after year," Mr. Powell has too many pullout drawings of daffodils. On its own, this image—stacks of identical primers with identical drawings of daffodils provided by a neglectful colonial bureaucracy—neatly encapsulates the dynamic of the "daffodil gap." Mr. Powell's students need new books; what they get are more daffodils. But out of these surplus daffodils he makes his art: "Mr. Powell was a lover of poetry. In his room provided for him by the parish council, behind the largest grocery store in the vicinity, he wrote poems about all manner of things. He decorated the walls of the room with his poems, printing them in black ink with his quill pen on the backs of the daffodil drawings he had been sent over the years. So when he lay on his bed, his own words were visible to him" (*Ab*, 85). Mr. Powell writes poetry out of the evidence of British colonial negligence and cultural hegemony. For amid the highly asymmetrical power dynamics, and in direct response to them, there is nevertheless artistic production.

With each pullout drawing that Mr. Powell rips from a primer and repurposes as writing paper, English daffodils and Jamaican poems become more inextricable and copresent—two sides of the same leaf. But in writing his poems, Mr. Powell also dictates the daffodils' disappearance: if he writes on the back of the drawings, his words can fill his room only when the daffodils face inward, flattened against the wall. What are his own words? They are beyond the scope of *Abeng*. Cliff reveals only that his poems are "about all manner of things," and they may well have nothing to do with Wordsworth on their surface. Yet it is, of course, precisely on their surface—the surface on which they are written—that they have something to do with Wordsworth. Pictures of Wordsworth's daffodils give Mr. Powell the paper he needs to make "his own words . . . visible to him," and it is daffodils whose presence he renders invisible—as they generally were in Jamaica—by displaying his own words. Perversely, for a teacher in preindependence Jamaica who wants paper for writing his own poems, pullout drawings of daffodils from unneeded student primers would be a fine and free source, one of the few leaves of paper in a book that is blank on its reverse and therefore usable as scratch paper. If daffodils represent to colonial readers a gap or a lack, the flowers also present a usable blank, a small expanse of valuable paper to be filled with poetry, an outline to be colored in deep hibiscus red or pumpkin orange. With this image of Mr. Powell in a room wallpapered with his handwritten poems, Cliff suggests that in Jamaica, Wordsworth's poetry can be simultaneously present and hidden, oppressive and repurposed, excessive and productive.

The dynamics of the "daffodil gap" are altered by the repurposings of Wordsworth that his poetry inspires or provokes. No longer a one-way exercise of colonial power, the gap becomes a space whose circulating currents, while never flowing free from the relations of domination and subordination that link Britain to its colonies, nevertheless travel to and fro "with the respirations of the tide," as Wordsworth puts it in *The Excursion*.[54] If Wordsworth provokes readers beyond Britain to write him into new existences, these writers provoke readers of Wordsworth to listen to him differently, as if he were engaged in an ongoing conversation with writers who interpolated him.

The remainder of this chapter turns to Kincaid's *Lucy* to model the methodology of reading the negotiations between Wordsworth and the authors who brought him to new life. Kincaid's bildungsroman is autobiographical and contains one of the most extensive postcolonial treatments of the daffodils' legacy. When Lucy first sees real daffodils, she is mostly grown, having left her native West Indies to work as an au pair for a wealthy white family in Manhattan. Tense discussions of the flower precede and immediately follow Lucy's encounter, and neither Lucy nor her well-meaning but naive employer, Mariah, can quite understand the other's reaction to daffodils: Lucy's anger and Mariah's delight are equally incomprehensible. For when Mariah rhapsodizes about spring and daffodils, Lucy remembers Wordsworth's poem. Or to be more precise, she remembers not the poem itself—neither

Wordsworth nor the poem's title is ever mentioned—but rather the act of memorizing and publicly reciting the poem in school. As a child, Lucy succeeds at her task, receiving accolades for her correct pronunciation and emphasis, like Mr. Powell's students who were expected to recite the poem "with as little accent as possible" (*Ab*, 85). But immediately the young Lucy vows to forget "line by line, every word of that poem" and, later that night, dreams that she "was being chased down a narrow cobbled street by bunches and bunches of those same daffodils that [she] had vowed to forget" (*L*, 18). The imagery is not subtle: Lucy ends up "buried deep underneath [the daffodils] and was never seen again," with the English flowers suffocating the colonized self. In memories and in dreams, Lucy experiences daffodils at a remove. Having never seen a real daffodil, she dreams about an image—perhaps a pullout daffodil drawing from a school primer—that is untied from the physical thing that it represents. To remember daffodils, then, is not to remember the poem but to remember memorizing the poem; it is not to remember the flower itself but to remember a dream about a flower she has only seen in a book. In this displacement, neither the poem, nor the flower, nor the poet is attached to Lucy's version of daffodils, which—as they are "emptied out of any real content"—become superfloral, capable of chasing down a young girl and piling on top of her.[55]

Again we have daffodils acting as a blank or gap that must be filled in: Lucy imagines the flowers as animate predators; elsewhere, her employers are daffodils, "two yellow heads" that "swam toward each other and, in unison, bobbed up and down" (*L*, 15). But let us transport this blank back to Wordsworth. For what is perhaps most surprising about the divorce of sign and content in Kincaid's rendering is how its resulting effacement of Lucy's dream self reveals a strikingly similar effacement in "I wandered lonely as a cloud." This similarity suggests that irony—the irony of reciting a poem about daffodils in a climate where none can grow—comprises only one level of meaning in the relationship between Wordsworth and Kincaid. Like most of his poems, "I wandered lonely as a cloud" exists in multiple versions. In 1807, the poem comprised three stanzas; by 1815, it had become four. In 1807, the poem went by its first line; by 1815, it was called "I wandered lonely." (Now it is often dubbed merely "Daffodils" or "The Daffodils," especially in anthologies.) But even beyond these sources of instability, there is a more profound decentering in the speaker himself, who by the end of the poem has left the poet's couch to join the host of daffodils and in this way bears some resemblance to Lucy, buried among the daffodils of her dream and "never seen again." The poem's conclusion, seen in this light, is surprising. "I wandered lonely as a cloud" is one of Wordsworth's most notorious poems, not just for postcolonial readers, but also for feminist critics, many of whom have noted the poem's silent dependence on Dorothy Wordsworth's journals. Read next to her entry about the daffodils, William's poem seems remarkable for its poetic egotism, its erasure of the convivial company that the Wordsworths actually enjoyed that day. Instead, the speaker is alone and can "discover something about himself and his profession as a poet through use of the external world."[56] But when read next to Kincaid's *Lucy*, the poem seems to revel in the power of the daffodils rather than the profession of the poet. These readings, in tension, are equally true.

In short, the similarities between Kincaid's and Wordsworth's treatments of daffodils emphasize something Wordsworth was very particular about: the agency of the flowers themselves. Starting with his first collected works in 1815, Wordsworth embarked upon a complex and thematic categorical system that would account for every poem included in the collection. Though groupings like "Poems on the naming of places" or "Poems proceeding from sentiment and reflection" may seem unnecessary, the divisions were crucial to Wordsworth, and he spent much of the "Preface" and "Essay, Supplementary to the Preface" distinguishing one category from another. (With this collection, then, Wordsworth became the first person to repurpose Wordsworth's poetry, placing his poems in new and different contexts that would necessarily affect how readers interpreted the verse.)[57] Perhaps unsurprisingly to Coleridge, who had been discussing theories of poetic inspiration with Wordsworth for almost twenty years, "Poems of the fancy" and "Poems of the imagination" were the most important of these categories, and Wordsworth could not decide in which of these categories the poem about daffodils belonged. Though he finally placed it in the category of imagination, the decision inspired a vexed footnote: "The subject of these Stanzas is rather an elementary feeling and simple impression (approaching to the nature of an ocular spectrum) upon the imaginative faculty, than an exertion of it."[58] In distinguishing between an "impression" on the imagination and an "exertion of it," Wordsworth makes a grammatical distinction with philosophical implications: an impression makes the imagination into a passive object, while an exertion promotes it to the level of subject. What disrupts the daffodils' inclusion in the category of imagination, then, is the lack of agency that they afford the poet's imagination. In Geoffrey H. Hartman's words, "The impact of the daffodils on his 'ocular spectrum' had been too strong."[59]

T. S. Eliot found little to like in this scheme: "If . . . the difference between imagination and fancy amounts in practice to no more than the difference between good and bad poetry, have we done more than take a turn round Robin Hood's barn?"[60] But Wordsworth's categorical system and the fussy footnote it inspired are important because they highlight the ability of the object—in this case, the daffodils—to act upon their viewer. By the time he categorized his poems, he had come to see the imagination as a particularly active and impressive force, "an endowing or modifying power" that "also shapes and creates."[61] We need not care very much about the line between imagination and fancy in order to take seriously Wordsworth's claim that the "imaginative faculty" has itself been impressed by some more active object rather than exerting the power of impression that is its birthright, in Wordsworth's understanding. At its most literal, Wordsworth's discussion of impression suggests that "I wandered lonely as a cloud" documents a moment when the imagination has been marked—that is, physically altered by an object that should bear the marks of impression itself. Here it is worth quoting the poem's conclusion in its entirety:

> The waves beside them danced, but they
> Out-did the sparkling waves in glee:
> A poet could not but be gay
> In such a jocund company:
> I gazed—and gazed—but little thought
> What wealth the shew to me had brought:
>
> For oft when on my couch I lie
> In vacant or in pensive mood,
> They flash upon that inward eye
> Which is the bliss of solitude;
> And then my heart with pleasure fills,
> And dances with the Daffodils. (*PW*, 2:216, lines 13–24)

The speaker here has little choice in his joy. As any poet would in such a situation, he "could not but be gay," a locution that students sitting for a matriculation exam in Allahabad were asked to explain but not analyze, a locution that makes joy into a reflex, an instantaneous response to the sight of daffodils and waves. Accordingly, the line drifts into monosyllables, continuing the poem's iambic tetrameter but with sonic simplicity.

This description of joy is in part what Wordsworth means when he refers to the poem as portraying a "simple impression . . . upon the imaginative faculty." In comparison to some of the more famous passages from *The Prelude*, for instance, "I wandered lonely as a cloud" doesn't aim to capture an especially complex response to the natural world. Daffodils dance, and the speaker responds with joy. Even his identification as "*a* poet" is couched in indefinition. The daffodils' agency escalates from this point, as the speaker thinks little and gazes much. In the poem's conclusion, we find him intentionally prone and passive, with the flowers reappearing to "flash upon that inward eye." While the homophonic *eye/I* trick directs our attention "inward," toward the speaker's individuated self, the final lines point elsewhere, outdoors, as the speaker's heart leaves the couch to "dance with the Daffodils." This is a happy move—the heart "with pleasure fills" amid "the bliss of solitude" that the speaker enjoys on his couch—but it is a move that orients our attention toward the daffodils rather than the speaker's self. It is also a move that depends on the daffodils' physical absence from the scene; they could not "flash" if the speaker did not first leave them behind. This, then, is the other part of the daffodils' power: their ability to withstand the poem's shift in setting from the lake of the first three stanzas to the couch of the final one. The daffodils, in defiance of their roots, prove mobile.

The poem's afterlives throughout the Anglophone world raise a question: What happens when it is not the speaker on his couch but someone else, far away—Lucy in her West Indian school auditorium—who is inundated with the vision of these absent flowers? Lucy's dream, which at first glance seems the singular invention of a young, harried girl, replays in a minor key the denouement of Wordsworth's poem. Both subjects disappear into a crowd of daffodils imbued with unexpected powers. For Wordsworth's speaker, of course, the move is desirable and deliberate; for Lucy, it spells her demise. Nevertheless, the agency of Lucy's dream flowers draws attention to Wordsworth's own efforts to delineate the precise force he believed his poetic object to have obtained. It would be difficult, I think, to attribute this similarity to Wordsworth's influence on Kincaid in any straightforward way. The scene ridicules Wordsworth's daffodils; it does not echo his voice or allude to lines of his poetry. So if there is any influence, it is of a different sort: Kincaid's influence on the critic. Her animated daffodils and the blank they fill ask me to carry them back and read them alongside Wordsworth's poem, where they set into relief the agency that the text and paratext of "I wandered lonely as a cloud" bestow on the absent daffodils.

The similarity between these writers' daffodils doesn't change the fact that for Lucy, the flowers are an enemy. When she finally sees the spring daffodils on a walk with Mariah, she reports that she "did not know what these flowers were" (*L*, 29). Her immediate reaction, though, is destructive: "I wanted to kill them." This wish is the nascent form of an argument that Kincaid posits in *My Garden (Book):* when she entitles a chapter about gardening and conquest "To name is to possess." Kincaid describes the "opportunity" that faced Carolus Linnaeus, originator of the Latinate binomial system of naming plants, who realized that "these new plants from far away, like the people far away, had no history, no names, and so they could be given names."[62] Naming implies knowledge—not just one's own knowledge of the object at hand but also the assumption of nonknowledge that others have of the object, the assumption that it is unnamed, and thus unstudied, without history.[63] (This unspoken assumption undergirds some of the poems in Wordsworth's "Poems on the naming of places," for instance.) Lucy does not know daffodils in the way that Mariah does—in her rhapsody about daffodils, Mariah describes spring "as if spring were a close friend, a friend who dared to go away for a long time and soon would reappear for their passionate reunion"—but bafflingly, Lucy knows the plant as one might know the face of a long-lost brother, subjectively and viscerally (*L*, 17).

The knowledge Lucy has is enough: "I wished that I had an enormous scythe; I would just walk down the path, dragging it alongside me, and I could cut these flowers down at the place where they emerged from the ground" (*L*, 29). Lucy's specificity in describing the location of her cut, "at the place where they emerged from the ground," is the strangest detail in this fantasy, both because it uses a wordy turn of phrase to describe a speedy cut and because it calls into question Lucy's desire to kill the flowers for good—for although the scythe is a potent image of death, it is also a real tool, one for harvesting grain or mowing grass. Reaping flowers with such a tool is thus symbolically ambivalent, as readers of Robert Frost know well: the scythe as symbol moves perpetually between harvest and death, between a predictable marker of agricultural circularity and the proverbial end of the line. But as with most perennials, daffodils "killed" with a scythe would grow back the next year: successfully killing daffodils would require ripping them up by the bulb, an act no less satisfyingly violent than reaping them with a scythe. There are a few ways to read this parody of a harvest. First, as a gardener, Kincaid knows how daffodils work, as do many of her readers. But Lucy does not, and her position as colonized subject is neatly encapsulated by her doomed effort at annihilating this representation of oppression. Second, the image of Lucy as a grim but ineffective reaper means that she destroys the flowers' current growth—their inexplicably recognizable appearance—while leaving the bulbs intact. Like Wordsworth's poem, which does not appear in the novel and instead lurks beneath its surface, the daffodils disappear while remaining immanent beneath the soil. This echo reverberates on the level of narrative structure. "I wandered lonely as a cloud" moves from the actual to the imagined, from lived experience in the first three stanzas to remembered experience on the couch in the fourth. So too does Lucy's harvest transform living daffodils into future blooms, into an absence that contains the ghostly potential for reappearance and regeneration. In the textual relationship that Kincaid forges with her repurposing, she and Wordsworth are not merely antagonists in a debate staged across time and space; they are also bound in a dialogue about human and floral ontology, jointly investigating the circumstances in which a self might begin to lose its edges amid the daffodils.

In the absence of daffodils, new varieties crop up: bright-red hibiscus-daffodil hybrids, daffodils drawn in the dirt, paper daffodils that flourish on walls, animated daffodils that run down cobbled streets. These proliferations are unpredictable, scattered, and distinct. As such, their significance lies not in their opposition of metropole and colony but in their rhizomic transplantations of British plant and poetic matter. But if these transplantations do not constitute a univocal "writing back," they do inspire a critical "reading back." The whole canon of daffodils must expand in order to accommodate these new species, "and so the relations, proportions, values of each work of art toward the whole are readjusted," as Eliot writes.[64] "I wandered lonely as a cloud" shifts slightly with the broadening of the genus *narcissus*; his solitude takes a step back, the image of his heart leaving the couch to join the daffodils moves into the foreground. So to isolate Wordsworth's daffodils from the global daffodils they generate artificially cements the genus in England, in 1807. His poem's afterlives hold the power to alter the meaning of daffodils—and with them, the meaning of Wordsworth.

NOTES

1 V. S. Naipaul, *The Overcrowded Barracoon* (Harmondsworth: Penguin, 1984), 24.

2 Cf. Marlon B. Ross, who sees lyric poems like "I wandered lonely as a cloud" as inherently imperial, not because of how they were disseminated, but because they helped "prepare England for its imperial destiny. They helped teach the English to universalize the experience of 'I.'" Ross, "Romantic Quest and Conquest: Troping Masculine Power in the Crisis of Poetic Identity," in *Romanticism and Feminism*, ed. Anne K. Mellor (Bloomington: Indiana University Press, 1988), 31.

3 Catherine Robson, *Heart Beats: Everyday Life and the Memorized Poem* (Princeton, N.J.: Princeton University Press, 2012), 11. As Robson has detailed, memorization as a pedagogical practice predated the arrival of mass education in the nineteenth century. In the late eighteenth and early nineteenth centuries, memorization was seen as a boon to the development of elocutionary and oratorical skills. Later in the nineteenth century, memorization "played an unrivaled role in the development of taste, in the refinement of the uncultured, in their elevation to a higher plane . . . memorized poetry brought every boy and girl in touch with the best that has been thought and said." In Britain, the practice of making students memorize poetry faded after the 1920s; in America, this decline occurred after the 1950s. In British colonies, the practice held on significantly longer (6–7).

4 Olive Senior, *Talking of Trees* (Kingston: Calabash, 1985), 26.

5 Helen Tiffin, "Cold Hearts and (Foreign) Tongues: Recitation and the Reclamation of the Female Body in the Works of Erna Brodber and Jamaica Kincaid," *Callaloo* 16, no. 4 (1993): 920n7.

6 For the history of English as a field of study in England, see D. J. Palmer, *The Rise of English Studies: An Account of the Study of English Language and Literature from Its Origin to the Making of the Oxford English School* (London: Oxford University Press, 1965); Chris Baldick, *The Social Mission of English Criticism, 1848–1932* (Oxford: Clarendon Press, 1983). Baldick emphasizes the importance of the Indian civil service exams to this formation. Gauri Viswanathan traces this formation earlier and locates it in India. Ian Reid has focused on the formation of English studies at the university level, and his book argues for Wordsworth's importance to that process. Viswanathan, *Masks of Conquest: Literary Study and British Rule in India* (New York: Columbia University Press, 1989); Reid, *Wordsworth and the Formation of English Studies* (Aldershot: Ashgate, 2004).

7 John Guillory, *Cultural Capital: The Problem of Literary Canon Formation* (Chicago: University of Chicago Press, 1993), 85–86. As Ian Michael describes in his meticulous survey of English textbooks, reading English literature was "a private activity" during the seventeenth century and only became more codified with the rise of school anthologies in the eighteenth century, though these anthologies tended merely to feature vernacular literature instead of teaching it. Not until the late eighteenth century did anthologies begin discussing the methodology of reading literature. Michael, *The Teaching of English: From the Sixteenth Century to 1870* (Cambridge: Cambridge University Press, 1987), 160.

8 *Classical Selections in Verse* (Liverpool: James Smith, 1808).

9 William Martin, *The Moral and Intellectual School Book* (London: Darton and Clark, 1838), iii.

10 Thomas Shorter, ed., *Poetry for School and Home* (London: T. J. Allman, 1861), iii.

11 Joseph Payne, *Studies in English Poetry*, 3rd ed. (London: Arthur Hall, Virtue, 1856), v.

12 *Selections from the British Poets*, 2 vols. (Dublin: Alexander Thom, 1855), 2:247.

13 Payne, *Studies in English Poetry*, v.

14 Edward C. Lowe, ed., *The Young Englishman's First Poetry Book* (London: James Parker, 1868), iii.

15 Michael, *Teaching of English*, 236. Michael warns against analyzing the contents of anthologies too closely because compilers rarely had a formal policy of selection or a wide knowledge of the available literature (169).

16 Mrs. Gething's volume is instead heavy on Felicia Hemans. Gething, *Selections from Modern Authors* (Darlington: J. Wilson, 1838).

17 *Readings in Poetry: A Selection from the Best English Poets*, 7th ed. (London: John W. Parker, 1843), 213; Martin, *Moral and Intellectual School Book*, 261.

18 Wordsworth's poems about Cambridge were especially popular. As Matthew Arnold notes, Wordsworth was "never, either before or since . . . so accepted and popular, so established in possession of the minds of all who profess to care for poetry, as he was between the years 1830 and 1840, and at Cambridge." See *CPW*, 9:36. In spite of the fact that Wordsworth was a mediocre student who enjoyed little about Cambridge, the association between poet and university was strong. Several decades after his death, a guide to Oxbridge for Indian students still cited him frequently in order to glorify the setting: "What indeed could be more picturesque than Wordsworth's description of his early Undergraduate days?" S. Satthianadhan, *Four Years in an English University*, 2nd ed. (Madras: Srinivasa, Varadachari, 1893), 49.

19 Viswanathan, *Masks of Conquest*, 6.

20 Joseph Hine, *Selections from the Poems of William Wordsworth, Esq.* (London: Edward Moxon, 1831), ix.

21 Hine, ix, iii.

22 Martin, *Moral and Intellectual School Book*, 261.

23 Martin, iii, emphasis mine.

24 Martin, 228.

25 Hine, *Selections from Wordsworth*, vii.

26 Martin, *Moral and Intellectual School Book*, 261.

27 Jhumpa Lahiri, *The Namesake* (Boston: Houghton Mifflin, 2003), 7, 9, emphasis in the original.

28 *The Allahabad University Matriculation Exam Papers from 1908 to 1909* (Allahabad: Ram Dayal Agarwala, 1911), 4.

29 Homi K. Bhabha, *The Location of Culture*, 2nd ed. (New York: Routledge, 2004), 153.

30 Michael, *Teaching of English*, 262.

31 See also the matriculation exams for University of London in 1878 and London University in 1880, both of which include papers on grammar but not literature. G. R. L. Marriott, *Papers Given in the London University Matriculation Examination* (London: Hirst Smyth, 1881); Richard Groombridge, *A Guide to the Matriculation Examination*, Groombridge's Guides to the Examinations of the University of London (London: Groombridge, 1878); Walter P. Workman, *The Questions Set at the Matriculation Examination of the London University, June 1880* (London: Joseph Hughes, 1880).

32 Robert Demaus, *English Literature and Composition: A Guide to Candidates in Those Departments in the Indian Civil Service* (London: Longmans, Green, 1866), vii.

33 C. M. Barrow, *The Poetical Selections Prescribed for the Matriculation Examination of the University of Madras* (Mangalore: C. Stolz, 1871).

34 Demaus, *English Literature and Composition*, 54, 132, 140. The few data points cited here support Viswanathan's assertion that "English literature appeared as a subject in the curriculum of the colonies long before it was institutionalized in the home country," but my aim is not a comprehensive record of how English literature infiltrated matriculation exams in England and in the British colonies (Viswanathan, *Masks of Conquest*, 3).

35 Some of these exams, set by British institutions for use overseas, include papers for students in specific colonies, and the questions in these sections are tailored to fit the students' context. A Cambridge school certificate examination from 1931, for example, includes a section for students in colonial Malaya and Western Africa and asks students to write a letter to a friend in another part of Malaya or correct a sentence about a boy named Ah Kow. *Cambridge School Certificate Examination Book of Question Papers Set in December 1931* (London: Cambridge University Press, 1932), 13–14.

36 I. L. Kandel et al., *Report of the Committee Appointed to Enquire into the System of Secondary Education in Jamaica* (Kingston: Government Printer, 1943), 11. For more on the role of Romantic poetry in twentieth-century colonial education in the West Indies, see Jocelyn Stitt, "Producing the Colonial Subject: Romantic Pedagogy and Mimicry in Jamaica Kincaid's Writing," *ARIEL* 37, nos. 2–3 (2006): 144–146.

37 *Guide to the Cambridge Higher Local Examination* (London: University Examination Postal Institution, 1899).

38 Kandel et al., *Report into the System*, 23. S. A. Hammond similarly critiqued secondary schools' tendency to focus "too little upon local interests." Similarly, another midcentury plan for secondary education in Jamaica recommended providing "literature, text and reference books, for reading and study which are written with a knowledge of West Indian conditions and for West Indian needs." Hammond, "Education in the British West Indies," *Journal of Negro Education* 15, no. 3 (1946): 442; *A Plan for Post-primary Education in Jamaica; Being the Report of the Secondary Education Continuation Committee* (Kingston: Government Printer, 1945), 18.

39 Thomas Babington Macaulay, *Prose and Poetry*, 2nd ed., ed. G. M. Young (Cambridge, Mass.: Harvard University Press, 1967), 722.

40 Hammond, "Education in the British West Indies," 442.

41 *Matriculation Examination Questions Set in the English Papers 1905–1922* (Cape Town: Juta, 1922), 123–125.

42 *Matriculation Examination Questions English, February 1932–December 1941*, 4th ed. (Cape Town: Juta, 1948), 93.

43 Jean Said Makdisi, *Beirut Fragments: A War Memoir* (New York: Persea Books, 1990), 111.

44 Jean Rhys, "The Day They Burned the Books," in *Tigers Are Better-Looking* (London: Andre Deutsch, 1976), 42.

45 In 1995, Joan Shelley Rubin had a query printed in the *New York Times Book Review* that asked readers to describe poems they memorized in school between 1917 and 1950 and reflect on both the experience of memorizing the poem in the first place and what the poem had meant to them since. The letters about Wordsworth's "Daffodils" range from a descendent of Nathanial Hawthorne, who described the physiological effects of memorizing poetry by stating, "They flash upon that inward eye / Which is the bliss of solitude," to a woman who said that recalling Wordsworth's poem helped her endure an abortion. Rubin suggests that the latter "was not primarily engaged in considering the delights of nature," but it would seem that the Hawthorne descendent wasn't either. (Or maybe they both were.) Rubin's point is that the line between a poem's inherent meaning and the meaning we give it once it lives in our minds is difficult to police. Rubin, *Songs of Ourselves: The Uses of Poetry in America* (Cambridge, Mass.: Belknap Press of Harvard University Press, 2007), 151, 153.

46 *Matriculation Examination Questions Set in the English Papers 1905–1922*, 123–124.

47 Lorna Goodison, *Turn Thanks* (Urbana: University of Illinois Press, 1999), 45.

48 Edwidge Danticat, *Breath, Eyes, Memory* (New York: Vintage, 1994), 21.

49 As Jana Evans Braziel has explained, daffodils here model creolized adaptation and not colonial imposition, as they do in *Lucy*. Braziel, "Daffodils, Rhizomes, Migrations: Narrative Coming of Age in the Diasporic Writings of Edwidge Danticat and Jamaica Kincaid," *Meridians* 3, no. 2 (2003): 113.

50 Tiffin, "Cold Hearts and (Foreign) Tongues," 920n7.

51 Mary Louise Pratt, *Imperial Eyes: Travel Writing and Transculturation*, 2nd ed. (London: Routledge, 2008), 7, emphasis mine.

52 *SI*, 36.

53 Cynthia James, "'You'll Soon Get Used to Our Language': Language, Parody and West Indian Identity in Andrea Levy's *Small Island*," *Journal of West Indian Literature* 18, no. 2 (2010): 57.

54 *E*, bk. 8, line 141.

55 Ian Smith, "Misusing Canonical Intertexts: Jamaica Kincaid, Wordsworth and Colonialism's 'Absent Things,'" *Callaloo* 25, no. 3 (2002): 816.

56 Susan M. Levin, *Dorothy Wordsworth and Romanticism* (New Brunswick, N.J.: Rutgers University Press, 1987), 33. See also Susan J. Wolfson, "Individual in Community: Dorothy Wordsworth in Conversation with William," in *Romanticism and Feminism*, ed. Mellor, 139–166.

57 According to Matthew Arnold, the effects were not good. The categories seemed "ingenious but far-fetched," and he warned that Wordsworth's poems "will never produce their due effect until they are freed from their present artificial arrangement" (*CPW*, 9:43–44).

58 William Wordsworth, *Poems (1815)*, 2 vols., ed. Jonathan Wordsworth (Oxford: Woodstock Books, 1989), 1:329.

59 Geoffrey H. Hartman, *Criticism in the Wilderness: The Study of Literature Today*, 2nd ed. (New Haven, Conn.: Yale University Press, 2007), 28.

60 T. S. Eliot, *The Use of Poetry and the Use of Criticism* (Cambridge, Mass.: Harvard University Press, 1933), 69. Eliot is talking about Coleridge's *Biographia Literaria* here, not Wordsworth's *Poems (1815)*, but Wordsworth had largely borrowed his conception of imagination and fancy from Coleridge.

61 *PrW*, 3:33. As David Rosen has pointed out, by 1815, *imagination* had come to mean "the transformation of everyday reality by mind," a definition that displaced Wordsworth's earlier theory of imagination, in which "the perceiving subject is so riveted by a particular object that the subject/object distinction falls away and the self is lost in relation." Rosen, *Power, Plain English, and the Rise of Modern Poetry* (New Haven, Conn.: Yale University Press, 2006), 70, 37.

62 *MGB*, 122.

63 Michel Foucault similarly associates this process of naming with the development of natural history as a field: "We must not see the constitution of natural history . . . as an experiment forcing entry, willy-nilly, into a knowledge that was keeping watch on the truth of nature elsewhere; natural history . . . is the space opened up in representation by an analysis which is anticipating the possibility of naming; it is the possibility of seeing what one will be able to say, but what one could not say subsequently." Foucault, *The Order of Things: An Archaeology of the Human Sciences* (New York: Vintage, 1994), 130.

64 T. S. Eliot, *Selected Essays* (New York: Harcourt, Brace, 1950), 5.

2

LANDSCAPE PEDAGOGY IN J. M. COETZEE, *THE PRELUDE*, AND THE LUCY POEMS

IN BETWEEN TWO SCENES OF sexual aggression in J. M. Coetzee's *Disgrace* (1999) appears one of pedagogical impotence. The novel's protagonist, David Lurie, is an adjunct professor of communications at Cape Technical University, where he is permitted to teach one elective course per year. The novel's plot moves from the city to the country—from the urban university to the South African farm—when Lurie's coercive sexual exploits with his student Melanie Isaacs go public, leading him to resign his position and flee the city. Aversion defines Melanie's role in their encounters: in one, she disentangles herself, "averting her face"; in another, "all she does is avert herself: avert her lips, avert her eyes" (*D*, 19, 25). In between these scenes of what the narrator dubiously calls "not rape, not quite that, but undesired nevertheless," Lurie meets with his elective course in Romantic poetry, butchering his lecture on William Wordsworth crossing the Simplon Pass in an attempt to communicate with Melanie. Having "never been much of a teacher," he is quick to fall off topic, comparing the speaker's dismay at Mont Blanc's "soulless image" to romantic infatuation: "Like being in love. . . . If you were blind you would hardly have fallen in love in the first place. But now, do you truly wish to see the beloved in the cold clarity of the visual apparatus?" (*D*, 4, 22). Knowing he's failed at his lesson, Lurie becomes "sorry for [Melanie] too, having to listen to these covert intimacies," and his lecture on *The Prelude* trails off into generalities: "Wordsworth is writing about the Alps. . . . We don't have the Alps in this country, but we have the Drakensberg, or on a smaller scale Table Mountain, which we climb in the wake of the poets, hoping for one of those revelatory, Wordsworthian moments we have all heard about" (*D*, 23).

The students prove uninterested. The Drakensberg is about nine hundred miles from their university. Table Mountain in Cape Town is more proximate, but it is, as Lurie admits, "on a smaller scale" than the Alps, its table-like appearance stunning but perhaps not sublime. On one level, Lurie's failure to engage his students proves what many critics have said about this scene—that "the European scenic tradition has come to seem irrelevant in the 'new South Africa,'" that those "Wordsworthian moments we have all heard about" are not as universal as Lurie implies.[1] Coetzee himself has said as much. In *White Writing* (1988), for instance, he points out that "Wordsworth called sublimity 'the result of Nature's first great dealings with the superficies of the earth,' not considering that plains, as well as mountains and oceans, resulted from these dealings" (*WW*, 52).[2] How does a geologic feature like Table Mountain, born of "nature's first great dealings" but lacking the grandeur of the Alps, fit into Wordsworth's rubric of the sublime? The seeming incompatibility of South African geography with the European landscape tradition leads Coetzee to wonder, "Is the very enterprise of reading the African landscape doomed, in that it prescribes the quintessentially European posture of reader vis-à-vis environment?" (*WW*, 62). The shift from the specific example of Wordsworth to the abstraction of "the quintessentially European posture" is smooth and proves fertile ground for interpreting the relationship between Africa and Europe.

The relationship between Africa and Europe is, of course, marked by centuries of European imperialism. But that simple fact does not make it easy to talk about South Africa's postcoloniality. There are reasons to do so: as residences of a former colony, "South Africans are hardly in a position to decline the term," writes one champion of postcolonial theory in South Africa.[3] Even theorists who find the appellation inaccurate recognize the power of thinking postcolonially: Annamaria Carusi, writing before the end of Apartheid, suggested that postcolonial theory helpfully "focused attention on the central position of cultural production in the attainment of those [liberatory] goals in real terms," which was significant in a nation that criminalized most other means of resistance.[4] Yet describing South Africa in postcolonial terms raises as many problems as it solves. Who is the colonizer and who is the colonized? How does South Africa's panoply of official languages and racial designations fit into the binary opposition of colonizer and colonized? When did the shift out of colonialism occur?

To be sure, these are the kinds of questions that plague any application of postcolonial theory to the complex realities of a nation reckoning with its colonial past. Laura Chrisman has warned of the danger in adhering to "an Oriental/Occidental binarism, in which continents and colonies which do not belong to this West/East axis are nonetheless absorbed into it"; Benita Parry has noted how "colonialism as a specific, and the most spectacular, mode of imperialism's many and mutable states . . . is treated as identical with all the variable forms."[5] But the dangers of generalization are particularly glaring in the context of South Africa. There is no clear date of independence to celebrate in South Africa, and each option posits a different identity for colonizer and colonized. The difference between 1931, when the Statute of Westminster gave British colonies full freedom, and 1994, when Apartheid officially ended, is more than just sixty-three years: it is the difference between seeing Britain or white South Africa as the colonizer. Consequently, gesturing at South Africa's two colonial powers, the British and the Dutch, only begins to clarify the situation. In 1963, two years after South Africa became a republic, the South African Communist Party suggested that the country was experiencing "colonialism of a Special Type," an internal colonization in which nonwhite South Africa could be considered "the colony of White South Africa itself."[6] Yet this distinction between white and nonwhite glosses over South Africa's more specific racial distinctions—English versus Afrikaner, Black versus Indian versus "Coloured"—not to mention economic ones. Even if one considers only white South Africans, the situation is complicated. After their defeat in the South African War, some Afrikaners considered themselves colonized by the British; thus "Afrikaners had a 'double' status in the course of South African history, that of being the colonizers as well as the colonized."[7] The victory of the National Party in 1948 would seem to solidify Afrikaners' status as colonizer, not colonized—the National Party promoted Afrikaner culture and oversaw the implementation of Apartheid—but the tension between British and Afrikaner culture never disappeared, ensuring that this "double" status had a long afterlife. Thus a foundational principle of colonial historiography like the distinction between settler and nonsettler colonies fails to describe the state of affairs: South Africa is a settler colony, but calling it that "requires maintenance of the binary colonizer/colonized as an essentially racial opposition," an opposition that Apartheid codified but that fails to account for South Africa's range of racial dynamics.[8]

The ill fit of postcolonial theory in South Africa also plays out in the realm of language, where the dominance of English (and, to a lesser extent, Afrikaans) has tended to promote a small canon of authors—what Louise Bethlehem refers to as "the Gordimer-Coetzee-Brink-Breytenbach dominant of 'South African Writing' packaged for international consumption."[9] I will say more about the battle between English and Afrikaans later on, but for now I want simply to note that neither is the most common first language spoken in South Africa. Yet they are, as Louise Viljoen points out, "institutionally privileged," and as a result, postcolonial scholars have historically paid little attention to "modes of appropriation and social hierarchies in pre-colonial African societies, or in oral forms of expression."[10] Add to this the fact that the linguistic demography of South Africa does not always correspond to race or ethnicity: many black South Africans speak Afrikaans as their first language, and the predominance of English has more do to with the rural/urban divide than with a specific European heritage. The dominance of Coetzee in the field of South African literary studies in some ways testifies to the particular status that certain languages enjoy over others in South Africa (Coetzee is Afrikaner; he writes in English). But in other ways, he is of his cohort the most removed from South Africa: his novels tend toward allegory rather than realism, he doesn't live in South Africa anymore, his cultural frame of reference is relentlessly European.[11] Given this remove, postcolonial critics' continued fascination with his novels typifies the strange place of postcolonial literary criticism in South Africa. This author, now a resident of Australia who hasn't published a novel set in South Africa since 1999, is still the one of the most discussed by critics interested in South Africa. As Bethlehem complains, "Coetzee has been so thoroughly domesticated by international criticism, that he functions . . . as a convenient point of reference through which to hone by-now predictable aspects of postcolonial theory in its metropolitan guises."[12]

Analyzing Coetzee's recourse to British Romantic poetry might seem like one of postcolonial criticism's predictable moves. Nevertheless, the present chapter does just that in order to dispute a predictable conclusion—namely, that Coetzee uses Wordsworth merely to critique the persistence of European cultural and aesthetic norms in South Africa. In *Disgrace*, the association of Wordsworth with the European scenic tradition only partly addresses what this Romantic poet is doing in the novel. Wordsworth is a constant, weathering the shift in mood and setting as *Disgrace* moves from Cape Town (where Lurie attempts to teach *The Prelude*) to the sparsely populated Eastern Cape, where an attack on Lurie's daughter, Lucy, evokes Wordsworth's "Lucy" poems. The first part of this chapter introduces Coetzee's relationship to Wordsworth in his autobiographical novel *Boyhood* (1997) before analyzing David Lurie's attempts to teach *The Prelude* in *Disgrace*. Like V. S. Naipaul's "B. Wordsworth," which parodies the English poet while detailing the applicability of certain Wordsworthian themes in Trinidad, *Disgrace*'s scenes of teaching do two seemingly contradictory things. First, Coetzee does use *The Prelude* in part to demonstrate how figures like Wordsworth are alien to the realities of students' lives in South Africa. Book 6 of *The Prelude*, better known for its rhapsodies on Alpine tourism than for its depiction of college life, is a wise choice for this demonstration. Second, in these scenes of teaching, *Disgrace*'s treatment of pedagogy and educational policy simultaneously echoes the other topic of book 6, Wordsworth's ambivalence toward his education at Cambridge, an ambivalence germane to students like Lurie's who are bored by their professor. This relevance prompts a question about *The Prelude* that I address in the chapter's second section: Why does book 6, "Cambridge and the Alps," unite those two disparate subjects, "Cambridge" and "the Alps"? Is it mere chronology that binds them together? By integrating the dual realms of book 6, the university and the Alps, *Disgrace* helps reveal a rhetorical relationship between those two settings that undermines Wordsworth's attempts throughout *The Prelude* to distinguish formal schooling from education through nature, the space of Cambridge from the space of the Alps.

Even if we read book 6 in its entirety, we probably would not call its placemaking "global." Wordsworth may construct Cambridge in relation to the Alps, but his representations of these settings do not develop the global sense of place that I argue characterizes later works like *The Excursion* and the *Guide to the Lakes*. The case is much the same with Wordsworth's Lucy poems, also from his "Great Decade" and alluded to throughout the second half of *Disgrace*. Yet returning to the Lucy poems after witnessing how they proliferate in Coetzee's depiction of the Eastern Cape changes how I interpret their representation of the natural landscape. The third section of this chapter contextualizes *Disgrace*'s shift from campus novel to farm novel with investigations of two twentieth-century historical trends in South Africa: the rise of "mother-tongue" education and the proliferation of the *plaasroman*, or South African farm novel. Finally, I argue that as *Disgrace* shifts into the genre of the farm novel, allusions to Wordsworth's Lucy poems shape the novel's critique of gender and the land in post-Apartheid South Africa. After she is raped by thieves on her farm, Lucy Lurie becomes a recognizably Wordsworthian figure, similar to his Lucy in her silence, her thoughts of death, and her affiliation with nature. Through these echoes to Wordsworth's early lyrics, notable for the contrast between Lucy's silence and the speaker's storytelling, the novel asks what it means to tell one's own story in South Africa, to tell stories in and about South Africa. The chapter concludes by analyzing Wordsworth in light of Coetzee, arguing that *Disgrace* draws attention to the way in which one of the Lucy poems, "I travelled among unknown men," subtly erodes its own depiction of England as isolated, picturesque, and dissimilar from foreign lands. Lucy Lurie's unwavering commitment to farming the land—and the affiliation with South Africa that this commitment underscores—highlights the bond between Wordsworth's Lucy and England in "I travelled among unknown men," a bond that reveals the boundaries of England to be imprecise and subjective contra the speaker's construction of the nation.

PEDAGOGICAL PERVERSIONS IN *DISGRACE*

Disgrace's use of *The Prelude* is highly ironic, though perhaps not in the way most scholars have suspected. On one level, as I have explained, David Lurie cannot engage his students in Wordsworth's vision of the Alps. A straightforward reading of this fact might conclude by suggesting the existence of a profound gap between the concerns of Wordsworth and the concerns of university students in post-Apartheid South Africa. Crucially, however, when Lurie flounders in the classroom with book 6 of *The Prelude*, his students are having an educational experience very similar to that of Wordsworth's earlier in book 6 of *The Prelude*—namely, finding oneself "detached / Internally from academic cares."[13] In a larger sense, then, the intellectually stultifying scene in Lurie's classroom echoes *The Prelude*'s interest in the practice and ramifications of two different pedagogies, education through nature and education through institutions. It thus becomes difficult to say that Wordsworth is irrelevant in the "new South Africa" (*D*, 23). Lurie's students may find the poet uninteresting, but the deadening pedagogy of their professor actually testifies to the continued importance of a poet like Wordsworth, who was deeply aware of how educational institutions can fail their students. To readers familiar with *The Prelude*, Wordsworth's seeming irrelevance in Lurie's college classroom becomes proof of his relevance.

That said, the role of Wordsworth in *Disgrace* is complex, even contradictory. Several of the novel's formal ticks make it difficult to forge conclusions with much precision. The voice is in the third person, but the narrative slips into free indirect discourse so frequently as to confuse the line between narrator and protagonist. Lurie's verbal habits, his polyglot slippages and his play with verb and adjective forms, mirror the narrator's. For example, Lurie, to no avail, distinguishes between *usurp* and the perfective *usurp upon* in his lecture on *The Prelude*; on a fantastical tangent into Flaubert, the narrator imagines Emma Bovary spying on Lurie's weekly appointment with his escort Soraya: "A moderate bliss, a moderated bliss" (*D*, 21, 6). The slippages also call into question the line between author and protagonist. As a professor of English in Cape Town, Lurie bears some resemblance to Coetzee, a former professor of English at the University of Cape Town, but the resemblance is a tease, characteristic of a satire rather than a roman à clef. Since at least the publication of his first autobiographical fiction, *Boyhood*, which features episodes "shared among Coetzee's life story and the novels," he has been notorious for finessing the relationship between identification and detachment with his protagonists.[14] (Elizabeth Costello from the *Elizabeth Costello* stories and Señor C. from *Diary of a Bad Year* are just two of Coetzee's doubles—not to mention the "John" of Coetzee's three autobiographical novels and the "John" of *The Lives of Animals*.)[15] Finally, the novel fictionalizes ground that Coetzee has explicitly addressed in nonfiction essays.[16] In obscuring the distinction among protagonist, narrator, and author, the novel inspires many different, and often contradictory, interpretive possibilities. Are we supposed to find it ironic or revelatory that Lurie calls Wordsworth one of his "masters"? Or both?

Coetzee's own experiences reading Wordsworth as a child ratify a sense of Wordsworth as a canonical yet impotent figure in *Disgrace*. In *Boyhood*, the young protagonist—a version of Coetzee rendered in the third person—first reads Wordsworth at the insistence of his father: "One day his father comes to his room with the Wordsworth book. 'You should read these,' he says, and points out poems he has ticked in pencil. A few days later he comes back, wanting to discuss the poems. 'The sounding cataract haunted me like a passion,' his father quotes. 'It's great poetry, isn't it?' He mumbles, refuses to meet his father's eye, refuses to play the game. It is not long before his father gives up." The boy's aversion has little to do with the actual content of Wordsworth's poetry: *Boyhood* offers no reading, either ameliorative or dismissive, of "Tintern Abbey." The problem lies with the father, the teacher, the conduit for Wordsworth, whom the boy "cannot imagine . . . reading poetry." An Anglophilic Afrikaner who spends most of his time at the bar, the father is an unconvincing proponent of Wordsworth. Indeed, his son "cannot see how poetry fits into his father's life; he suspects it is just pretence."[17] Appreciating the "sounding cataract" becomes less an aesthetic endeavor and more a vexed "game" between boorish father and recalcitrant son. In this light, the appearance of Wordsworth in *Disgrace* and *Boyhood* helps reveal the continued dominance of English culture and language in South Africa, a dominance that would seem to be under critique, given that Wordsworth is endorsed in these novels by David Lurie and young Coetzee's father, aging and corrupted disciples who prove ineffective at promoting their master to a new generation of South Africans. In these contexts, Wordsworth signifies as the English poet, tool of a cultural hegemony that is fast losing sway.

This vision of Wordsworth has little to do with the specific features of his poetry. Yet even in terms of content, the appearance of Wordsworth's verse in *Disgrace* is often parodic, as when the narrator bitingly associates *The Prelude*'s "Infant Babe" passage with David Lurie's sexual disgrace. Reading about his removal from the university in the newspaper, Lurie finds the following description of himself: "Lurie (53), author of a book on English nature-poet William Wordsworth, was not available for comment." The narrator immediately follows this characterization with another: "William Wordsworth (1770–1850), nature-poet. David Lurie (1945–?), commentator upon, and disgraced disciple of, William Wordsworth. Blest be the infant babe. No outcast he. Blest be the babe" (*D*, 46). In this passage of *The Prelude*, which at least one critic has called the "most explicit exposition of Wordsworth's pedagogical programme," the infant babe "Doth gather passion from his mother's eye," and

> day by day
> Subjected to the discipline of love,
> His organs and recipient faculties
> Are quickened, are more vigorous. (*P*, bk. 2, lines 243, 250–253)[18]

The contrast between Lurie and the infant babe is clear. The infant babe enjoys "the gravitation and the filial bond / Of Nature that connect him with the world," while

Lurie enjoys bonds of a less innocent sort and, as a result, is expelled from his world (*P*, bk. 2, lines 263–264). He is no nature lover, no infant babe: being a "disciple" of Wordsworth has very little bearing on how Lurie conducts his life.

At the same time, however, *Disgrace*—published in 1999 and written in the years immediately following the end of Apartheid in 1994—affiliates Wordsworth with the politics of its particular historical context. In its introduction of Lurie, the novel mentions that his "book on English nature-poet William Wordsworth" is about "Wordsworth and history." Titled *Wordsworth and the Burden of the Past*, Lurie's monograph might be read in two different ways: either Wordsworth is significant to the novel's treatment of South Africa's burdensome past or Wordsworth *is* the burden of the past (*D*, 4). Or perhaps both. *Disgrace* represents the "new" South Africa without much fanfare. (The word *Apartheid* is never mentioned.) Yet the novel frequently alludes to this long period of racial segregation by gesturing at "history," and it associates this term with the figure of Lucy, Lurie's daughter. At first, the association is neutral. As a farmer, Lucy strikes her father as a "throwback," and he reflects "perhaps it was not [her parents] who produced her: perhaps history had the larger share" (*D*, 61). Lurie interprets his daughter's farming less as an individual choice and more as a result of history, gesturing at the generations of white South Africans who farmed in the Eastern Cape. Following the rape of Lucy, however, the association between her character and history intensifies. After three black men assault and rob her, David Lurie repeatedly suggests that history is to blame: "It was history speaking through them. . . . A history of wrong. . . . It may have seemed personal, but it wasn't. It came down from the ancestors" (*D*, 156). A few pages later, he says to Lucy, "You wish to humble yourself before history" (*D*, 160). Though Lucy never accepts his reasoning, Lurie understands the rape as payment for a history of racial disenfranchisement and her unwillingness to report it as an attempt to atone for the sins of her white ancestors. In this formulation, both aggressor and victim lack agency, which is instead vested in history, in ancestors. When readers first encounter Lurie's monograph *Wordsworth and the Burden of the Past*, these events haven't transpired: the plot is young, and the title seems little more than a joking impersonation of academia. Yet the title also signifies proleptically: this is a novel in which the past will prove a burden, even putting aside the question of whether Lurie's understanding of his daughter's trauma is correct. It seems likely that in one sense, the title posits Wordsworth as a synecdoche for the "burden of the past," associating him with the cultural hegemony of British South Africa. But the title of Lurie's book is entirely plausible as an academic monograph about William Wordsworth: it wouldn't seem out of place on a bookshelf next to Alan Liu's *Wordsworth: The Sense of History* or David Bromwich's *Disowned by Memory: Wordsworth's Poetry of the 1790s*.[19] In another sense, then, we might take the title of Lurie's book seriously, for Wordsworth and Coetzee share a concern for the burden of the past, the burden of personal and political histories. Before Lurie's students are bored by *The Prelude*, before Lurie construes himself as a perversion of the "infant babe," *Disgrace* affiliates Wordsworth with "history": the history of Wordsworth's own life and of late eighteenth-century Britain but also, counterintuitively, the history of post-Apartheid South Africa. For to write about the burden of the past in South Africa during the Truth and Reconciliation Commission hearings is specifically to evoke the history of Apartheid.

This affiliation between Wordsworth and the burden of the past is important to the scene of Lurie in the classroom because it establishes Wordsworth's malleability: he can be simplistically weighted with the burden of South Africa's colonial past while simultaneously and contradictorily prefiguring the genuine questions the novel asks about a past, which—to borrow from Faulkner—isn't even past. Wordsworth proves similarly malleable for Naipaul in *Miguel Street* (1959), where the story "B. Wordsworth" centers on a poet who calls himself "Black Wordsworth," Trinidadian brother to the white English Wordsworth. The stories in *Miguel Street* are set in wartime Port of Spain, and each focuses on a single character as seen through the eyes of the first-person narrator looking back on his childhood. According to Black Wordsworth, the narrator is a poet like him, and the friendship between the two ends only when Wordsworth disappears, having admitted to the boy that he has not been writing "the greatest poem in the world," as he originally claimed.[20] Black Wordsworth is, on one level, an object of ridicule, a "fake and a failure," another in Naipaul's cast of deluded characters—the sort of people whom Naipaul "*hates*," according to Robert Haas.[21] Some of this ridicule flows upstream to poke fun at the White Wordsworth. When B. Wordsworth claims that he and his white brother "share one heart. I can watch a small flower like the morning glory and cry," the joke is on both Wordsworths, the Trinidadian poet who thinks that being a poet is all about crying and the English poet who wrote the "Immortality" ode that Naipaul is alluding to ("To me the meanest flower that blows can give / Thoughts that do often lie too deep for tears"; *MS*, 58). Naipaul's story, however, is rife with Wordsworthian themes. B. Wordsworth, like his namesake, must confront the impossibility of writing his great poem. His dwelling, a precious and unusual plot of land filled with so many fruiting trees that it "looked wild, as though it wasn't in the city at all," exists in opposition to the urban surroundings (*MS*, 59). In an echo of Wordsworth's *Michael*, his dwelling has vanished by the story's conclusion, the trees replaced with a two-story building, and no amount of memorializing on the narrator's part prevent it from seeming "as though B. Wordsworth had never existed" (*MS*, 65). It would be tempting to take some of these echoes of Wordsworth exclusively as parody were it not for the boy's attachment to B. Wordsworth, which the narrator never undercuts as he looks back on his former self (itself a Wordsworthian point of view). The narrative is peppered with short declarative sentences in which the boy affirms Wordsworth's insights: "He was right" (*MS*, 59); "I did as he told me, and I saw what he meant" (*MS*, 60); "I understood his story" (*MS*, 61); "The world became a most exciting place" (*MS*, 62); "I was filled with wonder" (*MS*, 63). In spite of Naipaul's notoriously disparaging attitude toward Trinidad and its inhabitants, the story is too genuinely elegiac for these affirmations to come off as delusional. Like *Disgrace*, Naipaul's story presents a Wordsworth who is strikingly relevant, who fits right in with the other fakes and failures of *Miguel Street*. The narrator, Black Wordsworth, and White Wordsworth share a heart attuned to both the necessity of memorializing and the impossibility of doing so as completely as one might desire.

Like "B. Wordsworth," the first half of *Disgrace* suggests the absurdity of transplanting Wordsworth so far from England, but it simultaneously nurtures the development of recognizably Wordsworthian themes in this distant setting. The narrator imagines Lurie's students complaining about Wordsworth, "A man looking at a mountain: why does it have to be so complicated, they want to complain?" Moments later, Lurie asks, "Where is the flash of revelation in this room?" (*D*, 21). There is no flash; Wordsworth remains a relic. On another level, however, Lurie is teaching poorly and he knows it, suggesting that his students' boredom is as much a commentary on the norms of university education as it is a referendum on Wordsworth's poetry. It is important to establish here the ways in which Lurie falters as a teacher because the failures of his classroom bring out of the shadows *The Prelude*'s representation of Cambridge.[22] This depiction begins in book 3, "Residence at Cambridge," which details Wordsworth's disappointments with and at Cambridge. (For example, professors seem to him and his peers "men whose sway, / And whose authority of office, served / To set our minds on edge, and did no more"; *P*, bk. 3, lines 569–571.) Book 6, "Cambridge and the Alps," turns its attention to Wordsworth's academic listlessness and the development of a "poet's soul" before moving to the Alps (*P*, bk. 6, line 55). I want to suggest that by teaching the half of book 6 about the Alps poorly—by inspiring in his students an academic listlessness—Lurie subtly but effectively teaches both halves of book 6, both Cambridge and the Alps.

His poor teaching takes two forms. Most egregious is Lurie's transgression of the standard ban on sexual relationships between teachers and students. The novel highlights this transgression by bookending the classroom scene with sexual encounters between Lurie and Melanie. In neither context is Lurie capable of striking the right note; he never fully separates the role of teacher from that of lover. During their first conversation, Melanie admits that she is "not so crazy about Wordsworth," and Lurie responds by chiding her: "You shouldn't be saying that to me. Wordsworth has been one of my masters" (*D*, 13). Later that evening, he engages her in a dialogue about whether she should spend the night. He concludes his argument with Shakespeare: "'From fairest creatures we desire increase . . . that thereby beauty's rose might never die'" (*D*, 16). The quotation does not have its intended effect. Melanie decides to leave, and Lurie reflects, "The pentameter, whose cadence once served so well to oil the serpent's words, now only estranges. He has become a teacher again, a man of the book, guardian of the culture-hoard." Within his realization, of course, lurks a humorous, stylistic reenactment of its content. The role of "teacher" is edited, "man of the book," and reedited, "guardian of the culture-hoard"—the repetitious flourish turning a basic description of Lurie's profession into a vaunted honorific. Lamenting the gulf between teacher and pupil becomes a means of widening the very gap he seeks to diminish: teacher takes over for lover. In the classroom, the situation is reversed. Lecturing on Wordsworth, he tries to command his students' attention by comparing Wordsworth's disappointment at Mont Blanc's "soulless image" to "being in love" (*D*, 22). Immediately, "a memory floods back: the moment on the floor when he forced the sweater up and exposed her neat, perfect little breasts. For the first time she looks up; her eyes meet his and in a flash see all" (*D*, 23). In comparison to his students, who suffer from "blank incomprehension"—a Wordsworthian phrasing—Melanie can "see all" and grasps that her professor is no longer talking about Wordsworth but has drifted into "covert intimacies." The roles Lurie inhabits are connected by his poor performance of each: "He has forgotten how to woo," and his class discussions inspire "silence" and "silence again" (*D*, 20, 21). Yet the roles of lover and teacher are bound more deeply by Lurie's muddling of their respective duties. Wooing means quoting Shakespeare like a teacher, while teaching means addressing "covert intimacies" to one student like a lover.[23]

Less morally egregious but perhaps more pertinent to *The Prelude* is Lurie's inability do more for his students than irritate them and "set [their] minds on edge," to borrow Wordsworth's description of his experience at university (*P*, bk. 3, line 571). For example, Lurie attempts to distinguish between the verb forms Wordsworth uses when encountering Mont Blanc:

> "Let us start with the unusual verb form *usurp upon.* Did anyone look it up in a dictionary?"
>
> Silence.
>
> "If you had, you would have found that *usurp upon* means to intrude or encroach upon. *Usurp,* to take over entirely, is the perfective of *usurp upon*; usurping completes the act of usurping upon." (*D*, 21)

Disgrace thrives on these uncomfortable moments in its first half, when it adheres to certain norms of the campus novel. To "usurp upon" is the ninth definition the

Oxford English Dictionary provides for the verb *usurp*, and the most applicable definition, "to encroach or infringe upon," is not radically different from the definition it provides for the perfective *usurp*, "to appropriate wrongfully to oneself."[24] Thus while Lurie's distinction is not false, it is also unlikely to inspire readerly joy in students who may not know what *usurp* means on its own, let alone that *usurp upon* is an unusual form of the verb. The atmosphere in the classroom never improves: "He has gone too far too fast. How to bring them to him?" His solution, comparing the passage to "being in love," is, as he admits, "hardly in Wordsworth": he has captured their attention but only by dropping the subject of the class (*D*, 22). It may seem ungracious to insist here on Lurie's faults as an educator—Who hasn't felt a little "sick at the sound of [one's] own voice" by the end of a challenging class (*D*, 23)?—yet Lurie's foibles are important for the way they echo and, to a large extent, prove relevant to Wordsworth's reservations about educational institutions in *The Prelude*. Ortwin de Graef has argued that Lurie remembers "only the harmonies of *The Prelude*, perhaps, forgetting its breakdowns."[25] Yet Lurie also replays, in an utterly different geographic and cultural context, the limitations that Wordsworth recognized as inherent in systematized education. Moreover, this scene's subtle integration of the dual realms of book 6—the university and the Alps, the institution of higher education and the font of the natural sublime—posits a deeper similarity between those two settings than even Wordsworth acknowledges.

BRIDGING CAMBRIDGE AND THE ALPS

Book 6 of *The Prelude* is titled "Cambridge and the Alps," yet it is not clear (nor have critics made it clear) what these two places are doing in the same book. The most basic explanation is chronological: Wordsworth and his friend Robert Jones took their tour of the Continent on a summer break from Cambridge. Wordsworth goes on to describe the relationship between the university and the grand tour as adversarial: "An open slight / Of college cares and study was the scheme" in setting off for the Continent (*P*, bk. 6, lines 342–343). Beyond these explanations, readers have not been compelled to make a case for any unity between these two locations. In part, this is because the second half of book 6 tends to overshadow the first. Cambridge is a less impressive subject than the Alps, and Wordsworth's performance as a student was less than impressive. There is only one sustained study of Wordsworth's time at Cambridge, and it was published sixty years ago.[26] Meanwhile, as Julia Sandstrom Carlson says, criticism of the Simplon crossing episode "has come to define generations of Romantic scholarship," and the passage is now one of the most frequently read pieces of verse in Wordsworth's oeuvre, perhaps because, as Alan Liu suggests, "the episode has become one of a handful of paradigms capable by itself of representing the poet's work."[27] To summarize the episode briefly, Wordsworth and Jones approach the Simplon Pass, a high passage in the Swiss Alps from which they may descend into Italy. Unsure of the precise location of the pass, they keep walking and find a peasant, from whom they learn that they "had crossed the Alps" already, without realizing it (*P*, bk. 6, lines 596–597).[28] At this moment of disappointment, the speaker launches into a paean to the imagination. (Critics are not of one mind about this transition from disappointment to apostrophe and find it perfectly reasonable, or a little strange, or inexplicably abrupt.)

Many of the passage's themes are touchstones for Wordsworth's poetry at large: the overwhelming sublimity of Mont Blanc, which the speaker and his traveling companion quickly abandon for the more ameliorative landscape of the Gondo ravine; the famous address to imagination, which triumphs over the poet's sense of being "lost; / Halted without an effort to break through"; the speaker's preference for a "living thought" over the "soulless" ocular impression that displaces it (*P*, bk. 6, lines 596–597, 526–527). Even though readings of the episode vary greatly, the Simplon crossing passage celebrates quite concisely the power of the imagination in the face of awful sublimity. For good reason, this passage, excerpted from *The Prelude*, appears in every anthology of Romantic poetry. Three factors, then, give this passage a special status in *The Prelude*: the amount of critical attention it has received, its ability to "represent the poet's work," and as a result, the way it lends itself to decontextualization in anthologies. Yet together these factors tend to overshadow any relationship this episode might have with the rest of book 6. I want to make the case for a structural, dependent relationship between the two settings of book 6, Cambridge and the Alps—the one a site of flawed pedagogy and mediocre performance, the other a font of overwhelming visuality and sublime disappointment—both yielding to abrupt assertions of imaginative, individual, and providential merit. It is not mere chronology that links one setting to the next, nor is it opposition, as Wordsworth implies with his reference to "an open slight of college cares and study." Rather, the association of both Cambridge and the Alps with this rhetorical pattern of disappointment and exultation constructs these settings not as discrete locales but rather as interconnected nodes, united by the revelations they inspire in Wordsworth's former self in spite of the distinction he draws throughout *The Prelude* between nature's education and the faulty pedagogy of educational institutions.

This distinction is most memorably developed in Wordsworth's description of the boy of Winander. With its juxtaposition of the boy's "natural" education and the more routinized education of a student whom Wordsworth calls the "dwarf man," *The Prelude* firmly distances itself from the rationalist educational techniques favored by contemporary reformers like Maria and Richard Edgeworth.[29] In "these too industrious times," Wordsworth laments, an accomplished child, a "dwarf man,"

can read
The inside of the earth, and spell the stars;
He can string you names of districts, cities, towns,
The whole world over, tight as beads of dew
Upon a gossamer thread. He sifts, he weighs,
Takes nothing upon trust. (*P*, bk. 5, lines 293, 295, 333–338)

As a result, "old Grandame Earth is grieved to find / The playthings which her love designed for him / Unthought of" (*P*, bk. 5, lines 346–348). The dwarf man who spends his youth memorizing the names of stars and towns has little time for the subtler lessons that lurk within nature's "playthings." The counterpoint to the dwarf man is the boy of Winander, evidence for *The Prelude*'s argument that nature's powers of education are superior to those of the schoolhouse. Instead of reciting "names of districts, cities, towns," the boy of Winander communes with owls. One of the more frequently analyzed episodes in *The Prelude*, the "Boy of Winander" immediately follows the discussion of the "Dwarf Man," in which Wordsworth wonders when teachers will learn

That in the unreasoning progress of the world
A wiser spirit is at work for us,
A better eye than theirs, most prodigal
Of blessings, and most studious of our good,
Even in what seem our most unfruitful hours? (*P*, bk. 5, lines 384–387)

This segue is significant because it characterizes the subsequent description of the boy of Winander as an example of nature's "wiser spirit," an antidote to the scathing description of "tutors of our youth" as "the wardens of our faculties / And stewards of our labour, watchful men / And skillful in the usury of time" (*P*, bk. 5, lines 376–379). Tutors, more akin to jailers and moneylenders than educators, are capable of creating only dwarf men.

In contrast, the boy of Winander enjoys a sublimely haphazard education. An accomplished birder, he spends his evenings with "both hands / Pressed closely palm to palm, and to his mouth / Uplifted," blowing "mimic hootings" to the owls across the lake (*P*, bk. 5, lines 395–397). The once "silent owls" reveal themselves, shouting "across the wat'ry vale . . . / Responsive to his call, with quivering peals, / And long halloos, and screams, and echoes loud, / Redoubled and redoubled" (*P*, bk. 5, lines 398–403). Eventually, silence falls:

And when it chanced
That pauses of deep silence mocked his skill,
Then sometimes in that silence, while he hung

> Listening, a gentle shock of mild surprize
> Has carried far into his heart the voice
> Of mountain torrents; or the visible scene
> Would enter unawares into his mind,
> With all its solemn imagery, its rocks,
> Its woods, and that uncertain heaven, received
> Into the bosom of the steady lake. (*P*, bk. 5, lines 404–413)

During the boy's seemingly "most unfruitful hours," amid the silence that "mocked his skill," nature enters his heart and mind "unawares," providing spontaneous intangibles like "the voice / Of mountain torrents" or "that uncertain heaven, received / Into the bosom of the steady lake" that a school could never deliver. Details like the unclear placement of "unawares" raise questions about Wordsworth's assignment of agency, questions with implications for our understanding of precisely how education through nature works in his theorization.[30] Yet I want only to point out here the intrinsic relationship between this episode and that of the "Dwarf Man," which suggests that the "Boy of Winander" episode is as much concerned with education as it is with language or the sublime, the themes that critics usually seize upon when analyzing the passage. Appearing back-to-back in book 5, the two passages present different sides of the same coin, the failures of one kind of pedagogy followed by the successes of another.

Coetzee has elsewhere called into question the relatively smooth shift in this scene from failure to edification, from the silence that "mocked [the boy's] skill" to the "visible scene" that enters his mind "with all its solemn imagery." In *White Writing*, Coetzee describes the plight of the South African writer, "the lone poet in empty space," alluding to the "Boy of Winander" but substituting a different outcome: "In the words he throws out to the landscape, in the echoes he listens for, he is seeking a dialogue with Africa, a reciprocity with Africa, that will allow him an identity better than that of visitor, stranger, transient" (*WW*, 8). But the reciprocal dialogue that the poet seeks with South Africa never materializes: "What response do rocks and stones make to the poet who urges them to utter their true names? As we might expect it is silence" (*WW*, 9). Coetzee's focus here on "echoes" and "silence" transplants the details of the "Boy of Winander" episode to an African setting, where the dynamic between poet and nature is stunted. For the boy of Winander, the silence that indicates the end his dialogue with the owls is merely the prelude to a more profound connection, characterized less by reciprocity than by the generosity of nature, which freely bestows its gifts on the passively receptive boy. For Coetzee's "lone poet," the silence is all. This poet is of "a highly problematical South African-colonial identity," and it is not clear whether from his subject position he "can speak to Africa and be spoken to by Africa" (*WW*, 8). The "echoes he listens for" never resonate; the silence of "rocks and stones" fails to usher in a "voice / Of mountain torrents" or any voice at all. While the boy and the English landscape become enmeshed in Wordsworth's vision, Coetzee's poet must remain "visitor, stranger, transient." Coetzee's reimagining of the "Boy of Winander" suggests that the relationship Wordsworth represents between silence and speech, paucity and bounty, cannot be realized in South Africa or in any colonial setting.

To reiterate, the relationship between the "Dwarf Man" and the "Boy of Winander" episodes is oppositional: the former presents the case against routinized education, while the latter argues for the nature's superiority as an educative power. Yet the deconstructionist analyses of Coetzee (and Paul de Man before him) make the divide between these educative forces less stable.[31] Explaining the linguistic problem that the poet faces in speaking to Africa, Coetzee rehearses a familiar argument about the unsuitability of the English language in South Africa, pointing out that "English carries echoes of a very different natural world—a world of downs and fells, oaks and daffodils, robins and badgers." (Daffodils are always a problem.) But he backtracks quickly, asserting that almost any language would pose the same problems, "since the language being sought after is a natural or Adamic language . . . a language in which there is no split between signifier and signified, and things are their names" (*WW*, 9). As Coetzee acknowledges, the gap between signifier and signified is endemic to all languages. Nevertheless, it seems a particular problem to English-speaking poets of South Africa: the natural world of the English language is "very different" from the natural world of Africa. Yet intensifying the gap between signifier and signified is precisely one of the effects in the "Boy of Winander" episode (though not in so many words). When de Man seizes on the "precariousness" of that episode, he cites Wordsworth's contradictory adjectives—"*gentle* shocks," "*mild* surprize," "*uncertain* heaven"—and concludes "that we have entered a precarious world in which the relationship between noun and epithet can be quite surprising."[32] Even without Coetzee's help in revealing the uncertainties that undermine Wordsworth's belief in education through nature, readers might find that belief, as expressed in the "Boy of Winander," rather unstable on its own terms. (What *is* a gentle shock?) The situation of Coetzee's poet thus becomes doubly precarious. Beyond the mismatch of language and geography lurks an old English poem—alluded to because of its ability to model dialogue and reciprocity between poet and landscape yet intent on disrupting the ready apprehension of its signifieds.

I have said that the distinction between Cambridge and the Alps suffers a similar fate, the two settings linked by a shared pattern of disappointment and revelation. Even before book 6, however, the die is cast, not just by the "Boy of Winander," but also by Wordsworth's attempts to separate luck from election, key concepts in the account of his poetic education. More specifically, these terms are important to Wordsworth's understanding of his time at Cambridge, where what is revealed on the path from disappointment to revelation is Wordsworth's election, his status as "chosen son." Nipping at the heels of this status, however, is the possibility that Wordsworth will not amount to much. Book 1 analyzes his choice of an autobiographical theme, pacing with agitation through other topics he could have chosen—"how Gustavus found / Help at his need in Dalecarlia's mines; / How Wallace fought for Scotland" (*P*, bk. 1, lines 211–213)—and concludes with a sentence that must seem uncomfortably familiar to anyone who has ever experienced writer's block:

> This is my lot; for either still I find
> Some imperfection in the chosen theme,
> Or see of absolute accomplishment
> Much wanting—so much wanting—in myself
> That I recoil and droop, and seek repose
> In indolence from vain perplexity,
> Unprofitably travelling toward the grave,
> Like a false steward who hath much received
> And renders nothing back. (*P*, bk. 1, lines 263–271)

The emphatic lack of "much wanting—so much wanting" laments Wordsworth's "lot" with pauses and repetitive stresses that depart from the neat, accomplished meter of the previous lines. I want to dwell for a moment on *my lot*, a term that connotes not just one's situation in life but also a method of random selection and thus the blind chance associated with the casting of lots. After worrying that he will "render nothing back," Wordsworth asks,

> Was it for this
> That one, the fairest of all rivers, loved
> To blend his murmurs with my nurse's song,
> And from his alder shades and rocky falls,
> And from his fords and shallows, sent a voice
> That flowed along my dreams? (*P*, bk. 1, lines 272–276)

How can it be that the education he received from nature—the "knowledge . . . of the calm / Which Nature breathes" that the river gave him—was for the sake of this, this sense of plodding mediocrely toward death (*P*, bk. 1, lines 284–285)? This question is a striking admission on Wordsworth's part, as it frets over the possibility that despite having "much received" from nature, his "lot" will be to "render nothing back." *The Prelude* tells the tale of the "Growth of a Poet's Mind," and that growth is largely attributed to nature's nurturing influence. Here, though, Wordsworth faces the possibility that he's wrong: whatever benefits he gleaned from his "natural" education, he may fail to write anything of merit.

Compare the connotations of this "lot" with the language Wordsworth more frequently uses to describe his relationship with nature. In book 1, he is a "favored being" of nature; in book 3, after arriving at Cambridge, he is "a chosen son" (*P*, bk. 1, line 364; bk. 3, line 82). These epithets, which evoke election and predestination, fit squarely within the tenets of Wordsworth's belief in education through nature.[33] The logic of election, though, requires that some are chosen while others are not. This is a problem for Wordsworth, not just because his chosen status makes it difficult to be merely "a man speaking to men," as he was a few years earlier in the preface to *Lyrical Ballads*. The tension between election and reprobation, providence and accident, the singular and the universal, does not merely pit Wordsworth against everyone else; it sets Wordsworth, chosen son, against a divergent version of himself—one who is disappointed with his lot, struggling to make good on the gifts he received. This distinction between past and present self has long been a crux in *The Prelude*.[34] Looking back at his younger self, Wordsworth can say that he was a "favored being"; looking squarely at the present task of writing, however, he must express the possibility that he will be unremarkable, that he will "render nothing back," that his successes will be due to his lot and not his election.

This possibility casts a shadow over the revelations that punctuate Wordsworth's time at university. Cambridge is a setting for both books 3 and 6, and in each book it is home to a rhetorical pattern familiar from Wordsworth's treatment of the Alps later in book 6: the transition from the Alps crossing to the apostrophe to imagination. If *Disgrace* imbricates the dual realms of book 6—Cambridge and the Alps, education and landscape aesthetics—book 6 suggests a deeper source of that imbrication. Beyond the physical characteristics that distinguish them, beyond the expanse of land and sea that separates them, "Cambridge" and "the Alps" are settings interconnected by a shared narrative function, their ability to foster sudden assertions of poetic revelation. On first arriving at Cambridge in book 3, Wordsworth finds that the institution "seemed more and more / To have an eddy's force, and sucked us in / More eagerly at every step we took" (*P*, bk. 3, lines 10–12). In comparison to the gentle "murmurs" of the Derwent, the "fairest of all rivers" from book 1, Cambridge in this metaphor assumes a more violent power, which intensifies in Wordsworth's description of the classroom:

> Of college labours, of the lecturer's room
> All studded round, as thick as chairs could stand,

> With loyal students faithful to their books,
> Half-and-half idlers, hardy recusants,
> And honest dunces; of important days,
> Examinations, when the man was weighted
> As in the balance; of excessive hopes,
> Tremblings withal and commendable fears,
> Small jealousies and triumphs good and bad—
> I make short mention. (*P*, bk. 3, lines 60–69)

The eddy moves into the classroom as Wordsworth pans across "the lecturer's room / All studded round" with fellow students, the long list of dunces and days and hopes only adding to the swirling effect. Nevertheless, the periodic sentence structure (appropriately learned and Latinate for its scholarly content) delays the subject and verb, "I make short mention," until the last moment, when they are free to parody the litany of objects that came before them: the "tremblings" and "fears" of the younger Wordsworth seem to his older self at least a little silly. Yet in spite of the ironic distance Wordsworth achieves by distinguishing the present narrating self from his younger self, intensity and excess define the scene: the totality of "all studded round, as thick as chairs could stand," the reiteration in "loyal students faithful to their books," the drama of "important days" and "excessive hopes."[35] In the subsequent line, these two selves merge—"Things they were which then / I did not love, nor do I love them now"—and this merging effectively removes the young Wordsworth from the academic fray, if only retroactively (*P*, bk. 3, lines 69–70).

Some ten lines later, Wordsworth arrives at one of his abrupt assertions of poetic providence. Though frequently "melancholy" and concerned with his "future worldly maintenance," Wordsworth reasons, "But wherefore be cast down, / Why should I grieve?—I was a chosen son" (*P*, bk. 3, lines 75–82).[36] Initially, these lines seem to be the interjection of his present self. Only as a thirty-four-year-old can Wordsworth look back on that melancholy student and know, definitively, that

> I had come with holy powers
> And faculties, whether to work or feel:
> To apprehend all passions and all moods
> Which time, and place, and season do impress
> Upon the visible universe, and work
> Like changes there by force of my own mind.
> I was a freeman, in the purest sense
> Was free, and to majestic ends was strong. (*P*, bk. 3, lines 83–90)

Like the boy of Winander, the speaker here is free but passive—or at least partly so. His is the power to "apprehend," while "time, and place, and season" possesses the power to "impress." Yet in turn, his mind grows authoritative, becoming a "force" that impels time and season to "work / Like changes there" (presumably, in the "visible universe"). Though no less thorny than the presentation of subject/object relations in the "Boy of Winander" episode, this passage tells a now familiar story about the kind of sustaining relationship Wordsworth sought and found with nature.

The insight that "I was a chosen son," however, does not remain the property of the older narrator and instead bleeds into the consciousness of Wordsworth's earlier self. Following immediately upon the assertion that he "was a freeman" comes the revelation that "'twas enough for me / To know that I was otherwise endowed"; a few lines later, he declares, "Let me dare to speak / A higher language, say that now I felt / The strength and consolation which were mine" (*P*, bk. 3, lines 92–93, 106–108). A variety of signals conspire to reveal that these sentiments belong to the young man—verbs of affect and epistemology (such as *know* and *felt*) rooted in the past, the insistent "now." Like the proclamation "I was a chosen son," these statements constitute a sudden break with the preceding disappointments: the anxieties about "future worldly maintenance" immediately give way to the knowledge of being "otherwise endowed." Moreover, these assertions are presented not as the hard-earned gains of a mature adult but as the perceptive glimmerings of a young mind. While it may be the narrating Wordsworth who calls himself a "chosen son," it is also the young man who knows and feels such designations to be true.

When Wordsworth returns to Cambridge in book 6, his narrative follows a similar pattern, first detailing the disappointments and worries associated with the university and then immediately countering these facts with self-possessed reflections on his status as poet. As in book 3, the older Wordsworth dismisses his university years as unworthy of much attention: "We need not linger o'er the ensuing time" (*P*, bk. 6, line 19). It suffices to say that he read many books and kept mostly to himself yet had "no settled plan," for he found himself

> detached
> Internally from academic cares,
> From every hope of prowess and reward,
> And wished to be a lodger in that house
> Of letters, and no more. (*P*, bk. 6, lines 29–33)

Wordsworth's state, "detached / Internally from academic cares," resembles that of David Lurie's students, disaffected and uninterested in their professor's thoughts on Romantic poetry. But while Lurie's students have no "flash of revelation," Wordsworth finds compensation amid his detachment. He briefly explains that he should have left Cambridge and devised his own plan of study but was reluctant to disappoint his family and—more to the point—too cowardly to make such a drastic change. The diction in this passage is unsparing: Wordsworth refers to the unchosen path as a "proud rebellion and unkind" to his family and disparages his "over-love / Of freedom" and the "indolence" that led him to ignore "regulations even of my own" (*P*, bk. 6, lines 41–47). Immediately, however, the tone shifts:

> And who can tell,
> Who knows what thus may have been gained, both then
> And at a later season, or preserved—
> What love of Nature, what original strength
> Of contemplation, what intuitive truths,
> The deepest and the best, and what research
> Unbiassed, unbewildered, and unawed?
>
> The poet's soul was with me at that time,
> Sweet meditations, the still overflow
> Of happiness and truth. A thousand hopes
> Were mine, a thousand tender dreams, of which
> No few have since been realized, and some
> Do yet remain, hopes for my future life. (*P*, bk. 6, lines 48–60)

Out of his younger self's detachment and indolence, the older Wordsworth spins an appealing possibility—that something was "gained . . . or preserved" during these two years of academic mediocrity, that "cowardise" was alchemically transformed into "love of Nature," "original strength / Of contemplation," and "intuitive truths" (*P*, bk. 6, line 43). This possibility appears as an epistemological black hole—"who can tell, / Who knows"—but the ensuing lines, where Wordsworth insists that the "poet's soul was with [him] at that time," turn the possible into the probable. As in book 3, Wordsworth consolidates his past and present selves, here through the figure of his youthful "dreams," some of which have been achieved and some of which remain to guide his "future life." But more important, the context of this "poet's soul" and all the trappings and poetic tools that accompany it—the "sweet meditations," the "overflow / Of Happiness and truth," the "thousand hopes"—is the disappointment that Wordsworth felt both in himself and in the education he was supposed to receive at Cambridge.

The transition from disappointment to poetic revelation is typically associated not with Wordsworth's college education—remarkable only for the fact that he completed it—but rather with *The Prelude*'s brushes with sublimity. The rationale for the journey that Wordsworth and Robert Jones took to the Alps was typical of spring breakers, what Ben Ross Schneider Jr. describes as "one more 'open slight' in a long series of open slights."[37] But while Wordsworth's reference to their "open slight / Of college cares" casts the journey as a break with the patterns of Cambridge, such a break is not forthcoming. As critics have long noted, the transition from crossing the Alps to addressing the imagination is abrupt, and overfamiliar as it may be, the passage is worth quoting in full. Wordsworth and Jones meet a "peasant" and inquire about their location:

> Hard of belief, we questioned him again,
> And all the answers which the man returned
> To our inquiries, in their sense and substance
> Translated by the feelings which we had,
> Ended in this—that we had crossed the Alps.
>
> Imagination!—lifting up itself
> Before the eye and progress of my song
> Like an unfathered vapour, here that power,
> In all the might of its endowments, came
> Athwart me. I was lost as in a cloud,
> Halted without a struggle to break through,
> And now, recovering, to my soul I say
> 'I recognize thy glory.' In such strength
> Of usurpation, in such visitings
> Of awful promise, when the light of sense
> Goes out in flashes that have shewn to us
> The invisible world, doth greatness make abode,
> There harbours whether we be young or old. (*P*, bk. 6, lines 520–537)

Out of the "deep and genuine sadness" of having crossed the Alps unknowingly emerges a reflection on the self, an assertion of individual merit: to his soul Wordsworth says "I recognise thy glory," a glory inherent in the imagination and "the might of its endowments" (*P*, bk. 6, line 528). For Geoffrey H. Hartman, this passage is foundational to the archetype of the "halted traveller," a figure he identifies throughout Wordsworth's early poetry as following roughly a "pattern of blankness and revelation." In the case of the Simplon Pass episode, Hartman fleshes out this pattern, describing how "disappointment becomes retrospectively a prophetic instance of that blindness to the external world which is the tragic, pervasive, and necessary condition of the mature poet."[38] Mark Reed sees a similar rhetorical pattern at work in the transition from disappointment to recovery at several key moments in book 6.[39] Indeed, the progression is a familiar one from far earlier with the "Boy of Windander," where disappointment at the owls' silence yields to the "gentle shock of mild surprise" that ushers in the voices and imagery of nature.

The pattern is also similar, as I have argued, to Wordsworth's rhetorical treatment of the failures of and at Cambridge, where disappointment over his cowardice and bewilderment at his place in the institution inspire sudden revelatory proclamations.[40] Thus the abrupt disjointedness of the Simplon Pass episode, which has long fascinated critics, is less an aberration and more an intrinsic feature of a repeated rhetorical pattern that binds together, somewhat unexpectedly, the university classroom and the Alpine summit, moments of academic disillusionment and reflections on the natural sublime.[41] When Coetzee associates Wordsworth with "the European posture of reader vis-à-vis environment," he is referring to the Wordsworth of the Simplon Pass, of Mount Snowdon—the Wordsworth whose poetry about these regions, following from Burke and Kant's theories of the sublime, helps codify a recognizable "posture" in which a male viewer may discover the glory of his soul amid the awful evidence of geologic force. But this posture is not just assumed in the face of European sublimity; Wordsworth also adopts it in the midst of his academic disenchantment. *Disgrace* helps reveal this similarity by situating the Alpine Wordsworth in a mediocre teacher's classroom. And while I don't think this was Coetzee's intention, the appearance of *The Prelude* in *Disgrace* thus underlines how Wordsworth's poem uses Hartman's "halted traveller" archetype to bind its construction of the Alps to its characterization of Cambridge, the spaces of sublimity to the spaces of institutional pedagogy.

Book 6 demonstrates that Wordsworthian revelations are not just the province of sublime landscapes and "natural" education; they also accompany experiences of academic disenchantment. What would happen if Lurie's students—or our students, for that matter—read this poetry of disenchantment alongside what Lurie calls "those revelatory, Wordsworthian moments we have all heard about" (*D*, 23)? His students would discover someone who, like many of them, worries about fitting in, passing his courses, disappointing his family, balancing the passions he wants to explore against the material he's required to study. They might discover that those revelatory, Wordsworthian moments bind not just the Alps to the Drakensberg but also Cambridge to Cape Technical. For it is possible that we simply don't know what Lurie's students have gained. As Coetzee points out, the sublime is not a category that lends itself to South Africa. But the realm of academic disenchantment is broad, common to most institutions of higher learning. Lurie expects his students to enjoy a "flash of revelation" when they read about Wordsworth's sublime experience in the Alps. But perhaps they have had a different Wordsworthian flash, the unexpected and abrupt flash of inspiration born of academic detachment and boredom in response to an awkward and uninspiring lecture about a mountain they have never seen.

CHAPTER 2

THE *BOERVROU* AND THE SOUTH AFRICAN FARM

In its first half, *Disgrace*'s use of Wordsworth treads a fine line, taking seriously Wordsworth's possible significance in South Africa while more visibly dismissing him as irrelevant. In its second half, which is also suffused with Wordsworth, there is no such clear critique, no evident arguments to make about Wordsworth's inapplicability in the new South Africa. There are two reasons for this shift. First, the novel's use of *The Prelude* is very different from its use of Wordsworth's Lucy poems. Lurie's scene of teaching names *The Prelude* outright and articulates the critique: "A man looking at a mountain: why does it have to be so complicated, they want to complain?" Meanwhile, the novel's use of the Lucy poems is allusive, and Wordsworth is only one of the writers alluded to. No character's trajectory is so fully structured by allusions as Lucy Lurie's. Like "coagulants at a wound," in the words of one critic, intertexts gather around her.[42] Mike Marais has focused on the allusions to Wordsworth's Lucy poems—in part because of Lucy Lurie's given name but also, and more importantly, because of her tendency to echo Wordsworth's quintessential dead child with statements like "I am a dead person and I do not know yet what will bring me back to life" (*D*, 161).[43] Yet Pamela Cooper sees not just Wordsworth but Yeats as well, and Gayatri Chakravorty Spivak spies *King Lear*, with Lucy playing Cordelia to Lurie's aging patriarch.[44] But in comparison to *The Prelude* and Byron's *Lara*, which Lurie discusses extensively with his students, *King Lear*, "Leda and the Swan," and the Lucy poems lurk just out of view, hailed not by direct references but rather by allusion. The more direct references in the novel's first part allow *Disgrace* to launch a clear critique of Wordsworth's dissemination around the Anglophone world.

Second, Wordsworth's Lucy poems occupy a very different position than the Simplon Pass episode in his corpus. That episode is, as I have mentioned, seen as being one of a few that might represent on its own Wordsworth's work. It is no wonder, then, that when Coetzee includes this passage in *Disgrace*, the discussion veers into generalizations about a monolithic version of Wordsworth and "those revelatory, Wordsworthian moments we have all heard about." In contrast, for all that critics have said about them, and in spite of their canonical status in his oeuvre, the Lucy poems remain essentially mysterious. (For instance, we still don't know who Lucy is or the precise significance of that gap in our knowledge.) While the Simplon Pass episode seems representative of Wordsworth, the Lucy poems are too gnomic to be representative, too figurative to inspire arguments about their relevance or irrelevance. Instead, the Lucy poems are important to *Disgrace* because they present and destabilize a female relationship to nature and the land, one that shapes how the second half of *Disgrace* critiques gendered affiliations with the land in post-Apartheid South Africa. This critique is founded on two interrelated historical discourses: the rise of "mother-tongue" education in white South Africa and the ideology of the *plaasroman*, or Afrikaner farm novel, a dominant genre in the first half of the twentieth century.

Coetzee is thus importing more than "Wordsworth," the English poet, when he evokes the Lucy poems in *Disgrace*. The similarities between Wordsworth's and Coetzee's Lucy figures are myriad: they share a voicelessness, an affiliation with death, a connection to nature. Yet while Wordsworth's Lucy enjoys a particularly English relationship with nature—or rather, a relationship with a version of nature that the poem's speaker thinks of as English—Lucy Lurie's connection to the land is complicated by her national heritage. As the daughter of an English professor and a Dutch mother, Lucy embodies South Africa's two colonial traditions. In turn, the historical tension between these colonizers inflects Lucy's status as woman and settler in transitional post-Apartheid South Africa. But it also inflects her textual relationship to Wordsworth's Lucy, particularly given the emphatic yet nebulous bond that the Romantic Lucy enjoys with the English landscape. When Lurie arrives at Lucy's farm, fresh from his disciplinary hearings at Cape Technical University, he finds his daughter "comfortably barefoot" (*D*, 59). After moving to the smallholding six years earlier and staying on far longer than her girlfriend or the rest of the commune, Lucy "had fallen in love with the place . . . she wanted to farm it properly" (*D*, 60). Lurie, not having seen his daughter since this transformation, realizes that she is "no longer a child playing at faming but a solid countrywoman, a *boervrou*." His recourse to Afrikaans at this moment is significant. Literally in touch with the land, with bare feet that "grip the red earth, leaving clear prints," Lucy is not a farmer but a *boervrou*, an Afrikaner, a farmer of Dutch descent (*D*, 62). This characterization makes sense given Lucy's heritage. But it seems here that her status as *boer* has more to do with her comfort and stability on the farm than with her family, for the term evokes not just the broad category of Afrikaners but more specifically the generations of Afrikaner settlers who farmed in South Africa. Lucy's ability to farm "properly" and her status as "this throwback, this sturdy young settler" qualify her for inclusion in the long line of Afrikaner settlers who preceded her (*D*, 61).

But she is a *boer* with a difference, as Lurie clarifies. She may be a "throwback," but she is also "a frontier farmer of the new breed," and this newness leads Lurie to ruminate, "History repeating itself, though in a more modest vein. Perhaps history has learned a lesson" (*D*, 62). Against Lucy's old-fashioned movement to the frontier, Lurie posits the possibility that history has accepted the sort of reeducation that Lurie himself refuses at his disciplinary hearing when a committee member suggests he seek counseling (*D*, 66). Lucy will not join the ranks of the "hereditary masters" whom Coetzee derides in his Jerusalem Prize acceptance speech (1987), whose "excessive talk, about how they love South Africa has been consistently directed toward *the land*, that is, toward what is least likely to respond to love: mountains and deserts, birds and animals and flowers."[45] Lucy, in contrast, exhibits the fraternity that Coetzee goes on to praise in his speech, making herself integral to a neighborly community composed of an old-guard German neighbor and the "dog-man" Petrus, an African farmer of the new South Africa. By the novel's conclusion, however, Lucy strikes a very different figure. In the aftermath of her assault, she decides to carry her pregnancy to term and agrees to become Petrus's third wife, if only in name, in exchange for protection. As a woman about to become a wife and a mother, Lucy's status as *boervrou* takes on new meaning. Literally translated as "farmer wife" or "farmer woman," the term *boervrou* comes to suggest that Lucy cannot, on her own, be a proper *boer*. She is always also a woman, and regardless of her own unvoiced desires—as Lurie explains to Petrus, Lucy has no interest in marrying a man—her status as a settler is so tenuous that she is willing to "be known as his third wife," "sign the land over to him," and "become a tenant" (*D*, 204). Her future status as mother will add a final layer of complexity to her relationship with the South African land, for historically, the battle between English and Afrikaner settlers that I described in this chapter's introduction was waged discursively in tropes of motherhood. These tropes were perhaps most visible during the early twentieth century, when educational norms centered on the question of language—or, as it was often framed, the question of the mother tongue.

Despite South Africa's eleven official languages, the question of language routinely boils down to a battle between Afrikaans and English even though the country's demographics favor neither of these colonial European groups.[46] The British may have claimed victory at the end of the South African War in 1902, but a virulent brand of Afrikaner nationalism became ascendant when the National Party was elected to power in 1948. Although South Africa remained part of the British Commonwealth until 1961, the cultural and political role that the British Empire played in the nation has not always been clear: "For much of the twentieth century, an exclusive form of white Afrikaner nationalism, with its explicit objective the capture of the state by the white Afrikaner 'nation,' has confronted its counterpart, a pan-South African black nationalism, which has sought the incorporation of Africans into the body politic."[47] It is against this balance—between Afrikaner nationalism on the one hand and black nationalism on the other—that British influence developed a niche. As Jonathan Jansen explains, "It is the memory of defeat at the hands of the English and the continued hegemony of English institutions and English power long after the South African War that in part explains the defense of the Afrikaans language" in the post-Apartheid era.[48] This defeat was especially violent: in the final years of the South African War, the British removed tens of thousands of Boer women and children to internment camps, destroying family homesteads, killing livestock, and rendering the land nonarable.[49]

In light of the minority stake that English holds in South Africa's panoply of languages, it is remarkable that "the most visible corpus of South African writing occurs in the English language."[50] Years after the end of Apartheid, and more than half a century after the Afrikaner Nationalist Party assumed power, English retains a cultural hegemony. But debates about the role of English in South Africa are not new by any means; education that emphasized the mother tongue was a priority for both early Dutch and British settlers.[51] For the choice of language is also the choice of culture: by the conclusion of the South African War, it was assumed that, as Colonial Administrator Alfred Milner expressed, controlling language also meant controlling "the values and traditions of which language is the medium": "Language is important, but the tone and spirit of the teaching conveyed in it is even more important."[52] In other words, the ideological intangibles that language could inculcate became more important than the language itself. It is this possession of "tone and spirit" that helps explain the turn that language education took in the 1920s, when dual-language education (which emphasized both English and Afrikaans) began to fall out of favor, especially among Afrikaners, many of whom worried "that when the two language groups were together in the same school, one culture would be swamped by the other."[53] The easy movement between language groups and the swamping culture they imply clearly belongs to the same line of thought that assumes language to inspire a distinctive set of values and traditions. In that formulation, language may be a medium, but it is a medium for a cultural hegemony that inheres in the language itself.

That cultural power is perhaps most evident in the discourse of the mother tongue, a phrase that historically has served as a shorthand for debates about language education in twentieth-century South Africa. It's telling, for instance, that while *mother tongue* most obviously invokes one's native language, it also has a more strictly pedagogical definition, one that has been particularly common in South Africa.[54] Historically, mother-tongue education—schooling that takes place in the student's native language—developed in reaction to the South African War. But subsequently, schooling became the primary method of denationalizing the battered Afrikaner population in the Transvaal: "English was made the sole medium of instruction. The Dutch language was to be taught only at the request of parents and then for not more than three hours per week." It's from this policy that historians date "the determination to have the principle of mother-tongue instruction enshrined in the matrix of all educational endeavour."[55] In the end, this determination found its way into the National Education Policy Act of 1967, which stipulated, among other things, that in state-run schools, "the mother tongue, if it is English or Afrikaans, shall be the medium of instruction."[56]

The memory of British enormities became an integral part of Afrikaner identity in the aftermath of the war (and to a certain degree, that history continues to inform Afrikaner culture in contemporary South Africa). Isabel Hofmeyr points to this memory when she discusses the cultural role Afrikaner women were called upon to play in the postwar era: "Women were after all the ones who were going to socialise children as Afrikaners, and it was not for nothing that Afrikaans was so frequently called 'the mother tongue.'"[57] Hofmeyr's statement further narrows the meaning of *mother tongue* in the context of South Africa—not just education in the child's native language but socialization in the Afrikaner tradition. In the twentieth century, then, English became less a potential mother tongue and more a requirement enforced from without. For "the supreme importance to developing communities of an 'access language'—a world language—unsettles the generally axiomatic proposition that a child should be educated in its mother-tongue."[58] Of course, this dynamic is partly a product of how the British and Dutch Empires developed and waned respectively in the late nineteenth and twentieth centuries, of the fact that English became a "world language" and Dutch did not. But the dynamic between Afrikaans and English also owes its staying power to the Afrikaner nationalism that grew out of the South African War and the persistence of a British cultural hegemony even in contemporary South Africa.

The role motherhood played in the cultural battle between English and Afrikaans is important to *Disgrace* because it underscores the change Lucy undergoes when she finds herself pregnant. Instead of a single, childless, queer individual who sells "flowers and garden produce" at the local market, Lucy becomes via motherhood a throwback of a different kind: a body on which is inscribed the historical tension between English and Dutch settlers, a cultural battle between dueling cultures and mother tongues waged by ideologies of motherhood (*D*, 61).[59] Moreover, as the white mother of a child who will be of mixed race, Lucy is freighted with further significance, becoming a diagram of South Africa's intersecting racial categories—as much a motif of diversity as a full-fledged character. Understandably, perhaps, this particular plot was not well received in South Africa. The African National Congress (ANC) faulted Coetzee for depicting "as brutally as he can the white people's perception of the post-apartheid black man," creating a world in which "the white women will have to sleep with the barbaric black men." Nadine Gordimer agreed, saying that in the novel, "there is not one black person who is a real human being."[60] Petrus might be a more real and interesting character than Gordimer allows, but the criticism stands. Coetzee paints a grim picture that trades on familiar stereotypes of black male sexuality, as Lucy's child will weave together divergent lines of white and black ancestry into a model of multiculturalism while also being the product of a rape that casts black men as animalistic violators of white femininity. Yet Lucy's fate is not quite the cynical and racist comment on diversity in South Africa that it might seem. Her pregnancy and her decision to marry Petrus alter her relationship to the land, sharpening the novel's commentary on the *plaasroman*. In alluding to Wordsworth's Lucy poems, *Disgrace* mirrors the *plaasroman*'s reliance on commonplace tropes of British Romanticism, revealing the tenacious and perverted grip of this outdated genre on a rapidly changing landscape.

As Coetzee explains in *White Writing*, "The Afrikaans novel concerned itself almost exclusively with the farm and *platteland* (rural) society" between 1920 and 1940 (*WW*, 63).[61] In the *plaasroman*, the relationship between farmer and farm achieved an idealized form, based less on the practical realities of land ownership and more on the affective bond of love, with the farmer acting as dutiful and monogamous husband to the land. Yet as Coetzee clarifies, the marriage is an institution that extends well beyond the life span of the farmer, for it unites not so much the farmer as his lineage to the feminized farm (*WW*, 86). Lineage is thus the major romantic partner to the land, and the farm is "inscribed with the signs of the lineage: with evidences of labour and with bones in the earth" (*WW*, 109). In the buried remains of his ancestors, in the daily labor he performs, and in the children he produces, the farmer unites past, present, and future in his bond with the farm. The farmer's awareness of his ability to link past and future is, in Coetzee's account, his "lineal consciousness," a consciousness that expands the farmer's self beyond the parameters of his own birth and death. (This account is a somewhat personal one for Coetzee. In *Boyhood*, he devotes many pages to his family's farm, insisting, "The farm is greater than any of them. The farm exists from eternity to eternity. When they are all dead, when even the farmhouse has fallen into ruin like the kraals on the hillside, the farm will still be here.")[62] So long as the farmer's lineage continues, and continues on the farm, his self may be thought to continue as well.

With its idealized relationship between man and nature, the *plaasroman* is, according to Coetzee, indebted to several of Romanticism's broad ideologies. (I should say that as someone who doesn't know Afrikaans, I am not in a position to assess Coetzee's association between the *plaasroman* and Romanticism and am thus merely interested in the frequency with which he mentions the association.) On a basic level, Coetzee senses that "into the myth of the good farmer and his marriage with his farm are drawn many of the energies of European Romanticism" (*WW*, 87). More specifically, in his chapter on the Afrikaner novelist C. M. van den Heever, Coetzee mentions Romanticism several times, suggesting that van den Heever's novels use the "Romantic commonplace about the recovery of man's truth in nature" to argue that "the Afrikaner will lose his independence and (eventually) his identity if he loses his base in landownership" (*WW*, 110). Coetzee similarly sees van den Heever's novels building toward moments of stillness "in which the truth comes to the subject," as in Romantic poetry, for which such moments "are of course the raison d'être . . . occurring as Wordsworthian 'spots of time' in the life of the soul" (*WW*, 97).[63] Based on such examples, it is not surprising to learn here that Coetzee's Romanticism is a Wordsworthian Romanticism. "Moments of stillness and intensity in which the truth comes to the subject" may as well be describing the "Boy of Winander" or the Simplon crossing passage. Similarly, Coetzee's description of Romanticism's tendency to "divide the world of the real into a realm possessed of significance (nature, the country, the farm) and a realm of chaos (the city)" presents a Romanticism centered firmly on *The Prelude* and not, for instance, on *Don Juan* or Keats's odes or *Eighteen Hundred and Eleven* (*WW*, 113). In Coetzee's view, van den Heever's novels are so indebted to Wordsworth that Wordsworth's major character types must be accounted for: "In the scheme of persons I have sketched [in van den Heever's novels], there is one hiatus. Where is the representative of Wordsworth's shepherd, a person unreflectively at one with nature?" (*WW*, 109). This commentary is not particularly important—or convincing—as a reading of Wordsworth: in *Michael*, it is arguable that the shepherd is "at one with nature," but his oneness hardly seems unreflective. As a reading of the *plaasroman*, however, the statement reveals that in Coetzee's conception, the genre is so Wordsworthian that he expects to see Wordsworthian figures at every turn.

With Lucy Lurie, Coetzee treads a fine line between rejecting and perverting the conventions of the *plaasroman*, a genre concerned with the relationship between specifically white men and the land—a genre, according to Coetzee, whose ideologies stem from not just Romanticism but Wordsworth's most canonical works in particular. I will discuss in the final section of this chapter how Coetzee's decision to echo Wordsworth's Lucy (as opposed to a Michael-like figure more "at one with nature") produces a new, if deeply troubled, model for imagining the relationship between women and the natural environment. Here, I want simply to point out how the details of Lucy Lurie's fate simultaneously underscore, warp, and circumvent the norms established by the *plaasroman*. Coetzee's earlier works foreshadow this variety of responses. While in *White Writing*, Coetzee assumes the voice of a relatively cool academic, eschewing the opportunity to critique overtly the political underpinnings of the farm novel genre, elsewhere he has been more open and, at the same time, more contradictory. As I have mentioned, in *Boyhood* the *plaasroman* provides the blueprint for his representation of his youthful affection for the family's farm, one as deeply felt as the love of one of van den Heever's protagonists. As he explains, "The secret and sacred word that binds him to the farm is *belong*," a word that leads him to think "*I belong on the farm*" and then "*I belong to the farm*." This final iteration is the most dangerous because *belong* "is misunderstood so easily, turned so easily into its inverse: *The farm belongs to me*."[64] These memories reveal the difficulty in achieving the sort of relationship with the land promoted by the *plaasroman*; exchanging the nouns in a sentence like "I belong to the farm" shifts a loving bond into a possessive one. At the same time, as Jennifer Wenzel explains, Coetzee is here "appropriating for his own life story some of the tropes of Afrikaner relationships to land that he has criticized in his earlier work."[65] As we have seen, Coetzee has little patience for those South Africans whose "excessive talk . . . about how they love South Africa has been consistently directed toward *the land*" rather than toward people capable of reciprocating love. It is easy to love the land, and it is easy to want to love the land. But according to Coetzee, it is also insufficient and almost beside the point to love the land in a nation that for decades legislated against love between races.

The critique is as just as complex in *Disgrace*. At first, Lucy seems specifically designed to repudiate the *plaasroman* marriage metaphor, in which marriage is necessarily heterosexual, binding together the patrilineal line of male farmer and his feminized land. Lucy is a woman—a woman who has, in the past, preferred women to men. At the beginning of the novel, then, Lucy's gender and her desire ensure that her relationship to the farm cannot take the form established by the *plaasroman*, which provides no model for imagining the ideal bond between a single, queer woman and the arable land. This renunciation of the genre's central trope also emerges in Lucy's reluctance to dub her land a farm: "This is not a farm, it's just a piece of land where I grow things" (*D*, 200).[66] However, the effects of the rape—the pregnancy Lucy chooses to carry to term, her fears for her future safety, her decision to marry a man—pervert the norms of the *plaasroman* rather than simply renouncing them. It is true that, as Jane Poyner has pointed out, Lucy's decision to accept Petrus "violates the sanctity of the Afrikaner *vrou en molder* (wife and mother) and the taboo of miscegenation."[67] Yet Lucy's reasoning reveals that marriage will allow Petrus, a black farmer, to enter into a relationship with the farm that was previously reserved for white Afrikaners, for the marriage that Petrus proposes numbers as its participants not Petrus and Lucy but rather Petrus and the farm. As Lucy bluntly states, "It is not me he is after, he is after the farm" (*D*, 203). She understands that what Petrus offers is not marriage but "an alliance, a deal" in which she "contributes the land" and in return is "allowed to creep under his wing." The imagery here suggests not just protection but also invisibility: under Petrus's wing, Lucy will be safe from future attacks because she will effectively disappear. This invisibility also emerges in Lucy's acceptance of a diminished and ambiguous role in her future family, in which she envisions a position somewhere between "third wife" and "concubine" (*D*, 204). The arrangement is, as Lurie protests, at the very least unorthodox, if not entirely self-abnegating. The threat of miscegenation and polygamy would seem to distance *Disgrace* from the *plaasroman*, which assumes the whiteness of its subjects and their dutiful monogamy. Indeed, toward the beginning of *Disgrace*, Petrus's position is rather low within the hierarchy of the farm. When Lucy first mentions him, she calls him her "new assistant," quickly correcting herself to "co-proprietor" to afford him a bit more authority (*D*, 62). By the novel's end, she directs her father, "Tell him I give up the land. Tell him that he can have it, title deed and all. He will love that" (*D*, 205). Petrus will love owning the land—holding the deed, Lucy says—but perhaps he might also love the farm itself.

By the novel's end, David Lurie has almost developed the lineal consciousness that Coetzee argues is characteristic of the *plaasroman*. Watching Lucy in the fields one day, he thinks, "Once she was only a little tadpole in her mother's body. . . . When he is dead she will, with luck, still be here doing her ordinary tasks among the flowerbeds. And from within her will have issued another existence, that with luck will be just as solid, just as long-lasting. So it will go on, a line of existences in which his share, his gift, will grow inexorably less and less" (*D*, 217). It is as close as Lurie gets to being content with his daughter's fate. She will keep living after he dies; her child will still live once she is gone. This continuation is the basis for the *plaasroman* marriage trope, which, as Coetzee reminds us, binds not the farmer but rather his legacy to the farm. Lucy's pregnancy and Petrus's offer of protection give Lurie a consciousness that most city boys never experience. Perhaps unsurprisingly, however, Lurie's lineal consciousness is incomplete. He ends his reverie by reflecting that "his share, his gift, will grow inexorably less and less." This is true but also irrelevant; what matters to the farm is not the individual but the family line. Yet Lurie's sense of becoming "less and less," as solipsistic as it is, should direct our attention to Lucy, a character who does become less and less in this lineage. As she disappears under Petrus's wing, Lucy fades out of the *plaasroman* that once seemed repudiated by her very existence. Lineal consciousness may include women, and may even depend on the reproductive capabilities of women, but it is not for women. The distorted *plaasroman* in which Lucy finds herself a minor figure is still, by definition, dominated by men: all discussions of marriage occur between Lurie and Petrus.

What Coetzee suggests in *Disgrace* is that old forms, like the *plaasroman* and the ideologies it reflected, cannot simply be cast off. Lucy certainly tries when she decides to farm the smallholding on her own. But continuing on the farm means entering into an imaginary whose outmodedness belies its staying power, an imaginary that might stretch to accommodate certain constituents of the new South Africa, like Petrus, while not embracing others, like Lucy. The debt that Coetzee thinks the *plaasroman* owes to Wordsworthian tropes should give us pause. What relevance can the theme of men finding truth in nature have in this rapidly changing nation, when the theme cannot be stretched to fit both black and female South Africans? Against such tropes, however, presses *Disgrace*'s use of Wordsworth's Lucy poems. As Lucy Lurie is hailed into a modern *plaasroman*, she evokes not Wordsworth's Michael, "at one with nature," but rather Wordsworth's Lucy, caught in the speaker's self-consciously inadequate system of representation in which her relation to nature and the nation is both fundamental and profoundly ambiguous. The bond between these female figures prevents Coetzee's Lucy from becoming merely an emblem of diversity and thus a cipher for South Africa: Lucy Lurie's character is built in conversation with the silence of Wordsworth's Lucy. The Lucy poems signify widely in *Disgrace*; each poem in the series earns its own echoes. But the complex relationship that Lucy Lurie has to her land, and to South Africa, directs our attention particularly to "I travelled among unknown men," the only Lucy poem to name the nation as England.

THE FINAL SURVEY OF ENGLAND

Whether or not it is wise for a Wordsworth scholar to name his daughter Lucy, Coetzee's repurposing of Wordsworth's lyrics begins with this fact: David Lurie, who counts Wordsworth among his "masters," has a daughter with the same name as Wordsworth's most famous dead girl. The two Lucys have much in common.[68] Yet the most significant overlaps are not on the level of content but rather form. As Mike Marais points out, the narrative structure of both Wordsworth's poems and *Disgrace* problematize Lucy's silence. In spite of the difference in point of view—the poems use a lyric "I" while *Disgrace* is narrated in the third person—neither Wordsworth nor Coetzee provide their readers with information beyond the consciousness of their protagonists. So when Lucy Lurie's refusal to report the rape to the police frustrates her father, it frustrates us as well; other characters, like Bev Shaw, may know more about Lucy's rationale, but the narrative is not focalized through Bev Shaw. When Lurie asks his daughter why she isn't "telling the whole story," she maddeningly replies, "I have told the whole story. The whole story is what I have told," quickly draining the content from Lurie's question with her repetitions (*D*, 110). And as Bev Shaw reminds Lurie, he wasn't there during Lucy's attack; locked in the bathroom and knocked unconscious, Lurie has no direct knowledge of what the "whole story" might be (*D*, 140). In Marais's view, "It is exactly this representational tension between presence and absence that the allusions to the Lucy poems in *Disgrace* invoke."[69] If the rape of Lucy Lurie exceeds the epistemology of *Disgrace*'s limited narrator, then in Wordsworth's poems, Lucy's death lies beyond the representational powers of the poems' speaker, as a lyric like "a slumber did my spirit seal" would suggest.

The break between these two stanzas is perhaps the most fraught in Wordsworth's corpus:

> A slumber did my spirit seal;
> I had no human fears:
> She seemed a thing that could not feel
> The touch of earthly years.
>
> No motion has she now, no force;
> She neither hears nor sees;
> Rolled round in earth's diurnal course,
> With rocks, and stones, and trees. (*PW*, 2:216, lines 1–8)

Many shifts occur in this poem, most of them, as de Man says, "hidden in the blank space between the two stanzas."[70] The past gives way to the present of "now," the speaker must revive from "slumber" to revise his initial assessment of what Lucy "seemed," Lucy becomes more truly a "thing" in death, dwelling "with rocks, and stones, and trees."[71] The second stanza is certainly light on plot: the speaker has achieved enough wisdom to recognize the error of his former judgment, but many blanks—the name of the girl, how she died—are never filled in. Nevertheless, by sequestering the speaker's mistaken understanding and his later realizations in separate, almost autonomous stanzas, the poem ensures that the gaps in the speaker's knowledge will exist not just as a feature of the poem's plot, such as it is, but as its overarching structure.

Such epistemological gaps are common in Wordsworth's early lyrics. "Old man travelling" (1798), for example, dramatizes the inability of the speaker, a confident peripatetic, to bridge the gap between himself and an aging passerby, whom the speaker interprets as "insensibly subdued / To settled quiet" and so patient that "patience now doth seem a thing of which / He hath no need" (*PW*, 4:247, lines 7–8, 11–12).[72] But the speaker's understanding is proven wrong when the man speaks: "Sir! I am going many miles to take / A last leave of my son, a mariner, / Who from a sea-fight has been brought to Falmouth, / And there is dying in an hospital."[73] The poem ends without further word from the speaker. The old man whom he understood to be "subdued" and peaceful is revealed—through the man's own words—to be in the midst of an arduous and mournful journey. It is precisely in the importance of the man's own words that "Old man travelling" parts ways with the Lucy poems. In "Old man travelling," the man is permitted to speak for himself with as little mediation as a first-person poem can muster when presenting the words of others.[74] In "A slumber did my spirit seal," wisdom is born not of any living voice but of the blank space between the stanzas. Voiceless and characterless, the unnamed Lucy never becomes more than a viewed object. She lacks "motion" and "force," or to be more accurate, she only achieves them passively, in death, as she is "rolled round in Earth's diurnal course." While the temporal "now" in the second stanza would seem to suggest that prior to her death, Lucy possessed some agency or activity, the first stanza hints at none. In fact, the only movement in the poem occurs in the grave, wherein Lucy is tossed "with rocks, and stones, and trees" as the days tick reliably by. The relationship of the speaker to Lucy in "A slumber did my spirit seal" thus remains that of a subject to an object, self to other.

Disgrace takes up this tension between speaking subject and silent object during one of Lucy and David's arguments about the attack. While the contents of "the whole story" that David exhorts Lucy to tell remain shadowy, Lucy approaches the construction of her violent history with the precision of a narratologist, analyzing the narrative rather than reporting the chronology of events: "You behave as if everything I do is part of the story of your life. You are the main character, I am a minor character" (*D*, 198). As Wordsworth's Lucy is the object to the speaker's subject, so Coetzee's Lucy is the secondary character to Lurie's protagonist, and she knows it. (Or to put this in the terms of the *plaasroman*, Lucy is a *vrou* in a novel interpolating the ghostly remnants of a genre uninterested in female characters.)

As many readers have noted, the task that Lurie undertakes in the second half of *Disgrace* is a sympathetic one: he must learn to identify with the parents of his student Melanie, with the dogs that he and Bev Shaw euthanize at her makeshift veterinary clinic, and most of all, with Lucy in the aftermath of her attack.[75] Imagining his daughter's assault, "he can, if he concentrates . . . be the men, inhabit them, fill them with the ghost of himself. The question is, does he have it in him to be the woman?" (*D*, 160). Lurie's question, whether he has it in him to "be the woman," would seem to be answered by the fate of his opera on Byron, which, by the novel's conclusion, has become an opera about Teresa, wife of Count Guiccioli, set long after the demise of her affair with Byron. By shifting focus from canonical Romantic poet to discarded and forgotten woman, Lurie shows some aptitude for the project of being the woman, or at least a willingness to try. And moments before querying the limits of his sympathy, Lurie succeeds in imagining what might have happened to his daughter as she was raped: "Lucy was frightened, frightened near to death. Her voice choked, she could not breathe, her limbs went numb. *This is not happening*, she said to herself as the men forced her down; *it is just a dream, a nightmare*" (*D*, 160, emphasis in the original). Yet the order of operations calls the education of Lurie's sympathetic imagination into question. It is only *after* he imagines Lucy's thoughts during her attack that Lurie wonders if "he [has] it in him to be the woman." And his subsequent task—writing Lucy a note in which he informs her "You are on the brink of a dangerous error" and "You wish to humble yourself before history"—hints that his ability to identify with Lucy remains limited. Like Wordsworth's peripatetic, convinced of the old man's patience and tranquility, Lurie misreads his daughter or, as she suggests in her response, he mis*sees* her: "All I know is that I cannot go away [from the farm.] You do not see this, and I do not know what more I can do to make you see. It is as if you have chosen deliberately to sit in a corner where the rays of the sun do not shine. I think of you as one of the three chimpanzees, the one with his paws over his eyes" (*D*, 161). Lucy's retort, which uses a variety of metaphors to demonstrate the poverty of Lurie's vision, connects the power of sight to the imaginative task that Lurie undertakes. The conclusion we might draw from Lurie's question—Does he have it in him to be the woman?—and his ensuing conversation with Lucy is that being the woman depends on sense of sight; to be reductive, the most apt cliché is not "walk a mile in her shoes" but rather "see the world through her eyes." Of all the senses, imagination in this formulation depends most on vision. And it is Lucy Lurie's emphasis here on the importance of sight that bends us back toward the Lucy poems, in particular "I travelled among unknown men," the only one of the series to imagine that a world, perhaps even a different one, existed through Lucy's eyes.

Composed in Germany two years after the other poems in the Lucy series, "I travelled among unknown men" was not published until 1807. (It is worth mentioning that Wordsworth did not group the poems in a series himself; we have Matthew Arnold, among others, to thank for that.)[76] Given its composition history, it is not surprising that it alone of the Lucy poems expresses national longing, addressing the nation directly and affiliating Lucy with not just nature but rather the natural world of England:

I travelled among unknown men,
    In lands beyond the sea;
Nor, England! did I know till then
    What love I bore to thee.

'Tis past, that melancholy dream!
    Nor will I quit thy shore
A second time; for still I seem
    To love thee more and more.

Among thy mountains did I feel
    The joy of my desire;
And she I cherished turned her wheel
    Beside an English fire.

Thy mornings showed, thy nights concealed,
    The bowers where Lucy played;

And thine too is the last green field
 That Lucy's eyes surveyed. (*PW*, 2:30–31, lines 1–16)

This poem is not the only in the series to introduce a third party into the relationship between speaker and Lucy. While "Three years she grew in sun and shower" interpolates the voice of nature, "I travelled among unknown men" pairs the speaker with two entangled loves, Lucy and England. But what exactly Wordsworth means to suggest with his references to England is unclear. For Frances Ferguson, England is "not the England of men, but the England of nature"—so much so that *nature* and *England* become almost interchangeable terms in her treatment of the poem.[77] For Pamela Woof, England is Great Britain, such that "the poet makes his vows of love . . . to a place, and to a nation," ending the poem on a note of "national and permanent piety."[78] It may seem obvious to say that England is probably a bit of both. Yet that imbrication of England as landscape and England as nation is precisely what we see if we understand Wordsworth's Lucy as an otherworldly precursor to Lucy Lurie, whose relationship with the land is always also a relationship with the nation.

"I travelled among unknown men" constructs its addressee, England, in direct opposition to other lands, fashioning it as ideally distinct and isolated. Yet when the poem's speaker begins to list the natural features of this England, the distinctness and specificity begin to fade. Key to the initial construction of England is Wordsworth's emphasis in the first two stanzas on the "sea" and "shore." In the next chapter, we shall see Wordsworth in *The Excursion* construing England as "the blessed Isle, / . . . the seat / Impregnable of Liberty and Peace," a familiar formulation in which England's status as "isle" is connected to her "impregnable" nature (*E*, bk. 8, 145–147). The sea isolates and protects. Similarly, here "unknown men" are sequestered in "lands beyond the sea," while the speaker vows, "Nor will I quit thy shore." He remains safely in England while other men and other lands lurk at a watery distance. The movement that water both embodies and enables makes it a shifty signifier, equally capable of signaling connectivity and isolation, and the symbolic valence of the sea—and waterways more broadly—morphed for Wordsworth during his career, as I detail in chapter 3. Yet here, in 1801, the sea is a separator, an imaginative waste and geographic barrier that makes England legible as a distinct national home.

At the same time, the natural features that Wordsworth finds lovable in England are sometimes so banal as to seem universal. Because of the direct address to England, all the elements of nature that Wordsworth mentions appear as possessions: "thy shore," "thy mountains." Fine: shores and mountains are distinctive features of England's geography, and the "bowers" and "green field" of the concluding stanza evoke a typically English picturesque landscape. But other English possessions in the poem seem more tenuous. What is English about "an English fire"? What about "thy mornings" and "thy nights"? Do they have some uniquely English quality beyond the ubiquitous ability of mornings and nights to show and conceal? In these moments, the Englishness of the scene becomes less a "plenitudinous presence" in its own right and more what Homi K. Bhabha refers to as the belated effect of England's contact with other nations and cultures: *Englishness* lacks a stable definition, a "plenitudinous presence," and instead exists only in contrast to the "other" of British India, in Bhabha's formulation (or Germany, in the case of this poem).[79] There is nothing particularly English about fires, mornings, and nights to make them recognizable and definitional features of a landscape. It is only after the difference between England and "lands beyond the sea" has been established that these natural features can appear as attributes of the speaker's beloved home. Defining occurrences as English is thus simultaneous with loving them: each action is only possible after the speaker has repudiated other lands.

In *Disgrace*, Lucy's resistance to the old tropes of relating to the land and thus to the nation do not prevent her from being interpellated into an ideology of male belonging that has outlasted the Apartheid state. She wants her farm to be not a farm so much as "a piece of land where I grow things," but a farm it is, and a farm it shall stay when it becomes the object of Petrus's duty and devotion. What, then, of Wordsworth's Lucy, her relationship to nature and thus to England? It is common to discuss the overlap between Lucy and nature: Geoffrey Hartman calls Lucy a "boundary being," nature and human but "not quite either," and Frances Ferguson construes nature as a "substitute lover" for the speaker in Lucy's demise.[80] This overlap becomes more complex in "I travelled among unknown men," where, as we have seen, it is also difficult to distinguish nature from England. The speaker loves England; the speaker loves Lucy. In this algebra, Lucy and England seem interchangeable, bound by their shared status as objects of the speaker's love. Or rather, this is the case until the poem's final stanza. To this point, the poem has been dominated by verbs that reveal the speaker's affect: *love, feel, cherish*. As it concludes, however, the poem shifts into the visual realm. Mornings show and nights conceal, presumably for the eyes of the speaker but also possibly for Lucy's. And with its last word, *surveyed*, the poem bestows upon Lucy, if posthumously, a sense of sight, a point of view distinct from that of the speaker.[81]

In its context, *survey* signifies little more than seeing. Yet within this visual realm, Wordsworth often deployed the term to signal the view an observer might achieve atop a hill or mountain.[82] This association between surveying and altitude is fitting during the era of Britain's first national ordnance survey, when mountain summits gave mapmakers the triangulations necessary for precise measurements.

As Ron Broglio writes, it is from a summit that land can be officially surveyed and thus brought "under the eye of the nation."[83] It is notable, then, that the survey Lucy enjoys at the conclusion of "I travelled among unknown men" benefits from no elevation. In the previous stanza, the speaker has bounded among mountains and has felt there "the joy of my desire." Yet Lucy lacks the elevation for such a survey, inhabiting lower altitudes, geographies that nurture bowers and fields. Unlike the speaker, whose desire for England reaches its apex when he is among her summits and can bring a vaster expanse of the landscape into view, Lucy's survey is limited and partial.[84] The "bowers where Lucy played" are continually hidden and revealed by earth's diurnal course, and the survey she achieves of the green field only occurs at the poem's very end, when the view is the last she sees before death.

And yet, of all the Lucy poems, "I travelled among unknown men" is the only one to afford Lucy the position of a viewing subject, however briefly. Like Lucy Lurie, who knows herself to be more than a secondary character in her father's narrative, more than an illegible object on whom interpretations can be attempted, Wordsworth's Lucy achieves sight and all that it often implies in Wordsworth's early lyrics: a subjectivity usually reserved for the speaker, the possibility of interpreting one's place in nature, and perhaps even what Coetzee calls the "quintessentially European posture of reader vis-à-vis environment" (*WW*, 62). It is insufficient, though, to refer to Lucy's sight in this poem as brief. It is more than brief, consisting of barely a breath in the time of the poem: "And thine too is the last green field / That Lucy's eyes surveyed." In the poem's version of events, Lucy's survey is coterminous with her death and is always already the last one, the event that signals her ceasing to exist.

Compared with the visions of Britain that Wordsworth developed later in his career, in *The Excursion* and the *Guide to the Lakes*, the isle of "I travelled among unknown men" seems uncomplicated: England is isolated, loveable, and green; it seems to exemplify Margaret Atwood's assertion that England's central, unifying symbol is "The Island."[85] But what feeling does Lucy bear for England? The content of her survey—what she actually sees, what it looks like to her, whether it is loveable or English—is simultaneously the poem's final concern and what it cannot record. The circumference has been tightly drawn around England, but through Lucy's eyes the view is uncharted, somewhere in the blank below the poem. The "whole story" that Lucy Lurie says she's told, what it means to "be the woman," is more than *Disgrace* can represent. But unrepresentable is not the same as nonexistent. The existence of Lucy's story, the tale we can only imagine it to tell about a woman loving the land in the new South Africa, is sharpened by, and sharpens in return, the last sight that Wordsworth's Lucy takes of England.

NOTES

1 Rita Barnard, "J. M. Coetzee's *Disgrace* and the South African Pastoral," *Contemporary Literature* 44, no. 2 (2003): 216. This line of thought is also pursued by Zoë Wicomb, "Translations in the Yard of Africa," *Journal of Literary Studies* 18, nos. 3–4 (2002): 216; and Kimberly Wedeven Segall, "Pursuing Ghosts: The Traumatic Sublime in J. M. Coetzee's *Disgrace*," *Research in African Literatures* 36, no. 4 (2005): 42.

2 Later in the essay, Coetzee points out how his aesthetic judgment is in line with other non-Europeans like William Cullen Bryant, whose 1832 poem "The Prairies" opens by describing the American prairies of the midwest as "gardens of the desert" "for which the speech of England has no name." Bryant, *The Poetical Works* (New York: D. Appleton, 1903), 130.

3 David Attwell, "Introduction," *Current Writing: Text and Reception in Southern Africa* 5, no. 2 (1993): 1. The other main proponent is Leon de Kock. Many critics have poked holes in their commitment to postcolonial theory; the clearest critique is in Nicholas Visser, "Postcoloniality of a Special Type: Theory and Its Appropriations in South Africa," *Yearbook of English Studies* 27 (1997): 84–89.

4 Annamaria Carusi, "Post, Post and Post: Or, Where Is South African Literature in All This?," *ARIEL* 20, no. 4 (1989): 81.

5 Laura Chrisman, "The Imperial Unconscious? Representations of Imperial Discourse," *Critical Quarterly* 32, no. 3 (1990): 40; Benita Parry, "Problems in Current Theories of Colonial Discourse," *Oxford Literary Review* 9, nos. 1–2 (1987): 34.

6 Quoted in Visser, "Postcoloniality of a Special Type," 79.

7 Louise Viljoen, "Postcolonialism and Recent Women's Writing in Afrikaans," *World Literature Today* 70, no. 1 (1996): 64. See also Carusi, "Post, Post and Post," 80; Rosemary Jolly, "Rehearsals of Liberation: Contemporary Postcolonial Discourse and the New South Africa," *PMLA* 110, no. 1 (1995): 22.

8 Jolly, "Rehearsals of Liberation," 22.

9 Louise Bethlehem, "In the Between: Time, Space, Text in Recent South African Literary Theory," *English in Africa* 27, no. 1 (2000): 152.

10 Viljoen, "Postcolonialism and Recent Women's Writing," 63; Kelwyn Sole, "South Africa Passes the Posts," *Alternation (Durban)* 4, no. 1 (1997): 145.

11 As Benita Parry argues, "The principles around which novelistic meaning is organized in Coetzee's fictions owe nothing to knowledges which are *not* of European provenance." Parry, "Speech and Silence in the Fictions of J. M. Coetzee," in *Writing South Africa: Literature, Apartheid, and Democracy, 1970–1996*, ed. Derek Attridge and Rosemary Jolly (Cambridge: Cambridge University Press, 1998), 150.

12 Bethlehem, "In the Between," 153.

13 *P*, bk. 6, lines 29–30 (citations from the 1805 version unless otherwise noted).

14 Jennifer Wenzel, "The Pastoral Promise and the Political Imperative: The *Plaasroman* Tradition in an Era of Land Reform," *Modern Fiction Studies* 46, no. 1 (2000): 105.

15 In a discussion of autobiographical fictions, Coetzee dubbed this technique "*autre*biography," in which the protagonist self is held at a safe remove, as much *autre* as self. In *Boyhood* and *Youth*, he achieves this distance partly through the use of third-person voice. See Coetzee, *Doubling the Point: Essays and Interviews*, ed. David Attwell (Cambridge, Mass.: Harvard University Press, 1992), 394.

16 Coetzee's essays on animals, for instance, or the South African landscape complement his treatment of these subjects in *Disgrace*. As Imraan Coovadia states, Coetzee "borrows the

themes of his narratives from questions raised in contemporary theory about such matters as signification, subjectivity, and colonial subordination." Coovadia, "Coetzee in and out of Cape Town," *Kritika Kultura* 18 (2012): 109.

17 J. M. Coetzee, *Boyhood: Scenes from Provincial Life* (New York: Viking, 1997), 105.

18 Pieter Vermeulen, "Wordsworth and the Recollection of South Africa," in *J. M. Coetzee in Context and Theory*, ed. Elleke Boehmer et al. (London: Continuum, 2009), 52.

19 Alan Liu, *Wordsworth: The Sense of History* (Stanford, Calif.: Stanford University Press, 1989); David Bromwich, *Disowned by Memory: Wordsworth's Poetry of the 1790s* (Chicago: University of Chicago Press, 1998).

20 *MS*, 65.

21 Aaron Eastley, "Naipaul's Children: Representations of Humor and Ruin in 'Miguel Street,'" *Journal of Caribbean Literatures* 5, no. 2 (2008): 52–53; quoted in Scott Winokur, "The Unsparing Vision of V. S. Naipaul," in *Conversations with V. S. Naipaul*, ed. Feroza F. Jussawalla (Jackson: University Press of Mississippi, 1997), 118.

22 Other critics interpret Lurie's pedagogy more generously than I do. See Gary Hawkins, "Clerk in a Post-religious Age: Reading Lurie's Remnant Romantic Temperament in *Disgrace*" and Daniel Kiefer, "Sympathy for the Devil: On the Perversity of Teaching *Disgrace*," in *Encountering Disgrace: Reading and Teaching Coetzee's Novel*, ed. William E. McDonald (Rochester, N.Y.: Camden House, 2009), 148–172; 264–275.

23 This perversion is especially acute in light of the educational reforms of the post-Apartheid era. The Higher Education Act of 1997 (passed two years before the publication of *Disgrace*) focused in part on "developing a new kind of 'institutional culture' which is learning centred, eschews racism and sexism, and guarantees the safety of all (but with special attention to women) on campus." The language of this act is standard for a nondiscrimination policy. Yet its particular attention to racism and the safety of women draws attention to Lurie's transgression because Melanie, whom he prefers to call "the dark one," is a Coloured student. Teboho Moja and Fred M. Hayward, "Higher Education Policy Development in Contemporary South Africa," in *Implementing Education Policies: The South African Experience*, ed. Yusuf Sayed and Jonathan D. Jansen (Cape Town: University of Cape Town Press, 2001), 118.

24 *OED Online*, s.v. "usurp," http://www.oed.com/view/Entry/220720 (accessed November 7, 2016).

25 Ortwin de Graef, "Suffering, Sympathy, Circulation: Smith, Wordsworth, Coetzee," *European Journal of English Studies* 7, no. 3 (2003): 329.

26 Ben Ross Schneider Jr., *Wordsworth's Cambridge Education* (Cambridge: Cambridge University Press, 1957).

27 Julia Sandstrom Carlson, "The Map at the Limits of His Paper: A Cartographic Reading of *The Prelude*, Book 6: 'Cambridge and the Alps,'" *Studies in Romanticism* 49, no. 3 (2010): 376; Liu, *Sense of History*, 4.

28 In the 1850 version of the *Prelude*, Wordsworth italicizes the revelation "that we had crossed the Alps," intensifying the pique.

29 Inspired by Anna Laetitia Barbauld's *Lessons for Children*, Maria and Richard Edgeworth wrote school primers designed, for instance, to teach "the elements of reading through a rationalized alphabetical system (different vowel sounds indicated by diacritics, silent letters marked by a vertical bar, and so forth)." Barbauld, *Lessons for Children of Two to Three Years Old* (London: J. Johnson, 1778); Alan Richardson, *Literature, Education, and Romanticism: Reading as Social Practice, 1780–1832* (Cambridge: Cambridge University Press, 1994), 130.

30 The conversation between Geoffrey Hartman and Paul de Man in regards to this passage, which addresses the placement of this adjective, continues to provide an illuminating guide to the scene's perplexities. See Hartman, *Wordsworth's Poetry 1787–1814* (1964; repr., Cambridge, Mass.: Harvard University Press, 1987), 19–22; de Man, "Time and History in Wordsworth," *Diacritics* 17, no. 4 (1987): 4–17.

31 Also contributing to this instability is the fact that in *The Prelude*, the "Boy of Winander" episode ends with a twist: the boy is dead, and the speaker stands by his grave. (In its earliest form, the poem was autobiographical; only later did the speaker become an observer at the boy's grave.) Richardson has argued that the boy's untimely death signals "the contradiction underlying Wordsworth's ideal of a 'natural' education, for education can only distance us from an imagined natural existence, and remaining one with nature means, in Wordsworth's poetry, never to grow out of childhood." Hartman reads the boy's death more figuratively, suggesting that it "mak[es] an incident out of an inward action," which gives double meaning to Wordsworth's long pause at the boy's grave: "He looks not only at something external, a grave, but also at something within, his former heart." Richardson, *Literature, Education, and Romanticism*, 130; Hartman, *Wordsworth's Poetry*, 21.

32 de Man, "Time and History in Wordsworth," 7, emphasis in the original.

33 Mary Jacobus has shown that Wordsworth's focus on providence, particularly in book 6, is indebted to both John Newton, whose antislavery *Authentic Narrative* features a God who "personally oversees the redemption of a single sinner," and Isaac Newton's *Principia*, "in which God oversees the entire universe." Jacobus, *Romanticism, Writing and Sexual Difference: Essays on the Prelude* (Oxford: Oxford University Press, 1989), 82.

34 See, for instance, Mark Reed, who describes Wordsworth's "frequently interjected expressions of what appear to be the personal emotions or circumstances of the literal William Wordsworth either only shortly before or immediately in the act of writing" as a "problem" that interferes with the task of treating *The Prelude* "as [a] poem." Reed, "The Speaker of 'The Prelude,'" in *Bicentenary Wordsworth Studies in Memory of John Alban Finch*, ed. Jonathan Wordsworth (Ithaca, N.Y.: Cornell University Press, 1970), 278–279.

35 It is likely that in addition to Wordsworth's complaints about the academic climate at Cambridge, he also struggled socially: "He was a north-countryman and a sizar, circumstances which placed him just one step above the college servants, in the eyes of those with whom such matters counted." Schneider, *Wordsworth's Cambridge Education*, 40.

36 This claim is not present in the 1850 version of *The Prelude*, where Wordsworth merely says he was "endowed with holy powers / And faculties" (*P*, bk. 3, lines 88–89).

37 Schneider, *Wordsworth's Cambridge Education*, 174.

38 Hartman, *Wordsworth's Poetry*, 40–41.

39 Reed, "Speaker of 'The Prelude,'" 283–289. For more on the structure of this transition from the Alps to the imagination, see Kenneth Johnston, *Wordsworth and "The Recluse"* (New Haven, Conn.: Yale University Press, 1984), 149–158; Robin Jarvis, *Romantic Writing and Pedestrian Travel* (London: Macmillan, 1997), 122–123; John Elder, *Imagining the Earth: Poetry and the Vision of Nature* (Urbana: University of Illinois Press, 1985), 98.

40 Keith Hanley notes a similarity between these two sections as well, but the similarity is on the level of diction, and Hanley doesn't make much of it. The solace Wordsworth finds in his address to "Imagination!" shares a vocabulary with Wordsworth's disappointing professors at Cambridge—both are "unfathered." While imagination is an "unfathered vapour," Cambridge represents a place where professors pore over their tomes "like caterpillars eating out their way / In silence, or with keen devouring noise / Not to be tracked or fathered" (*P*, bk. 3, lines 465–467). Hanley, "Crossings Out: The Problem of Textual Passage in *The*

Prelude," in *Romantic Revisions*, ed. Robert Brinkley and Keith Hanley (Cambridge: Cambridge University Press, 1992), 121.

41 Harold Bloom actually found little troubling about this transition and was able to explain it straightforwardly: "Imagination usurps the place of the baffled mind, and the light of sense momentarily goes out." But more readers have found the break notable. Max Wildi called it a "geological fault and abrupt change of layer"—"a volcanic eruption." Thomas Weiskel described the apostrophe as "dialectically confronted," and not in a good way: the passage "is simply not the way Wordsworth writes or thinks, not his kind of greatness." Bloom, *The Visionary Company: A Reading of English Romantic Poetry* (Ithaca, N.Y.: Cornell University Press, 1971), 153; Wildi, "Wordsworth and the Simplon Pass II," *English Studies* 43, no. 5 (1962): 374, 375; Weiskel, *The Romantic Sublime: Studies in the Structure and Psychology of Transcendence* (Baltimore: Johns Hopkins University Press, 1976), 204, 197.

42 Pamela Cooper, "Metamorphosis and Sexuality: Reading the Strange Passions of *Disgrace*," *Research in African Literatures* 36, no. 4 (2005): 32.

43 Mike Marais connects this statement to the final lines of "Strange fits of passion have I known": "'Oh mercy! to myself I cried / 'If Lucy should be dead!'" Marais, "J. M. Coetzee's *Disgrace* and the Task of the Imagination," *Journal of Modern Literature* 29, no. 2 (2006): 86.

44 In the scene of Lucy's rape, "with its 'sudden blow' of seizure, its inscription of penetration as historical necessity, and of transgressive intercourse as the act which ushers in a new age," Pamela Cooper hears "Leda and the Swan." Richard Russell suggests that *Disgrace* also alludes to "Leda and the Swan" with Lurie's violation of Melanie. Cooper, "Metamorphosis and Sexuality," 32; Russell, "The Yeatsian Intertexts of Coetzee's *Disgrace*," *Journal of Commonwealth and Postcolonial Studies* 2, no. 2 (2014): 7; Gayatri Chakravorty Spivak, "Ethics and Politics in Tagore, Coetzee, and Certain Scenes of Teaching," *Diacritics* 32, nos. 3–4 (2002): 20.

45 Coetzee, *Doubling the Point*, 97.

46 As Leon de Kock says, "Unlike 'settlers' in certain other colonies . . . the South African 'settlers' of European origin have remained in the minority throughout the country's history." De Kock, "South Africa in the Global Imaginary: An Introduction," *Poetics Today* 22, no. 2 (2001): 272–273.

47 Shula Marks and Stanley Trapido, *The Politics of Race, Class, and Nationalism in Twentieth-Century South Africa* (New York: Longman, 1987), 1.

48 Jonathan D. Jansen, *Knowledge in the Blood: Confronting Race and the Apartheid Past* (Stanford, Calif.: Stanford University Press, 2009), 32.

49 The British constructed many more camps for black Africans than they did for white Afrikaners, but the Boer concentration camps remain significantly more notorious.

50 de Kock, "South Africa in the Global Imaginary," 265.

51 For instance, confirmation in the Dutch Reformed Church was a social necessity for early Dutch settlers, one that "implied the ability to read the Bible, recite the catechism or articles of faith, and write one's own name." Similarly, for the British at Cape Colony, education was an imperative, and in 1822, English became the official language of the colony; teachers were to be employed "for the purpose of facilitating the acquirement of the English language to all classes of society." Abraham Leslie Behr, *New Perspectives in South African Education: A Review of Education in South Africa, 1652–1984* (Durban: Butterworths, 1984), 4, 6.

52 Brian Rose and Raymond Tunmer, eds., *Documents in South African Education* (Johannesburg: Donker, 1975), 161.

53 Behr, *New Perspectives*, 25.

54 *OED Online*, s.v. "mother tongue," http://www.oed.com/view/Entry/122678?redirectedFrom =mother+tongue (accessed April 12, 2013). The third definition reads, "Designating the teaching of, or teaching carried out in, the native or first language of students": of the five records of this use that the *OED* includes, three are from South Africa.

55 Behr, *New Perspectives*, 15–16.

56 See the National Education Policy Act (1967) in Elizabeth Dean et al., *History in Black and White: An Analysis of South African School History Textbooks* (Paris: Unesco, 1983), 129. English and Afrikaans are presented as the only two options because the National Education Policy Act defined education as the instruction of white pupils. Previous acts, like the Bantu Education Act (1953), the Coloured Persons Education Act (1963), and the Indian Education Act (1965) enforced Apartheid segregation and addressed students of other racial categories.

57 Isabel Hofmeyr, "Building a Nation from Words: Afrikaans Language, Literature and Ethnic Identity, 1902–1924," in *The Politics of Race, Class and Nationalism in Twentieth Century South Africa*, ed. Shula Marks and Stanley Trapido (New York: Longman, 1987), 113.

58 Rose and Tunmer, *Documents in South African Education*, 150.

59 The tension between Afrikaans and English informs Coetzee's memoirs, not to mention earlier novels and his translations from Afrikaans. As Rita Barnard argues, "One of the earliest of Coetzee's doubles . . . is the Afrikaans boy and thus the Afrikaans man that he never became, but who nevertheless once presented himself as a shadowy alternative, as a subject position consciously refused—one that had to be refused, in fact, since in this refusal lay the possibility of a career as a cosmopolitan writer and intellectual." Barnard's argument is useful here in its juxtaposition of "the Afrikaans man" and the "cosmopolitan writer and intellectual"—English as an "access language" allowed Coetzee a cosmopolitanism that he could not have sustained in Afrikaans. Barnard, "Coetzee in/and Afrikaans," *Journal of Literary Studies* 25, no. 4 (2009): 87.

60 Quoted in Rachel Donadio, "Out of South Africa," *New York Times*, December 16, 2007, http://www.nytimes.com/2007/12/16/books/review/Donadio-t.html (accessed June 28, 2016).

61 Olive Schreiner's *Story of an African Farm* (1883; repr., Oxford: Oxford University Press, 1992) is one of the few British contributions to the genre, though it significantly predates the popularity of the genre in Afrikaans and thus lacks many of the genre's standard tropes.

62 Coetzee, *Boyhood*, 96.

63 This thesis, that Afrikaner identity depends on Afrikaner landownership, had clear political correlates. There were several proposals for independent Afrikaner states in the 1980s, and one of these proposed states, Orandee, relied on a justification similar to that of Israel "in the belief that all Afrikaners would feel more secure if they possessed a homeland in which their culture and language would be preserved by law." A. J. Christopher, *The Atlas of Changing South Africa*, 2nd ed. (London: Routledge, 2001), 100.

64 Coetzee, *Boyhood*, 95–96, emphasis in the original.

65 Wenzel, "Pastoral Promise," 92.

66 In addition to the "primal stuff of the Afrikaner *plaasroman*," Lucy might also be rejecting the farm's association with the Great Trek of the nineteenth century—a mass emigration of Afrikaner farmers to the interior of South Africa, celebrated throughout the height of Afrikaner nationalism in the twentieth century. Jane Poyner, *J. M. Coetzee and the Paradox of Postcolonial Authorship* (Burlington, Vt.: Ashgate, 2009), 156–157.

67 Poyner, 159.

68 Jerome McGann is a rare voice of dissent on this point, saying that in spite of the deliberate allusions to the Lucy poems, "Lucy [Lurie] is no Wordsworthian figure." McGann, "Is Romanticism Finished?," in *The Cambridge History of English Romantic Literature*, ed. James Chandler (Cambridge: Cambridge University Press, 2009), 654.

69 Marais, "Task of the Imagination," 86.

70 Paul de Man, *Blindness and Insight: Essays in the Rhetoric of Contemporary Criticism*, 2nd ed. (Minneapolis: University of Minnesota Press, 1983), 225.

71 As Frances Ferguson explains, "Lucy is too integral a part of nature and too self-integrated for responsiveness." She is not *like* "rocks, and stones, and trees" but *with* "rocks, and stones, and trees," fully enmeshed in a "diurnal course" that the speaker cannot access. Ferguson, *Wordsworth: Language as Counter-spirit* (New Haven, Conn.: Yale University Press, 1977), 193.

72 The poem, like many others, fell victim to Wordsworth's incessant revisions. In later versions, it concludes immediately after the speaker issues these confident and slightly condescending assumptions, becoming a touching but ultimately slight character sketch of an old man who is indeed "insensibly subdued" and patient beyond all measure.

73 *PW*, 247n "*After* 14" (I have quoted the concluding lines of the 1802 version).

74 As Saree Makdisi puts it, in this moment, "the mediating speaker disappears, in fact, leaving us, the audience alone with the old man, who is now addressing us directly, speaking out of the pages of the volume." Makdisi, *Making England Western: Occidentalism, Race, and Imperial Culture* (Chicago: University of Chicago Press, 2013), 110.

75 See Geoffrey Baker, "The Limits of Sympathy: J. M. Coetzee's Evolving Ethics of Engagement," *ARIEL* 36, nos. 1–2 (2005): 27–49; Marais, "Task of the Imagination"; Kate McInturff, "Rex Oedipus: The Ethics of Sympathy in Recent Work by J. M. Coetzee," *Postcolonial Text* 3, no. 4 (2007): 1–20; Michael G. McDunnah, "'We Are Not Asked to Condemn': Sympathy, Subjectivity, and the Narration of *Disgrace*," in *Encountering Disgrace: Reading and Teaching Coetzee's Novel*, ed. William E. McDonald (Rochester, N.Y.: Camden House, 2009), 15–47.

76 Mark Jones, *The "Lucy Poems": A Case Study in Literary Knowledge* (Toronto: University of Toronto Press, 1995), 7.

77 Ferguson, *Language as Counter-spirit*, 186.

78 Pamela Woof, "The 'Lucy' Poems: Poetry of Mourning," *Wordsworth Circle* 30, no. 1 (1999): 35.

79 Homi K. Bhabha, *The Location of Culture*, 2nd ed. (New York: Routledge, 2004), 153.

80 Hartman, *Wordsworth's Poetry*, 158; Ferguson, *Language as Counter-spirit*, 187.

81 In the Lucy poems, most everything about Lucy is posthumous: she "commonly arrives just in time to leave; indeed her naming is her departure." John Powell Ward, "'Will No One Tell Me What She Sings?' Women and Gender in the Poetry of William Wordsworth," *Studies in Romanticism* 36, no. 4 (1997): 612.

82 For example, in "To——, on Her First Ascent to the Summit of Helvellyn," the speaker tells the addressee (Dorothy) to "inherit / Alps or Andes" and "survey their bright dominions" (*PW*, 2:287). In *Guilt and Sorrow*, the female speaker describes how "from the last hill-top, my sire surveyed, / Peering above the trees" (*PW*, 1:108). In *The Borderers*, Oswald describes having "from the top of Lebanon surveyed / The moonlight desert." William Wordsworth, *The Borderers*, ed. Robert Osborn (Ithaca, N.Y.: Cornell University Press, 1982), 239.

83 The project of mapping the nation progressed in fits and starts throughout the late eighteenth century, with the first maps of the Corps of Royal Military Surveyors and Draughtsmen

printed in 1801. Ron Broglio, "Mapping British Earth and Sky," *Wordsworth Circle* 33, no. 2 (2002): 71.

84 Compare James M. Garrett's argument about Wordsworth's Black Combe poems—that he attempts to "transcend local differences by subjecting the landscape to the 'prospect view,' the abstract imperial gaze available from the mountain summit." Garrett, *Wordsworth and the Writing of the Nation* (Aldershot: Ashgate, 2008), 70.

85 Margaret Atwood, *Survival: A Thematic Guide to Canadian Literature* (Toronto: House of Anansi, 1972), 27.

3

GLOBALIZING ENGLAND

Lydia Maria Child and *The Excursion*

THERE ARE SEVERAL OPTIONS FOR pinpointing the date of William Wordsworth's decline into poetic bombast and moralizing conservatism. Perhaps the descent began sometime after the publication of his *Poems, in Two Volumes* in 1807. Maybe it began even sooner, after Wordsworth had finished the final version of the preface to *Lyrical Ballads* in 1802. Most attractive, though, is the possibility that with the publication in 1814 of *The Excursion*—a meandering epic hated by Francis Jeffrey, bemoaned by Matthew Arnold, and rarely read today—Wordsworth had sunk irrevocably into political and aesthetic apostasy. *The Excursion*, unlike earlier publications, proves rather than foreshadows decline. Even many scholars of Romantic poetry avoid it, and those who do write about the poem are obliged to rehearse its seemingly eternal unpopularity. Yet for all the jabs (Jeffrey's review opened by declaring "This will never do"), *The Excursion* was easily Wordsworth's most popular poem during the nineteenth century and even some of the twentieth. It cemented his reputation as the English poet, not only in England, but in America and the British colonies as well. What did those readers like in a poem that we find so difficult to tolerate or even acknowledge today?

During Wordsworth's life, *The Excursion* was not read as evidence of his waning powers: Jeffrey, for one, had been suspicious of Wordsworth's poetry since at least 1807. If anything, at its publication, *The Excursion* signaled Wordsworth's ascension to the role of serious poet, one who described the condition of England in sober blank verse (rather than a poet who, for instance, described a potentially murderous mother in the voice of a loquacious retired ship captain). Indeed, *The Excursion* was read as a particularly moral poem in both England and America. In this light, it makes sense that the poem came to hold a certain moral capital across the Atlantic, with quotations from it mustering support of issues as diverse as abolition, unionization, and environmental protection. What makes less sense is that a poem so vocally concerned with the specific condition of England—namely, the effects of rapid industrialization on Britain's countryside and its subjects—could have made such moral capital available to the Anglophone world at large. This chapter will focus on the case of American abolitionist Lydia Maria Child, who cited Wordsworth—particularly *The Excursion*—frequently in her political tracts and newspaper articles, in order to explore how an understanding of Wordsworth as a global, moral poet developed across the Atlantic. Child's political repurposing of Wordsworth in America did not result from a misreading or co-opting of *The Excursion*'s content. The surprising appearances of *The Excursion* in American abolitionist writing make visible how the poem in fact lays the foundation for its own broad moral utility, a utility whose range only seems to contradict the poem's outward concern for the "native Briton," the "English ground," and the scourge of industrialization that plagued both (*E*, bk. 8, line 298; bk. 1, line 117).

If *The Excursion* does represent a turning point in Wordsworth's career, it marks not just a shift from good poetry to bad or revolutionary engagement to apostasy. *The Excursion*'s afterlife in America also helps uncover Wordsworth's multivalent representation of England not only as a contained, aloof isle and an expansive, dynamic nation beset but also as undergirded by global networks of trade and imperialism. In the previous chapter, I suggested that the Wordsworth of *The Prelude* is a figure whom J. M. Coetzee can invoke as representative of a narrow and Eurocentric aesthetic tradition (even while *Disgrace* shows that characterization to be but half of the story). In contrast, the Wordsworth of *The Excursion* is, for Child, a poet whose highly local concerns do not prevent him from assuming a transnational moral authority. With the publication of his now unloved epic poem, he became an exemplar of Englishness and simultaneously a tool of American social progress whose regional specificity could be imaginatively interpreted beyond England's shores. This turn of events changes how I read *The Excursion*. Child's repurposing across the Atlantic underscores the global dimensions of Wordsworth's construction of England. Child—and, as I will suggest in the next chapter, Jamaica Kincaid—thus herald the possibility that Wordsworth's representations of his local English setting can do more than alienate readers and writers for whom that geographic radius is a terra incognita. These representations can, on one level, unify readers and writers who see in Wordsworth's local commitments a harmonious echo of their own. But on another—and this is the focus of the present chapter—Wordsworth does not depict *The Excursion*'s English settings as purely English. Rather, in his representation, particular English landscapes and laborers are marked by the worldwide movement of people, products, and culture thanks to the growth of British imperialism and global trade. To Arnold, another Wordsworth fan writing a decades after Wordsworth's death, Wordsworth was a moral poet because he talked about "how to live," a question that, in Arnold's view, English poets addressed better than any other nation's. But if Wordsworth's attention to "how to live" made Arnold think of England, it made an abolitionist like Child think of America.

It is difficult to overstate the personal and professional changes that Child experienced when she published her controversial *Appeal in Favor of That Class of Americans Called Africans* in 1833. Her substantial audience, composed of readers on both sides of the Atlantic who admired the romances, cookbooks, and home-economy manuals that had made her famous, viewed her first overt foray into national politics with something less than anticipatory zeal. Her Boston benefactors, scared off by their association with a newly born radical, abandoned her. Her family and friends, many of whom did not share her abolitionist stance, avoided her company.[1] From this point on, Child's career was defined by her participation in the antislavery movement, and though she continued to write romances, they were overshadowed by her subsequent abolitionist monographs and her editorship of the *National Anti-Slavery Standard*. But even though readers both then and now have tended to see her *Appeal* as distinct from her own literary productions, its literary vestiges—its inclusion of poems, its penchant for narrative interpolations, its epigraphs from Coleridge, Cowper, Montesquieu, Sterne, and Shakespeare—belie such a distinction. Some epigraphs seem more apropos than others, however, and some of the more puzzling selections come from *The Excursion*, a poem that appears twice in Child's antislavery text but that is not known for saying anything on the subject of slavery.

While Child argued in the *Appeal* that the burgeoning industrialization of New England would help solve the problem of slavery and allow for total emancipation, *The Excursion* is concerned with the destruction that industrialization brought to the English countryside. Such an incongruity raises the question of what purpose Child found in her references to Wordsworth and thus, in a larger sense, of what use Wordsworth could have been to the American antislavery movement. Paradoxically, the very traits that provided the foundation for Wordsworth's apolitical reputation in America—his literariness and his Englishness—are the tools that Child mobilizes in her creation of a politically potent global Wordsworth. She emerges from this repurposing as an influential American critic of Wordsworth, one whose understanding of his poetry went beyond the heartfelt but bland praise offered by the periodicals that helped popularize him in America—one who seemed to realize that for Wordsworth, the line between "England" and "the earth" at large was permeable.

Wordsworth's importance to nineteenth-century American writers has been of interest to literary scholars since well before the inauguration of transatlantic studies as a field, and this interest continued after the publication of Robert Weisbuch's foundational *Atlantic Double-Cross* (1986), which took inspiration from Harold Bloom's *Anxiety of Influence* in investigating the relationships between canonical

American authors and their English predecessors and peers.[2] But in spite of books like Paul Gilroy's *The Black Atlantic* (1993) and Joseph Roach's *Cities of the Dead* (1996), which focus on the complex networks connecting the United States, the Caribbean, Africa, and Europe, nineteenth-century transatlantic scholarship tends to follow in Weisbuch's footsteps by centering on a binary and often antinomian relationship between Britain and the United States.[3] When critics imagine influence crossing the Atlantic, it tends to flow from east to west: as Lawrence Buell explains, "We form the habit of picturing Hawthorne as leading to Melville rather than to, say, George Eliot, even though nothing in the Melville canon follows a Hawthornian pretext more faithfully than *Adam Bede* follows *The Scarlet Letter*."[4] In the last decade, critics like Elisa Tamarkin have shown that anxiety over British influence was not the only feeling—or even the dominant feeling—animating American writers. American abolitionist writers were particularly inclined to venerate British antislavery activists, who had already helped usher in the abolition of the slave trade in Britain.[5] The present chapter builds on this strain of thought in transatlantic studies, holding that culture flows back and forth along many different currents and that the desire to fashion an American literary culture distinct from that of Britain was not a unilateral concern. Child's desire was the abolition of slavery, and she found in the Wordsworth of *The Excursion* an unlikely ally. In turn, it is the very unlikeliness of this match that influences how we understand Wordsworth's depiction of England—its isolation and its concomitant porousness—in *The Excursion*.

Wordsworth's relationship to the abolition movement in America is largely unstudied, perhaps for understandable reasons.[6] With the exception of his sonnets on the abolitionist Thomas Clarkson and the Haitian revolution leader Toussaint L'Ouverture, Wordsworth didn't write much about slavery directly. (Indeed, in terms of volume, he wrote much of his poetry after Great Britain abolished the slave trade in 1807.) And when he did address the topic, the results were deflating. Child would not have known Wordsworth's avowal in *The Prelude*, which remained unpublished until 1850, that the fight for abolition

> had wanted power
> To *rivet* my affections; nor did now
> Its unsuccessful issue much excite
> My sorrow; for I brought with me the faith
> That, if France prospered, good men would not long
> Pay fruitless worship to humanity,
> And this most rotten branch of human shame,
> Object, so seemed it, of superfluous pains
> Would fall together with its parent tree. (*P*, bk. 10, lines 254–262, 1850 version)

This is Wordsworth's most notorious statement about slavery, and as Debbie Lee writes, when Wordsworth says it, "we tend to believe him." But perhaps we should not: as Lee points out, Wordsworth discussed the condition of black women with surprising frequency in his poetry, and as Joel Pace has shown, Wordsworth did care about American abolitionism, contributing a poem to an American anthology of antislavery poetry even though he had denied a similar request from an English antislavery anthology years earlier.[7] Add to this Wordsworth's antislavery sonnets, and it seems less of a stretch for Child to quote Wordsworth in her antislavery *Appeal*.

The first section of this chapter provides the historical context of Child's references to Wordsworth by detailing what cultural capital he held in America in 1833. In American newspapers and magazines, *The Excursion* appeared frequently in excerpts and was reviewed as an especially moral and English poem. If these descriptors sound capacious and vague, they were. But they appear in lieu of an adjective that was *not* applied to Wordsworth in American periodicals: *political*. The second section turns to Child's editorship of the *National Anti-Slavery Standard*, which frequently reprinted Wordsworth's poems, to demonstrate that Child recognized moral points of contact between the abolitionist cause and Wordsworth's concerns about industrialization. In this way, Child had a more specific understanding of Wordsworth's morality than her peers. The third section treats Child's *Appeal in Favor of That Class of Americans Called Africans* and Wordsworth's *Excursion* in dialogue. I argue that Child's management of the epigraph as literary convention is inseparable from the transnational approach she brings to the abolition of slavery. But in light of the political use that Child finds for *The Excursion* in America, how do we understand *The Excursion*'s depiction of England and its current condition? Wordsworth's poem attempts to distinguish two opposed versions of England: (1) Albion, inviolable isle, land of hardworking Britons and (2) Great Britain, globalized, industrial nation of the racialized poor. Yet the many speakers of *The Excursion* ensure that this binary doesn't hold. The speaker who longs to preserve the country of his youth is contradicted by one who insists that the England of the past was no better than the England of the present; the Briton who labors in the fields is as inscrutable as the racialized beggar. *The Excursion*'s vision of the nation is changeable and thus resists summary, but suffice to say here that it is a vision familiar from recent debates about Brexit: the poem's representation of trade and imperial fantasy, and its recourse to a planetary scale, suggest the porousness of Britain's boundaries, undercutting the isolationist vision of England that the poem simultaneously holds up as an ideal. The chapter concludes by comparing Child with a later American industrialist and Wordsworth fan, Henry Ford, whose use of Wordsworth in his Amazonian rubber plantation pushes the logic of Child's use to its extreme. Comparing the two repurposings makes Child's recourse to Wordsworth seem all the more remarkable: Child saw not only that Wordsworth could have political capital but also that it was applicable to what was by 1833 a singularly American fight—all without divorcing that capital from the literary Englishness that defined it.

AN "ENGLISH ENGLISH" POET: WORDSWORTH IN ANTEBELLUM LITERARY CULTURE

In 1833, what did it mean to quote Wordsworth in America? A decade earlier, it meant nothing good. The *Port-Folio*, a popular literary and political periodical established in Philadelphia at the turn of the century, posed the question snidely. If, as the periodical surmises, good poetry gets quoted frequently, then "Who quotes Wordsworth?"[8] Such a question can be seen as a distant cousin to Sydney Smith's query from 1820, "Who reads an American book?"—a question that, like the *Port-Folio*'s, silently offers up its own answer: no one.[9] Yet the question was a good one: Who *was* reading and quoting Wordsworth in the years before Child's *Appeal* and why? It is difficult to generalize about Wordsworth's reception in any context because, as David Simpson writes, Wordsworth "has always been a contested rather than a universally accepted author."[10] It is not surprising, then, that American periodicals were often at odds about him, a fact that did not escape their own notice. H. T. Tuckerman equitably reasoned in 1841 that it was "the fortune of Wordsworth, like many original characters, to be almost wholly regarded from the two extremes of prejudice and admiration."[11] Yet some trends do emerge. *Lyrical Ballads* was unpopular—many found the collection to be a conglomeration of poems most notable for "their grossness, their childishness and their vanity" that could only be enjoyed with a "qualified and temporary approbation."[12] But this review (along with several other scathing condemnations) appeared in the 1820s, two decades after the *Lyrical Ballads* appeared on American shelves and in American journals, suggesting that that the distaste for Wordsworth's earlier productions sprang from the critics' general preference for his subsequent blank-verse creations. (Indeed, for many readers, "Tintern Abbey" was the only good thing about *Lyrical Ballads*.) *The Excursion* was more successful: particularly after the American publication in 1824 of Wordsworth's collected works, newspapers and periodicals frequently printed long excerpts from *The Excursion*.[13] It was during this period that Wordsworth started to become a monolithic figure, "key to the construction of a literary canon in America," and periodicals that printed Wordsworth's poetry largely oversaw this construction.[14] Their Wordsworth had two key characteristics: he was English and his poetry was beautiful—but not political.

Although these tendencies fully emerged after the publication of *The Excursion* in America, the consolidation of Wordsworth's Englishness began earlier. Only one American periodical was publishing Wordsworth at the turn of the century, and that was the *Port-Folio*, established by Anglophile Joseph Dennie, a man "reactionary in politics, conservative in outlook, and intensely concerned with developing a national culture closely akin to that of England."[15] In the first month of the periodical's existence in 1801, long before its contributors began wondering if anyone quoted Wordsworth anymore, Dennie reprinted "Simon Lee," originally published in the 1798 edition of *Lyrical Ballads*, and introduced it as belonging to "a collection remarkable for originality, simplicity, and nature, to which Mr. Wordsworth, of St. John's college, Oxford, is a principal contributor."[16] That Wordsworth actually attended St. John's College at Cambridge, not Oxford, is beside the point: for Dennie, both institutions seem to signify the same Englishness. (In England, Wordsworth's Oxbridge affiliation was rarely mentioned, even though he, more than other major Romantic writers like Coleridge and Shelley, earned the affiliation by actually taking a degree.)

Although such glowing recommendations did not persist after the Philadelphia publication of the *Lyrical Ballads* in 1802—one critic's "so truly worthless" will stand in here for many other critiques—Dennie's appreciation is remarkable not just for its rarity but also for its introduction of Wordsworth as a product of a markedly English educational system.[17] In an editorial note of about sixty words, "St. John's college, Oxford," is the only biographical information offered up to interested readers, beating out any mention of his birthplace, current residence, or family. Such a focus is perhaps to be expected of an editor devoted to fashioning an American culture "akin to that of England," and indeed, as Leon Howard notes, "Dennie consistently identified Wordsworth with Oxford."[18] But that the first man committed to reproducing Wordsworth for an American public should have been so intent on simultaneously reproducing (if inaccurately) his very English credentials establishes that from the beginning, Wordsworth was presented in America as not just a poet of possible interest but also an "English English" poet, to borrow from black American abolitionist Alexander Crummell.[19]

Crummell was talking about English universities, not English poets, but his reduplication captures both the vagueness and the emphasis of Dennie's biographical note. Of Crummell's designation, Tamarkin writes, "'English English,' as opposed to what?"[20] Repeating the term *English* proves easier than defining it.[21] For as Tamarkin notes, Crummell construes England as "a repository of less tangible, more imaginative contributions," based not on specific knowledge of how English and American universities differed but rather on a well-wrought collection of attributes and attractions. To many English subjects, there is a difference between

Oxford and Cambridge, between an Englishman and, as Olaudah Equiano dubs himself, "almost an Englishman." To many Americans, spatially removed from the locales that Ian Baucom explains as helping identify Englishness, those differences are less legible.[22] So it's difficult to pinpoint exactly what struck nineteenth-century American readers of Wordsworth as so English. Wordsworth entered American literary culture as an "English English" poet not because of his degree from Cambridge but because of his association with Oxford or Cambridge or whichever it was—so long as it evoked England, home of the Dover Cliffs and afternoon tea.

As time passed, Wordsworth's Englishness also came to depend on his poetry's silent avoidance of the Orientalized subject matter that many other major Romantic poets addressed. This version of Englishness is not more specific than the version imposed on Wordsworth by Joseph Dennie, but it appears under the aegis of an Occidentalism with which American reviewers of Wordsworth could identify. (In this way, it functioned differently than Wordsworth's affiliation with Oxbridge.) The *United States Literary Gazette*, for instance, liked Wordsworth's "resolute and confident adherence to truth," an accolade that lacks a certain desirable specificity until the reviewer compares Wordsworth to poets who write "Eastern fictions filled with creatures that never lived before but in Eastern minds." The implication is that Shelley and Byron have been Orientalized, their minds turned "Eastern" by their subject matter. To be clear, the reviewer *likes* poets such as Shelley and Byron who author these fictions but cannot ignore that the characters inhabiting these worlds "are impossible beings, made up of irreconcilable parts, bound, not blended, together; and their thoughts, and emotions, and purposes, are all alien to the nature of man."[23] In contrast, among the English poets, Wordsworth is notable for his "adherence to truth," a designation that makes him simultaneously more authentically English than Byron and Shelley and more universal in his intimacy with the "the nature of man." More than any other explanation of Wordsworth's Englishness, the fact that Wordsworth seldom wrote about such "Eastern" subject matter has had the longest afterlife and is still one of the reasons he rarely seems central to current discussions of global Romanticism.

His Englishness had one final source in addition to his biography and the content of his poetry: the development of a canon of English literature. When American reviewers wanted to praise Wordsworth, they reached for their Milton. No poet embodied England—and English literature—quite like Milton. So when a reviewer decided to assert that Wordsworth's best poems were "as exquisite specimens of melodious versification, beautiful imagery, and noble thoughts, as the whole circle of English literature can afford," he also might say that this poetry contained "more true and manly poetry . . . than can be found in almost any other poem published since the great English Epic was given to the world."[24] Similarly, a reviewer of Hazlitt's *Lectures on the English Poets* writes, "No poet since Milton seems so thoroughly imbued with old English and the truly poetical language, as Mr. Wordsworth."[25] Some even thought that Wordsworth's talent was incomparable: "We know no English poet who has written more melodious verses."[26]

Today, the genealogy that connects Milton to Wordsworth may seem too familiar to be remarkable, so it is worth saying that Byron, for instance, developed a different reputation. It is not surprising that reviewers seldom placed Byron in a lineage going back to Milton; Wordsworth's poetry, particularly in blank-verse works like *The Excursion*, is more Miltonic than Byron's poetry is. But more significant than poetic style is the fact that Milton could represent England, as this hit piece on Byron makes clear: "With the names of Spenser, Shakspeare [*sic*], Milton, we associate the idea of our nature in its earthly perfection. . . . We are proud of England, because she produced them. . . . In all [Byron's] writings, how little is there whose object it is to make us reverence, virtue, or love our country!"[27] There's a strange ambiguity in the reviewer's use of the first-person "*our* country," which must indicate the United States even though Byron, as the reviewer knows, is not an American. (This slippage speaks perhaps to the reviewer's belief that he too belongs to the Occidental world encapsulated by England.) But more important is the reviewer's association of Spenser, Shakespeare, and Milton with English national pride and the concurrent assertion that Byron enjoys no such affiliation. Byron may be an English poet, but in comparison with Wordsworth, he is not an *English* English poet.

As this praise of Wordsworth suggests, *The Excursion* fared better than the *Lyrical Ballads* in the hands of American periodicals. Full reviews of the poem were rare though; while many American periodicals printed a notice or, in some cases, reprinted an English review, when *The Excursion* was first published in 1814, only a few magazines stepped up to review the poem when it appeared in the American edition of Wordsworth's collected works in 1824.[28] Those critics who did feel compelled to comment on Wordsworth's epic often focused on how much better it was than the "beggar-ballads and daffodilly-ditties" that preceded it or else refuted the negative reviews of the poem that appeared shortly after its publication in Britain: in a belated repudiation of Jeffrey's condemnation, one critic insists "that it ought to do, and inevitably must do—in despite of the criticism."[29] The *Atlantic Magazine* was so taken with the 1824 American collection that the review spanned two issues, with fifteen pages of "lucubrations" in each.[30] What American readers had disliked about the *Lyrical Ballads*—the proudly deliberate attention to low subjects, the simple diction and marked rhythms of the nursery—they did not find in *The Excursion*, and to them, the poem was better for it.

If many periodicals failed to publish an original review of *The Excursion*, they made up for it in excerpts, publishing small portions of the poem without introduction or editorial. In the years before Child's *Appeal*, a page from *The Excursion* routinely appeared in journals both general and literary, and these excerpts not only testify to the poet's popularity in America but also signal the periodicals' willingness to cut the epic into manageable, printable pieces. Such willingness is not necessarily remarkable—*Don Juan* was excerpted too—but it does help illustrate how *The Excursion* was read in America. Without access to the full poem, many Americans read it piecemeal and out of its original context. In this mode, the fragment generates its own context, a context free from a stable original, or else garners a new one amid the ephemera of the periodical's pages. The *National Recorder*, printing excerpts in an article simply entitled "Excursion," goes so far as to mash together verse paragraphs from books 1, 2, and 4. Though the editors acknowledge their selections to be "detached passages," the layout makes the fragments look like a linear poem.[31] Though Emerson may have consumed *The Excursion* in its entirety, for those readers whose familiarity with Wordsworth came from widely disseminated periodicals rather than from a collection devoted solely to his verse, fragments were the rule. Of course, reading *The Excursion* in America is different from reading it in England, just as reading "I wandered lonely as a cloud" in Antigua or India is different from reading about daffodils in England. But in this case, *The Excursion* actually looked substantially different in American periodicals. More important, it was condensed into a sort of wisdom literature that contained solemn, moral, and beautiful musings but no visions of child labor or other miserable factory workers. Like many editors before and since, antebellum American editors preferred a specific version of Wordsworth, and in reproducing the English poet, the *National Recorder* made his poem unique to America.

This fragmentation is important because reviews rarely considered the possibility that in writing *The Excursion*, Wordsworth wanted not just to communicate certain aesthetic and philosophical truths but also to represent the condition of England. (They especially did not consider the possibility that these goals were inseparable to him.)[32] *The North American Review* printed the entirety of Wordsworth's sonnet "Thought of a Briton on the Subjugation of Switzerland" without commenting on its content—the reference to the "tyrant" Napoleon and the "holy glee" of his opponents—and focusing instead on the poem's "sublime personification."[33] The *Literary Gazette*, which in 1824 refuted the *Edinburgh Review*'s condemnation of the epic, acknowledged that *The Excursion*'s topics were "of a more solemn cast" than Wordsworth's previous works but settled on a familiar refrain by quoting excerpts that feature his "religious musings," "the exquisite beauty of the poetry," and "the majesty of its versification."[34] The *Analectic Magazine* was able to recognize *The Excursion*'s "strange mystical morality" but neglected to specify what this morality entailed and ended its short appraisal by deeming the poem "full of eloquence and nature."[35] The *National Recorder* thought the poem would delight the "lover of nature and the muses" and arouse "the sympathies of the devotional reader," while the *Atlantic Magazine* was convinced the poem would join "the other grave and seriously didactic poems of this author" and secure "his claims upon the admiration of posterity."[36] One month earlier, the same periodical praised the poem's "extraordinary beauty," asserting that it included "more true and manly poetry, more beautiful embodying of pure and noble thoughts, more definite revealing of the secret influences which so wonderfully sway or complicated being" than any poetry since Milton.[37] The reviews, though effusive, are far more impressed by what is "moral" and "mystical" about the poem than by what is explicitly condemnatory. To be fair, the poem doesn't lend itself to summary; it rather "frustrates any expectations we might have entertained of narrative progression," in Alison Hickey's words.[38] But the poem is also not nine straight books of wisdom literature. There are characters, walks, positions taken and abandoned, and few of these details make it into American reviews of *The Excursion*.

This myopia is not true of the verses that Child included in her *Appeal* or in the *National Anti-Slavery Standard*, where she proved herself familiar and comfortable with the blend of nature poetry and political verse in Wordsworth's body of work. What Child did take from periodical culture was the freedom to fragment the "English English" poet. In the context of the periodicals I have cited, her willingness to sever Wordsworth's verse from its surrounding context is not unique. How Child differed was in her manipulation of Wordsworth's vague if reified Englishness, a designation that like his supposed mysticism and morality made his poetry seem distant and elevated. In Child's transnational approach, it is Wordsworth's very Englishness that makes his poetry germane to a treatise concerned with a distinctly American dilemma, suggesting that compared to her contemporaries, Child had a very different sense of what it meant to be an English poet. She seems to have recognized that what other readers identified in Wordsworth's poetry as a particularly English morality was broad enough to warrant a much wider relevance.

FASHIONING WORDSWORTH IN THE *NATIONAL ANTI-SLAVERY STANDARD*

To be clear, Child knew and liked the familiar Wordsworth, the moral English poet. But she also saw his poetry as political and, moreover, understood that the English Wordsworth and the political Wordsworth were one and the same. In 1841, eight years after she published the *Appeal*, Child assumed the editorship of the *National*

Anti-Slavery Standard, a newspaper that had existed only a year. Like most antislavery newspapers, the *Standard* included a poetry section in every issue. According to Carolyn L. Karcher, the inclusion of poetry was key to the newspaper's success: during Child's two-year tenure, the circulation rose from 2,500 to 5,000 subscribers, while during the same period, William Lloyd Garrison's antislavery periodical *The Liberator*, founded in 1831, lost subscriptions.[39] Such an increase stems from Child's manipulation of what had become the standard form of antislavery newspapers so that her paper might accommodate a wider readership. As editor, her aim was to produce a "family newspaper," one with a higher "proportion of literary and miscellaneous matter" on its back page.[40] This goal presents an interpretive problem: if the *Standard*'s literary matter was included to entice a wider readership, then the connection of that literary matter to the newspaper's larger goal is far from given.

Generally speaking, some of the newspaper's poetry does straightforwardly reflect the newspaper's antislavery agenda. Lydia Sigourney's antislavery poems appeared frequently, as did Garrison's and Robert Southey's. But the newspaper also presented poems like William Cullen Bryant's "To a Waterfowl," which does not explicitly address the antislavery cause, among many now forgotten apolitical verses of poets like Sigourney (whose "On visiting the grave of Sir Walter Scott, at Dryburgh Abbey" merited inclusion) and Southey (who was represented on one occasion by "On a picture by J. M. Wright, Esq."). While Wordsworth was in heavy rotation both before and after Child assumed her post, the newspaper's wide-ranging approach to poetry selection means that interpreting his inclusion is rather difficult. Clearly Child was an admirer (in the two months following her advancement to editor, poems by Wordsworth appear five times, far more often than in the whole of the previous year), but it remains hard to say if this flurry of Wordsworthian reprints signifies something other than an aesthetic appreciation of poetic style. After all, though a poem like "To a Waterfowl" and its assertion that "soon that toil shall end" would have a special meaning for abolitionist and enslaved American alike, one could as easily argue for its inclusion as part of "the garland of imagination and taste" that Child intended to balance out some of the paper's drier material.[41] This example raises a question: Was Wordsworth reprinted because his poetry was gaining popularity in America or because it spoke to the newspaper's cause?

Both, it seems. While it is clear that the proliferation of Wordsworth in the *Standard* during Child's editorship signals her admiration of his poetry, this explanation is only part of the story, for the specific layout of poems in the *Standard* reveals the moral correspondence Child sees between American chattel slavery and English labor practices. What I find interesting—and on a more subjective level, likeable—about Child's use of Wordsworth in the *Standard* is that it enacts this correspondence without diminishing Child's own ability to participate in the emotional and philosophical responses to Wordsworth's poetry that defined most American criticism. That is, her recognition of political fraternity coexists with her sheer enjoyment of the verse—with the power it has to inspire thoughts on the themes of memory, nature, imagination, and childhood that continue to feed conversations that modern enthusiasts have on first encountering a poem like "Tintern Abbey." This might seem like an overblown way of saying that for her, the personal was political, but I hope to show that her catholic use of Wordsworth in the *Standard* is of a piece with her use of Wordsworth in the *Appeal*, where she avoids characterizing the expressly political implications of *The Excursion* as essentially different and separable from the rest of his verse. A nondualistic approach like hers is all the more remarkable in consideration of the binaries that have seemed—and still do seem, in some cases—so applicable to Wordsworth, some for good reason: the radical and the conservative, nature and the city, the boy and the man, the crowd and the self, the ballad and the blank verse, the good poetry and the bad.

A few examples will illustrate my point about Child's fluid movement between the political and the philosophical Wordsworth (or, in other words, that category composed of the "strange" and "mystical" bits of Wordsworth's verse that American periodicals liked best)—a move whose ease suggests there is some folly in distinguishing between these categories too scrupulously. One year before Child assumed the editorship, she wrote a short article entitled "Thoughts" for the *Standard*. The piece begins with an epigraph from "Tintern Abbey," where the speaker's comparison of his boyhood appreciation of nature—immediate, physical, mingling pleasure with pain—with the more mature sense of "a presence that disturbs me with the joy / Of elevated thoughts" serves as the basis for Child's musings on a species of false memory that makes the unfamiliar seem like home (*PW*, 2:261–262). In fashioning her own spot of time, Child begins as we might expect, describing how "the day was closing in, and as I sat watching the scarcely moving foliage of a neighboring elm, my mind gradually sank into a state of luxurious repose, amounting to total unconsciousness of all busy sights and sounds of earth." In this daydream, she suddenly finds herself "seated by a calm, deep lake" and reports, "The landscape differed from any thing I had ever seen," and yet "I felt *at home*; and could I see a painting of it, I should know it as readily as the scenes of my childhood."[42] Child's occult familiarity with the unknown landscape leads to a series of questions that forms the rest of the article: "Have we indeed formerly lived in a luminous and shadowless world, where all things were light as a garment?" "Are not our soul's [*sic*] wandering in the spirit land while our bodies are on earth?" and to conclude, "Does Infancy owe to this angel crowd its peculiar power to purify and bless?" The article ends with five lines from Wordsworth's "Immortality" ode—"Heaven lies about us in our infancy!"—as if to suggest that Wordsworth might help answer questions about infancy and the shadowless world.

A second example appears in the *Standard* a year later, after Child had become editor. In the issue's poetry column appears an excerpt from Wordsworth's "Humanity" (1829) detailing his impassioned response to Cowper's claim in *The Task* that

> "Slaves cannot breathe in England"—a proud boast!
> And yet a mockery! if, from coast to coast,
> Though fettered slave be none, her floors and soil
> Groan underneath a weight of slavish toil,
> For the poor many, measured out by rules
> Fetched with cupidity from heartless schools,
> That to an idol, falsely called "the wealth
> Of nations," sacrifice a people's health,
> Body and mind and soul; a thirst so keen
> Is ever urging on the vast machine
> Of sleepless labor, 'mid whose dizzy wheels
> The power least prized is that which thinks and feels.[43]

Heroic couplets are not standard Wordsworthian fare, nor is palpable anger. Though the lines' enjambment softens the insistent thrum of the couplet form, the movement from repeated exclamation to mocking quotation to the emphatic polysyndeton of "body and mind and soul" sharpens the passage's rhetorical fervor, revealing a province of Wordsworth's poetic outpourings that is almost always excluded from the canon. These lines explicitly equate the experience of the "fettered slave" with the "slavish toil" of young factory workers, an equation that the *Standard* echoes by following these verses with an anonymous poem titled "The Little English Factory Girl," a rollicking trimeter ballad that ends with the death of the title character (see figure 3.1).

The spatial proximity of these poems on the printed page inspires a few insights. First, the proximity recognizes and ratifies the comparison Wordsworth makes between chattel slavery and English labor practices—the placement of one poem above the other in an antislavery newspaper points to the "Factory Girl" as proof of the similarity Wordsworth claims between the two conditions. Second, it argues that the comparison goes beyond identifying a shared vocabulary on which both of these critiques depend. It is not simply the case that Wordsworth's diction is also well suited to a discussion of American slave labor or that Child is more interested in the pathos used to describe factory workers than with the details of their plight. Rather, the proximity of the two poems insists that readers of the *Standard* who sympathize with the condition of enslaved Americans should also sympathize

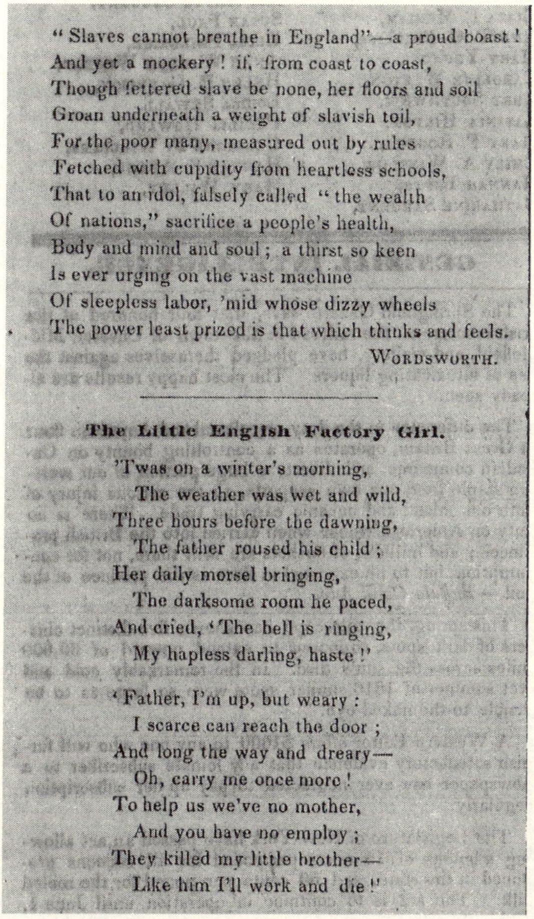

"Slaves cannot breathe in England"—a proud boast!
And yet a mockery! if, from coast to coast,
Though fettered slave be none, her floors and soil
Groan underneath a weight of slavish toil,
For the poor many, measured out by rules
Fetched with cupidity from heartless schools,
That to an idol, falsely called "the wealth
Of nations," sacrifice a people's health,
Body and mind and soul; a thirst so keen
Is ever urging on the vast machine
Of sleepless labor, 'mid whose dizzy wheels
The power least prized is that which thinks and feels.
WORDSWORTH.

The Little English Factory Girl.

'Twas on a winter's morning,
The weather was wet and wild,
Three hours before the dawning,
The father roused his child;
Her daily morsel bringing,
The darksome room he paced,
And cried, 'The bell is ringing,
My hapless darling, haste!'

'Father, I'm up, but weary:
I scarce can reach the door;
And long the way and dreary—
Oh, carry me once more!
To help us we've no mother,
And you have no employ;
They killed my little brother—
Like him I'll work and die!'

FIGURE 3.1. "Humanity" and "The Little English Factory Girl," *National Anti-Slavery Standard*, June 1841, 208. Courtesy of Beinecke Rare Book and Manuscript Library, Yale University.

with the little English factory girl—the comparison is necessarily moral as well as linguistic.

Excerpts from Wordsworth in the *Standard* always appear amid other poems, so there is some danger in reading too deeply into the placement of poems on the page. The closing lines of "Lines Left upon a Seat in a Yew-Tree" do not become political when they appear directly after a rousing poem celebrating the dedication of new abolitionists.[44] But the case of "Humanity" and "The Little English Factory Girl" is different: both poems address the same subject. And while it remains impossible to assert definitively that Child herself was responsible for the selection and placement of poems in this issue of the *Standard*, Karcher believes that "every department of the *Standard*—from the news on the front page to the literature and miscellany on the back page . . .—bore her impress and served to attract as broad a readership as possible."[45] I pair this example with Child's "Thoughts" from a year previous to argue that during a time when Wordsworth was thought to sate the palate of the "lover of nature and the muses" but was not widely recognized as germane to any sort of political advocate, Child herself was both of these readers.[46] She was the solitary nature lover and the public political activist, and her singular embodiment of their supposedly heterogeneous tastes refuses to acknowledge the two as dualistically opposed. The Wordsworth she reveals is simultaneously a familiar one, the Oxbridge poet of mystical morality, and one that her readers would not yet have known.

It was not until 1879 that Matthew Arnold glossed morality—a strength of English poetry, in his view—as the knowledge of "how to live." But nearly half a century earlier, Child already grasped the prescriptive moral value of Wordsworth's poetry and did so in a text recommending specific political action. That is, she demonstrated that the ability to tell others "how to live" was just as much an American trait as an English one while at the same time relying on Wordsworth's reputation as an English sage to support her own explicit prescriptions. In comparison, Arnold's sense of morality is imprecise, circling around a scatterplot of key terms: "The question, *how to live*, is itself a moral idea; and it is the question which most interests every man, and with which, in some way or other, he is perpetually occupied. A large sense is of course to be given to the term *moral.* Whatever bears upon the question, 'how to live,' comes under it" (*CPW*, 9:45). "How to live" is a moral question; *moral* means whatever addresses the question "how to live." The connection does not solidify beyond this point. But perhaps what is most precise about Arnold's definition of morality is that it emerges in the introduction to his selection of Wordsworth's poems, an essay where Arnold vociferously defends Wordsworth, insisting that he "is one of the very chief glories of English Poetry; and by nothing is England so glorious as by her poetry" (*CPW*, 9:55). To Child, what made Wordsworth so moral was his treatment of England. To Arnold, what made Wordsworth so English was his treatment of morality.

Arnold is quick to establish Wordsworth's place in English and continental literary history; just below Shakespeare and Milton but better in "real poetical achievement" than Chaucer, Dryden, or Pope; Voltaire, Racine, or Hugo (*CPW*, 9:41). From this high point of adoration, the path speeds downhill. Wordsworth's reputation—insufficient, in Arnold's opinion—has been marred not by a fluke of history or cultural dissemination but rather by the quantity of bad writing he produced. Arnold's disappointment abounds: the "mass of inferior work" is responsible for "imbedding the first-rate work and clogging it, obstructing our approach to it, chilling, not unfrequently, the high-wrought mood with which we leave it" (*CPW*,

9:42). Wordsworth has not been properly recognized and lauded because his good work has always been tainted by the proximity of the bad; extracting the worthy words from the clogged mire of "poetical baggage" is too much to ask of most readers. Indeed, the *Atlantic Magazine* made the same observation in 1824, wishing for "another edition of his works, purged of the *parvae maculae* that now serve only to deter the ignorant, to grieve the friendly, to detach the doubtful, and disgust the squeamish."[47] But Arnold has performed this cleansing chore, and the result is a collection that finally demonstrates Wordsworth's "powerful and beautiful application of ideas to life"—which, for Arnold, is a long way of saying his morality (*CPW*, 9:6). For in the opinion of Arnold, this morality is what makes English poetry great.

Borrowing from Voltaire, whom he quotes as saying that "no nation has treated in poetry the moral ideas with more energy and depth than the English nation," Arnold makes a two-pronged argument (*CPW*, 9:45). First, great poetry is moral—it tells us "how to live" without falling into overt didacticism. Second, "how to live" is a question that England as a nation excels at answering, at least poetically. The question of "how to live" is a very broad one, and it is thus quite a coup to turn some native sensitivity to the question into a particularly English asset. It follows that although Arnold provides examples from Keats and Shakespeare that support his argument, he never explains satisfactorily why the English poets are so good at telling their readers how to live or what the effects of this facility might be. Indeed, morality only balloons as the essay continues until Arnold has concluded that "a poetry of revolt against moral ideas is a poetry of revolt against *life*; a poetry of indifference toward moral ideas is a poetry of indifference toward *life*" (*CPW*, 9:46, emphasis in the original). He does, however, build on Voltaire's praise to clarify that the English nation is not necessarily more moral than other nations; rather, it treats morality "with more energy and depth." In other words, the association of Englishness with morality depends on theory, not practice; on "the application of ideas to life," not life itself. There is a level of remove here: English poetry is great because it talks with power and beauty not about a particular life but about how to live. That remove might begin to explain the role that Wordsworth's poetry filled in British colonial matriculation exams, for example, where it could inspire introspection into the *how* of living rather than the *what* (which must vary from Britain to Pretoria to Hong Kong).

But Child transports Wordsworth's morality to America without divesting it of the specificities that distinguish Britain from its former colony. In fact, those specificities are precisely what constitute Wordsworth's morality in her hands—not the "application of ideas to life" but life itself, not the diction of moral outrage but the suffering of actual laborers. It might seem unexpected to find two poems explicitly concerned with the condition of England in a newspaper like the *National*

Anti-Slavery Standard whose name announces in more than one way its strictly American concerns. But this is part of the point: her political agenda, though concerned with an American plight, was fed by a morality that had little interest in national boundaries.

LYDIA MARIA CHILD'S *APPEAL* AND *THE EXCURSION*'S GLOBALIZED ALBION

An Appeal in Favor of That Class of Americans Called Africans, a text that developed out of years of research, has received almost no attention in current literary studies. When it was published, reviewers saw the *Appeal* as a stark departure from form: Child's prior publications included the interracial romance *Hobomok* (1824)—which, like most of her romances, has garnered much recent notice—and the tomes of home economy, *The Frugal Housewife* (1829) and *The Mother's Book* (1831). Child herself was aware of this generic shift, and in the preface to the *Appeal* she dares her reader to "read it, from sheer curiosity to see what a woman (who had better attend to her household concerns) will say upon such a subject."[48] However, the shift was not as momentous as readers (and even Child herself) made it out to be. *Hobomok*, the romance that launched Child into literary fame, features a headstrong female protagonist bent on challenging patriarchal authority. Child's *Juvenile Miscellany*, a children's periodical that she founded in 1826, routinely made reference to the evils of slavery and did so with increasing frequency after Child met Garrison in 1831—indeed, "many of the facts and arguments Child amassed for her juvenile readers would appear in her 1833 *Appeal*, often repeated verbatim."[49] Fans of her novels may have seen her as a novelist; devotees of her home economy held her as a paragon of "good sense" and a "decided utilitarian."[50] But for all these perceptions, Child had been a publicly political writer since 1828, when she published *The First Settlers of New England*, a tome that staunchly defended American Indian rights.[51] The *Appeal* did not inaugurate Child's activism but rather made it impossible to ignore.

The *Appeal* addresses the history, economics, and politics of slavery from a global standpoint, and although Child borrowed from antislavery precursors like Thomas Clarkson, David Walker, and Abbé Grégoire, her text is unique in its breadth. Its chapters include a comparative history of slavery with its economic and political effects, an examination of the morality and intellect of enslaved people and the prejudices of white Americans, and a plan for peaceful emancipation. It is also unique in its rejection of the colonization movement, which in Child's words sought to end slavery "by gradually removing all the blacks to Africa" and that largely dominated antislavery discourse when the *Appeal* was published (*A*, 117).[52]

Stymied by the objections of slavery apologists, Child undertook the research and writing of a treatise that would silence their previously unanswerable questions, and this undertaking resulted in a textbook—a decidedly unfeminine genre in the view of many readers, especially compared to her previous publications. In writing this textbook, Child was aware "of the unpopularity of the task" but insisted, "Though I *expect* ridicule and censure, I cannot *fear* them" (*A*, 5, emphasis in the original). Indeed, the *Appeal* received its fair share of ridicule and censure, but it also thrust Child to the forefront of the abolitionist cause, "elevating her to a position of unparalleled political influence for a woman."[53] The *North American Review*, which had dubbed Child "the first woman in the republic" just one month before the *Appeal*'s publication, did not foresee how apropos that honorific would become.[54]

In her *Appeal*, Child chooses epigraphs that are almost exclusively literary in origin, a fact that in itself is not surprising. What is surprising is that none of these epigraphs come from American authors: while Child describes slavery as a uniquely American problem, no American authorities appear in her epigraphs.[55] Such selectiveness can be explained in part by the fact that the antislavery verses of Coleridge in "Fears in Solitude" (1798) or Cowper in "The Negro's Complaint" (1788), both of which appear in the *Appeal*, had no contemporary American correlate: there were few famous American writers to choose from in 1833 and little widely circulating American abolitionist poetry in the late eighteenth and early nineteenth centuries. But Child's selectiveness also requires us to understand the relationship between body text and epigraph, a dynamic in which the paratext foreshadows and comments on the body text that follows—as a relationship that is national as well as textual—in which English and continental writers assume a visually authoritative position in regards to the examination of American policy and practice that follows.

Although the epigraph is, in Gérard Genette's words, "a mute gesture whose interpretation is left up to the reader," it is a gesture whose place on the page affords it an aura of influence, an authority that reframes the seeming passivity of its silence and isolation as textual power.[56] In appearance it is always fragmentary but can come garnished with quotation marks, or without, or in italics, or with the author's name in parentheses, or in capital letters, "and so forth," for as Genette admits, "I do not think a norm has been established for these matters, at least in France."[57] For all his irreverence, Genette takes seriously the "ways in which . . . paratextual devices can be both conventional in their form and highly original in their deployment," and this means taking seriously forgery and inaccuracy, two major sources of such originality.[58] Writers, after all, are free to fabricate quotations and attribute them to any author they choose, real or imagined.[59] Or, more subtly, an epigraph may be "authentic but inaccurate," either because the epigrapher remembers the source imperfectly, or because he or she "wishes to make the quotation fit its context better." This "fit" is what we try to decipher when reading an epigraph, which, deprived of its original context, is supposed to comment on or even presage a new and different context. So while forgery and inaccuracy are possible, decontextualization is guaranteed: as a fragment, the epigraph is always missing whatever text came before and after.

The relationship between the epigraph and the text that follows is both paramount and mystifying; writers often neglect to mention the epigraph at all, let alone explain its place in the text as a whole. In light of the epigraph's definitional and fragmentary silence, the ones from Wordsworth demand interpretation not because they too are decontextualized and unexplained but because their absent context stands in opposition to the plan Child proposes for ending slavery in America: she chooses epigraphs that describe the suffering of factory workers in a treatise that advocates drastically increasing the number of factory workers. This disconnect is particularly thorny because the passages Child selects did not routinely appear in the periodicals that reviewed Wordsworth, suggesting that Child had read *The Excursion* in its entirety and was familiar with its condemnation of factory labor. Even so, she was not above altering epigraphs to fit her purpose and could have taken far greater liberties with Wordsworth: in the epigraph to her second chapter, she quotes from an epilogue to Irish playwright Isaac Bickerstaff's *The Padlock*, "written by a very worthy Clergyman" and published in the *Gentlemen's Magazine*. The original says, "Then all nations in your code may see, / The British Negro, like the Briton, free"; Child switches out the last line for her own: "That, black or white, Americans are free" (*A*, 36).[60] This willingness to replace the quotation's British context with an explicitly and falsely American one not only recalls Genette's reminder that the authenticity of the epigraph is never guaranteed but also makes Child's more scrupulous treatment of *The Excursion* noteworthy. What use did Child find in a poet who did not say much about slavery and who abhorred the practice of industrialization that she championed?

Genette's investigation of epigraphs suggests that although their very status as epigraphs guarantees a modicum of obscurity to the *Appeal*'s selections from *The Excursion*, they owe the remainder of their murkiness to the specific context that the epigraph form removes. That is, epigraphs are always decontextualized and blurry, but these are especially so. One of the two epigraphs for the first chapter of the *Appeal* comes from Cowper and the other from book 8 of *The Excursion*, in which the Wanderer, the Recluse, and the Vicar amble and discuss, among other things, the encroachment of industrialization. It describes the factory workers' predicament:

> The lot is wretched, the condition sad,
> Whether a pining discontent survive,

And thirst for change; or habit hath subdued
The soul depressed; dejected—even to love
Of her close tasks, and long captivity. (*A*, 7)

Child's habit (a common one) is to cite the author of the epigraph but to give no further information about the epigraph's location within a specific text. Spoken by the Wanderer, who is usually taken as Wordsworth's spokesman, these five lines betray nothing that might upset their inclusion in an abolitionist tract. In accordance with Child's topic ("Brief history of Negro slavery.—Its inevitable effect upon all concerned in it"), the epigraph details individual suffering—the potential for "pining discontent," the soul "dejected" by the influence of subduing "habit." However, arriving in *The Excursion* a few pages after the Wanderer's lament that

I have lived to mark
A new and unforeseen creation rise
From out the labours of a peaceful Land
Wielding her potent enginery to frame
And to produce, with appetite as keen
As that of war, which rests not night or day,
Industrious to destroy! (*E*, bk. 8, lines 89–95)

the epigraph's anti-industrial context becomes clear. In Wordsworth's hands, industrialization has the ability "to frame / And to produce," but these verbs take no direct object, making industry seem strangely unproductive in spite of the latent femininity in "her potent enginery," which suggests a fecundity without end and a perverted mimicking of nature.[61] What matters more than the products of industry is its appetite, warlike and destructive. As this context comes into focus, so too does Child's decision to crop the epigraph as she did: the image of the factory's hunger "as keen / As that of war" has no place in an argument for the peaceful emancipation of the American South.

In order to foreground the otherwise cryptic work of Child's epigraphs, I would like to take a brief detour into the afterlives of Wordsworth's sonnet on L'Ouverture. Child quotes this sonnet in the body of her *Appeal*, in a paragraph about the importance of L'Ouverture, and integrates it with the barest of sentences: "Wordsworth addressed the following sonnet to Toussaint L'Ouverture" (*A*, 159). The sonnet, first published in 1807, is Wordsworth's most famous treatment of slavery and the fight for abolition:

Toussaint, the most unhappy man of men!
Whether the whistling Rustic tend his plough
Within thy hearing, or thy head be now

Pillowed in some deep dungeon's earless den;
O miserable Chieftain! where and when
Wilt thou find patience? Yet die not; do thou
Wear rather in thy bonds a cheerful brow:
Though fallen thyself, never to rise again,
Live, and take comfort. Thou hast left behind
Powers that will work for thee; air, earth, and skies;
There's not a breathing of the common wind
That will forget thee; thou hast great allies;
Thy friends are exultations, agonies,
And love, and man's unconquerable mind. (*PW*, 3:112)

The sonnet is not a perfect tribute—one might wish that Wordsworth hadn't advised the leader of the Haitian Revolution to wear his bonds with "a cheerful brow"—but the poem is a genuine attempt to make good on its assurance that L'Ouverture's name will not die with him.[62] In Child's hands, the sonnet's sole purpose is to support the warm biography she provides for the leader. Appearing in a chapter called "Intellect of Negroes," the sonnet is treated less as a poem than as an objective fact: like the other evidence arranged in support of the revolutionary leader, it directly addresses L'Ouverture's role in the Haitian Revolution and praises his influence.

In the hands of Claude McKay, who included the whole sonnet on L'Ouverture in his picaresque novel *Home to Harlem* (1928), the poem was a more vexing artifact, for McKay was ambivalent about the role Wordsworth's speaker fashions for himself as a purveyor of L'Ouverture's fame. In McKay's novel, two men—both black, both working class—discuss L'Ouverture, and one of them, the Haitian intellectual Ray, is inspired to recite Wordsworth's sonnet. That the novel interpolates the sonnet in its entirety is notable—the only other texts quoted at length are songs popular at Harlem clubs—and Ray's introduction of the sonnet similarly places Wordsworth in a vaunted position. According to Ray, L'Ouverture "was honored by a great enigmatic poet of that period. And I honor both Toussaint and the poet by keeping in my memory the wonderful, passionate lines."[63] In this formulation, reciting Wordsworth's poem means honoring the poet as much as the revolutionary whom Wordsworth was trying to honor. The balance here is somewhat discomfiting. Why is a Haitian intellectual, displaced from his home country by the U.S. occupation of Haiti in the early twentieth century and working as a waiter on the railroad, as keen to honor Wordsworth as L'Ouverture? As if to intensify this question, McKay makes the scene overtly didactic, with Ray acting as teacher to his American friend Jake, who has never heard of Haiti: Jake sits "like a big eager boy," learns "many facts about Hayti," and "plies his instructor with questions" (*HH*, 131–132). According to Leah Read Rosenberg, scenes like this one hint at "McKay's failure to imagine a bond of equality between the poet Ray and the worker Jake," a failure that she associates with McKay's debt to British Romanticism (and particularly Wordsworth's separation of the artist from the people in the preface to *Lyrical Ballads*).[64] Yet the dynamic between Ray and Jake is less an imaginative failure on the part of McKay than a conscious choice. Ray loves Wordsworth but is cynical about the level of education that his love of Wordsworth reveals. Modern education is an "anachronism," he says, something "we Negros" get "like our houses. When the whites move out, we move in and take possession of the old dead stuff. Dead stuff that this age has no use for" (*HH*, 243). Wordsworth, part and parcel of the "dead old stuff" that Ray decries, shapes Ray's connection to L'Ouverture, and it is a shaping that Ray could do without. He is, in his own words, "a misfit with my little education and constant dreaming" (*HH*, 274). And yet it is through Wordsworth's sonnet that Ray disabuses Jake of his prejudices, turning him into an adherent of pan-Africanism. When Ray finishes his recitation of Wordsworth, "Jake felt like one passing through a dream, vivid in rich, varied colors. It was a revelation beautiful in his mind." No longer can Jake "look askew at foreign niggers" from the West Indies and Africa; now he feels "like a boy who stands with the map of the world in colors before him, and feels the wonder of the world" (*HH*, 134). The knowledge of Wordsworth separates Ray from Jake, but the lesson that Jake takes from Wordsworth draws him closer to Ray.

In short, Ray has a complex relationship to Wordsworth's sonnet: he is pleased that a canonical poet wrote beautifully about a Haitian hero, but Ray's subject position is so distant from that of Wordsworth that he cannot but resent the influence of the English poet, representative of "dead old stuff" and an education that ill suits his role in the United States. In contrast, Child's use of Wordsworth's sonnet is simple because her political aims are visibly in concert with his; he writes in praise of the revolutionary leader and so does she. In the epigraphs of her tract, however, her relationship to Wordsworth is more ambiguous, and it is in this paratextual space of decontextualization that she chooses to stage her negotiation. Here, Child invokes the Wordsworth of *The Excursion*, a poet whose support she implicitly claims, whose concerns do not neatly align with her own, but whose poetry is, in fact, as global as Child implies.

On the surface, it would seem that Child's second epigraph from Wordsworth has as straightforward a job as the sonnet to L'Ouverture: to echo the disgust Child expresses with the duplicity of public discourse. To introduce chapter 3, "Free labor and slave labor.—Possibility of safe emancipation," Child places a quotation from the book of Jeremiah alongside one from book 5 of *The Excursion*:

> Who can reflect, unmoved, upon the round
> Of smooth and solemnized complacencies,
> By which, on Christian lands, from age to age
> Profession mocks performance. Earth is sick,
> And Heaven is weary, of the hollow words
> Which States and Kingdoms utter when they talk
> Of truth and justice. (*A*, 72)

The meaning is clear enough: states and kingdoms are not to be trusted. Wordsworth's solution differs politically from Child's—he recommends that we "turn to private life / And social neighbourhood; look we to ourselves" in order to cope with the hypocrisy of political discourse, while Child is far more interested in public solutions to such hypocrisy (*E*, bk. 5, lines 381–382). They share, however, a belief that "Earth is sick" and current political structures are untrustworthy.

More troubling is the fact that Child reaches similar heights of outrage during her impassioned defense of Northern manufacturing a chapter later, where she addresses the political tension between the North and the South and memorably asserts that "if one man were to knock another down with a broad axe, in the attempt to brush a fly from his face, and then blame him for not being sufficiently thankful, it would exactly illustrate the relation between the North and the South" on the subject of commerce and industrialization (*A*, 109). Child goes on to describe how after protectionist tariffs were passed in 1816 and 1824, Northern manufacturing prevailed over the obstructionist efforts of Southern interests: "Neat and flourishing villages rose in every valley of New England. The busy hum of machinery made music with her neglected waterfalls. All her streams, like the famous Pactolus, flowed with gold. From her discouraged and embarrassed commerce rose a greater blessing, apparently indestructible. Walls of brick and granite could not easily be overturned by the Southern *lever*, and left to decay, as the ship timber had done. Thus Mordecai was again seated in the king's gate, by means of the very system intended for his ruin" (*A*, 110, emphasis in the original). This earth is not sick. Industrialization here is responsible for drawing nature out of her hiding spots and harmonizing with her in its own droning hum, a hum without which waterfalls are "neglected," devoid not just of gold but also of human care. Similarly, Child's references to the book of Esther and the myth of Midas elevate industrialization above its sheer materiality, affiliating the factory with the higher influences of religion and mythology. But it's hard to imagine Wordsworth conceiving of this landscape as anything other than sick, let alone capable of music.

As jarring as this disconnect is, it would not have been apparent to most American readers of Child's *Appeal.* American periodicals were not inclined to print the excerpts Child chose for her epigraphs before 1833; as I've shown, they most often chose long natural descriptions or philosophical ruminations. So while readers may have been accustomed to a piecemeal appreciation of this English epic, those who did not own the American 1824 edition of Wordsworth's collected poems were most likely unfamiliar with the fragments that Child included in her *Appeal* and thus also unfamiliar with their surrounding context. To these readers, there would have been no appearance of contradiction; out of the context of *The Excursion*, none of the Wordsworth verses that Child quotes seem out of place in a tract that praises industrialization. Though it is difficult to generalize about the familiarity of Child's readers with the entirety of Wordsworth's epic, newspaper reviews suggest that the epic's political agenda often went unnoticed. The epigraphs from Wordsworth, then, would have demanded little more explanation than the explicitly antislavery epigraphs from Cowper and Coleridge.

In more than one way, however, Child knew what she was doing when she invoked Wordsworth's *Excursion*. First, the seeming disagreement between Wordsworth and Child is largely due to the differing historical realities of factory labor in England and America. As Child's inclusion of "The Little English Factory Girl" in the *Standard* implies, industrialization in England was more advanced and more exploitative than factories in 1830s New England. America lagged behind in its development of factories in part because of England's stringent laws prohibiting both the export of machines and drawings and the emigration of skilled men who could potentially re-create the machines in a competing economy. But when factories did start opening their doors in New England in the 1820s, many of them thrived, and they did so without the conditions that made England's factories notorious.[65] As Amanda Claybaugh notes, Harriet Martineau, whom Child discusses in her *Appeal*, confessed that "industrial workers in Britain were as oppressed, and agricultural laborers as ignorant, as slaves in the United States," echoing the comparison of the two plights that Wordsworth and others made.[66] Though Child does not detail the conditions of New England's factories, the seeming disjuncture of her Wordsworthian epigraphs fades in light of the attitude she and Wordsworth share toward the alienation of their respective countries' poorest workers. Child quotes at length from the "Great Compromiser," statesman Henry Clay, who proposes, "That labor is best, in which the laborer knows that he will derive the profits of his industry, that his employment depends upon his diligence, and his reward upon this assiduity" (*A*, 74), and as if offering a mournful portrayal of what happens when "the profits of his industry" are seized, the Wanderer bemoans how "this organic frame, / So joyful in its motions, is become / Dull, to the joy of her own motions dead," detailing how the textile factory, its workers dabbed "with cotton-flakes / Or locks of wool," succeeds in transforming the "organic" into the "dull" (*E*, bk. 8, lines 322–324, 309–310). Neither the enslaved worker nor the factory worker benefits directly from his labor, a divorce that deadens both workers to the "joy" of their motion. Thus in regards to manufacturing as it was practiced in England, Child and Wordsworth were of one mind despite the appearance of dissent, and both were similarly comfortable equating the experience of English factory workers with the suffering of enslaved Americans.

Second, Child's strategic repurposing of Wordsworth outside of England shows *The Excursion*'s global context to inhere not just in the poem's afterlives but also in the poem itself. To be clear, it is not the case that reading *The Excursion* in light of Child's *Appeal* means discovering that *The Excursion* is concerned with the plight of laborers worldwide or that the poem's interest in the condition of England is a microcosm for the condition of the global sphere. Rather, the careful nuance of Child's repurposing encourages us to pay closer attention to how *The Excursion* describes the nation that American readers so consistently associated with its author. What we find is an England that is global in several different but imbricated ways. England is earth and air, evoking a planetary environment of which it is but a part. It is both unified and carved up by national and transnational transit networks, the result of British colonial expansion and trade. It shall export its cultural boons to its colonial holdings. At the same time, it is being effectively colonized from within and does not fully possess those cultural boons it is supposed to export. In spite of its national specificity, *The Excursion* cannot address the condition of England without conjuring England's vexed place in an ever-expanding global network.

The remainder of this section dwells in one of the books Child quotes in her epigraph, book 8, where Wordsworth imagines these competing versions of England. But typically, critics interested in Wordsworth's occasional treatment of a more global sphere focus on book 9 of *The Excursion*, where the Wanderer imagines England as a beehive from which British colonials will spread abroad to inhabit new locales, "even till the smallest habitable rock, / Beaten by lonely billows, hear the songs / Of humanised society" (*E*, bk. 9, lines 387–389).[67] The Wanderer goes on like this at length. Colonial expansion is underwritten by nature, "as the element of air affords / An easy passage to the industrious bees / Fraught with her burdens," and overpopulation ceases to be a problem, as "the wide waters, open to the power, / The will, the instincts, and appointed needs / Of Britain, do invite her to cast off / Her swarms" (*E*, bk. 9, lines 369–378). There are reasons to think that this imperial fantasy might not reflect Wordsworth's own attitudes. David Simpson points out how even within the scope of book 9, the poem ironizes the Wanderer's fantasy by following his speech with some jovial plant hunting so that "we have here a group of intelligent and articulate lovers of rural life, 'seemingly' secure in a space protected from the 'restless world,' who themselves act as agents of disturbance and molestation within the local economy of that very same space."[68] My focus, however, is on how book 8, with its conflicting visions of England, denies support to an imperial project in which Britain is capable of exporting "humanised society" and "civil arts" (*E*, bk. 9, lines 389, 390). In short, book 8 seeks but cannot find the line separating past from present, civilized from savage, georgic from industrial, and in a larger sense, England from Britain.

These distinctions collapse amid *The Excursion*'s discussion of two related subjects: landscapes and laborers. At first, it appears that this argument runs counter to the poem's prevailing vision of England, a place we might call English England, to borrow from Alexander Crummell, or else Albion, to use Wordsworth's language from book 9 (*E*, bk. 9, line 393). An emphatic nostalgia for an England that is no more imbues book 8 of *The Excursion* and is voiced by nearly all the poem's characters. The Wanderer, who does most of the talking, pines for the wandering of his earlier years, when he was welcomed in a "straggling burgh, of ancient charter proud, / And dignified by battlements and towers / Of some stern castle" (*E*, bk. 8, lines 101–103). The town's age and dignity—not to mention its castle—cast it as an ideal and idealized locale that is located irrevocably in the past; now, when the Wanderer wanderers, it is "with fruitless pains" (*E*, bk. 8, line 95). His purview soon broadens to encompass the whole country, "the blessed Isle, / Truth's consecrated residence, the seat / Impregnable of Liberty and Peace," and the alliance of England with the qualities of truth, liberty, and peace becomes inseparable from the nation's "impregnable" status, its firm isolation from neighbors (*E*, bk. 8, lines 145–146). The Wanderer is not the only speaker who develops this nostalgic vision of England. The poem's first-person speaker soon seizes the baton and falls into a mood of moral conservatism, detailing how he and his compatriots "revere" and "preserve" a host of endangered traits: "The old domestic morals of the land, / Her simple manners," not to mention "the character of peace, / Sobriety, and order, and chaste love, / And honest dealing, and untainted speech, / And pure good-will, and hospitable cheer" (*E*, bk. 8, lines 234–242). The similarities between this list and the one begun by the Wanderer are striking: truth, liberty, and peace become "peace," "honest dealing, and untainted speech." Moreover, these similarities suggest that the disappearance of these traits is lamentable not simply because they are universal goods but because they are particularly English, as the Wanderer has established by associating them with "the blessed Isle." Meanwhile, the flight into polysyndeton raises the rhetorical barometer, inspiring the Wanderer to exclaim that these characteristics are "fled! . . . Fled utterly!" (*E*, bk. 8, lines 252–253). Now half of the peripatetic party is mourning a stable, isolated, and ideologically coherent England.

This vision of England is commonly associated with Wordsworth's later works, and for good reason. (Writes one American reader, "His love for England and English institutions was too undiscerning.")[69] But it is not the only vision of

England that book 8 presents; rather, the characters weave back and forth between reverence for old English England and detailed representations of the contemporary landscape, which they recognize as imbricated within a global sphere. In this way, as Simpson argues, "any unified (or reified) image of the ideal country life is pre-empted," sequestered irretrievably in the past.[70] Immediately after his lament for towns girded by a "stern castle," the Wanderer shifts focus to describe one of these more globalized landscapes, noting that wide roads have come to replace smaller paths:

> The foot-path faintly marked, the horse-track wild,
> And formidable length of plashy lane,
> (Prized avenues ere others had been shaped
> Or easier links connecting place with place)
> Have vanished—swallowed up by stately roads
> Easy and bold, that penetrate the gloom
> Of Britain's farthest glens. The Earth has lent
> Her waters, Air her breezes; and the sail
> Of traffic glides with ceaseless intercourse,
> Glistening along the low and woody dale;
> Or, in its progress, on the lofty side,
> Of some bare hill, with wonder kenned from far. (*E*, bk. 8, lines 105–116)

This vista features two types of circulation that work in unexpected concert: on one hand, the circulation of transport networks (roads and traffic), and on the other, the more planetary circulation of natural materials shared by landscapes across the globe (waters and breezes). The Wanderer's distaste at broad roads that somewhat violently "penetrate the gloom / Of Britain's farthest glens" is reminiscent of Wordsworth's later attacks on the railroad and his cranky complaints about modish houses that I describe in the next chapter. But what strikes me here is how quickly the Wanderer expands his purview from "Britain's farthest glens" to "the Earth," who "has lent / Her waters, Air her breezes" to this nation. England here is not an "impregnable" isle. On the contrary, in these lines it is the beneficiary of earth and air, no longer Albion or Britain but a plot of bedrock, a portion of the "grounded entity" represented by the planet.[71] The capitalization personifies these natural elements, making their products—waters and breezes—seem more like gifts and their lending an act of generosity. England here may be "blessed," as the Wanderer has insisted, but it is also just another corner of the planet, a planet that is, in Gayatri Chakravorty Spivak's words, part of "the species of alterity, belonging to another system; and yet we inhabit it, on loan."[72] In these passages, then, the immediate transition from this planetary sphere to "the sail / Of traffic" is abrupt—almost as abrupt as the previous transition, from the newfangled "stately roads" to the beneficence of earth and air. (At this historical moment, *traffic* refers to commerce or trade rather than a line of coaches plugging the road.) The Wanderer shifts rapidly between subjects and tones, enveloping his graceful description of England's planetary context in descriptions of infrastructure—roads, waterways, trade routes—that suggest an entirely different and yet apparently related sort of global context. The "waters" and "breezes" lent by earth and air mean that "the sail / Of traffic" can actually sail.

The tone throughout this passage is mixed. Wide roads are almost predatory in their ability to "penetrate the gloom" of forests and "swallow up" more spirited avenues like the "horse-track wild" and "plashy lane." It makes sense that this tone of critique falls away when the Wanderer moves on to the generosity of earth and air. But when "waters" and "breezes" lead into "the sail / Of traffic" that "glides with ceaseless intercourse," the tone remains positive: traffic is seen "glistening along the low and woody dale," generating "wonder" in far-off spectators. While the sail imagery is successful in that it makes traffic seem like an aesthetic boon, it operates rather strangely: "The sail / Of traffic" has made its way inland amid hills and dales with no mention of a river. The image thus reverses a dynamic that Gillian Beer has noted, where "the sea offers a vast extension of the island, allowing the psychic size of the body politic to expand, without bumping into others' territory," for here the sea and its ships appear to be infiltrating the mainland.[73] This description is surprising. The Wanderer's speech is about how the landscape has changed for the worse since the advent of "an Inventive Age" defined by industrialization and population growth (*E*, bk. 8, line 87). What is an aesthetically pleasing description of commerce doing here? Why is the ceaseless sail of traffic any better than the stately roads? The effect is rather like Wordsworth's sonnet on Westminster Bridge, where London's cityscape is naturalized and aestheticized so that its "ships, towers, domes, theatres, and temples" can supersede the beauty of "valley, rock, or hill" (*PW*, 3:38). Like London at sunrise, traffic in this passage somehow becomes pretty. Yet in "Composed upon Westminster Bridge," the city's built environment is only beautiful when London's inhabitants are asleep—when no smoke or sounds pollute the air. In *The Excursion*, it is the traffic (and as we will see, the smoke) that glitters, inspiring wonder. There are some chinks in the armor. The enjambment in "the sail / Of traffic" creates just enough suspense for *sail* to sound like the more expected term, *sale*, given the context of trade. In that light, the "glid[ing]" of traffic, which needs the image of the sail in order to appear effortless, loses a bit of its aesthetic sheen. And perhaps the repetition of *ease*—"easier links" and "roads / Easy and bold"—worms its way into the "c*ease*less intercourse," suggesting that the traffic is reduplicated and excessive, a result of overly "easy" trade routes. But overall, the impression is that this landscape's picturesque beauty, its mix of hill and dale, is not marred by the incursion of traffic; it is actually improved by it. As the argument of book 8 predicted, there are "favourable effects" from "changes in the Country from the manufacturing spirit" (*PW*, 5:265).

In these descriptions of the landscape, the "manufacturing spirit" has rendered certain sights and views obsolete. Yet this spirit has also managed to harmonize with the existing landscape: like Child, who described how "the busy hum of machinery made music with her neglected waterfalls," the Wanderer spies glistening beauty in the "sail of traffic." These glimpses do not atone for the working conditions in factories, the souls "depressed; dejected," as Child quotes in one of her *Excursion* epigraphs (*E*, bk. 8, line 295). But I don't think the Wanderer intends to make a list of industrialization's pros and cons. Rather, his multifaceted depiction of the changes wrought by industrialization makes it difficult to cling to a tidy conception of an isolated Albion, simple and honest. The seemingly purer, ameliorative forces of earth and air crisscross national borders, like the "ceaseless" trade that they physically support.

The mixed tone continues when the Wanderer discusses laborers and their dwellings. He mourns how urban growth threatens the land but simultaneously describes clouds of smoke in not unpleasant terms:

> at social Industry's command,
> How quick, how vast an increase! From the germ
> Of some poor hamlet, rapidly produced
> Here a huge town, continuous and compact,
> Hiding the face of earth for leagues—and there,
> Where not a habitation stood before,
> Abodes of men irregularly massed
> Like trees in forests,—spread through spacious tracts,
> O'er which the smoke of unremitting fires
> Hangs permanent, and plentiful as wreaths
> Of vapour glittering in the morning sun. (*E*, bk. 8, lines 117–127).

The rate of production in this scene is excessive. Like the earlier description of the "inventive age," never resting, "wielding her potent enginery to frame / And to produce," the hamlet has rapidly become a "huge town" (*E*, bk. 8, lines 92–94). The natural imagery does little to naturalize this growth. Though the comparison between houses and trees might seem positive, Wordsworth shows his hand with the reference to "spacious tracts." Like plantations of larch trees—which, as we will see in the next chapter, are a source of ire for Wordsworth in the *Guide to the Lakes*—these metaphorical tree tracts are planted and artificial, prefiguring suburban housing tracts. But these complaints lead again into a "Westminster Bridge" dynamic, an aestheticization of the smoke hanging over the houses, "plentiful as wreaths / Of vapour glittering in the morning sun." Perhaps the Wanderer is being facetious. But it seems instead that even in this hastily assembled and smoky town, there is something "glittering," worthy of admiration. As Alison Hickey and Sally Bushell point out, the dialogic structure of *The Excursion* means that no one character holds absolute authority or a consistently discrete ideological position.[74] As Hickey writes, "The 'sides' to which book 8 refers are not simply ascribed to different voices . . . but mingled in the same voice."[75] These complex, even inconsistent representations of contemporary England—ugly and beautiful, at once under the thumb of planetary currents and the incursions of global capital—stand in stark contrast to the stable vision of England, "truth's consecrated residence, the seat / Impregnable of Liberty and Peace," that book 8 of *The Excursion* simultaneously develops.

So far, we have seen many versions of England: Albion, industrialized Britain, mercantile Britain, the planetary isle. These versions are porous: the Wanderer, for instance, sees that trade depends on a transportation network of roads and waterways, some of which are in turn buttressed by the planetary forces of earth and air. Let us add to the list imperial Britain, equally imbricated in this matrix of Englands. Britain's imperial destiny depends on a stable and idealized vision of Albion, as the Wanderer suggests during his imperialist speech from book 9: "From culture, unexclusively bestowed / On Albion's noble Race in freedom born, / Expect these mighty issues" (*E*, bk. 9, lines 392–394). Albion's inhabitants may not have sole possession of "culture," but their freedom, when combined with this gift of culture, enables Britain to spread "humanised society" to "the smallest habitable rock" (*E*, bk. 9, lines 387–389). In book 9, oceans are the medium for this dissemination; as Samuel Baker describes, the sea allows Wordsworth to "reconfigure the world into Britain writ large."[76] But in book 8, the sea creeps inland. British colonialism and British trade mingle in the Wanderer's depiction of England's shores: "Hence is the wide sea peopled,—hence the shores / Of Britain are resorted to by ships / Freighted from every climate of the world / With the world's choicest produce" (*E*, bk. 8, lines 133–136). This is the solution to the threat of overcrowding: the population boom brought on by British industrialization leads directly to a meditation on the global transport of both people and products. Britain peoples the seas while enjoying the "choicest produce" from afar. Yet the seas, or rather what they portend, do not stay put: the Wanderer describes how Britain is inundated with a "spectacle of sails / That, through her inland regions, to and fro / Pass with the respirations of the tide, / Perpetual, multitudinous!" (*E*, bk. 8, lines 139–142). Like the "sail of traffic" carried aloft by earth's breezes, these boats are as natural as breathing, sensitively staging their incursions with the tides. But their presence is accompanied by the threat of violence. The Wanderer concludes his description of this maritime landscape with an ode to the navy, a "dread arm of floating power" that will protect the nation from "those who would approach / With hostile purposes" (*E*, bk. 8, lines 143–145). The connection between British industrialization and global, mercantile, and potentially hostile incursions is not clear from the Wanderer's meditation, but what I want to emphasize here is the connection itself, not its rationale. While the ravages of industrialization were, as I argued earlier, seen as exclusive to Great Britain at this time, the Wanderer here cannot discuss the British factory system and its effects on the appearance of England without invoking the global sphere of air and sea, natural forces that propel ships overseas while also carrying them into the heart of England.

With his descriptions of the countryside, the Wanderer brings emblems of global movement—ships and roads, air and water—into England. With his descriptions of England's poor, he is doing something similar but making clear the stakes. The "sail of traffic" can be aesthetically integrated into a vista of English hills and dales. In the Recluse's descriptions of Britain's poor, however, certain classes are clearly racialized, evidencing a sort of internal colonization that is absent from the incursions the Wanderer describes with regards to the landscape. This racialization emerges in the Recluse's comparison of the "ragged Offspring" of the English countryside with "Britons born and bred within the pale / Of civil polity" who work in the fields (*E*, bk. 8, lines 348, 392–393). These two figures, the ragged offspring and the laboring Briton, occupy the same physical space while epitomizing a binary between self and other most often associated with *Lyrical Ballads* and book 7 of *The Prelude* in Wordsworth's corpus. And yet, as we shall see, the Britons "bred within the pale" are no more integrated into Britain's "civil polity" than the ragged offspring in spite of the circumstances of these Britons' birth.

The "ragged Offspring" are

> Naked, and coloured like the soil, the feet
> On which they stand; as if thereby they drew
> Some nourishment, as trees do by their roots,
> From earth, the common mother of us all. (*E*, bk. 8, lines 354–358)

Earth is not a mother sufficiently "common" to prevent these children's soil-colored skin from distancing them from the speaker, who admits a line later that "figure and mien, complexion and attire, / Are leagued to strike dismay" (*E*, bk. 8, lines 358–359). These children are beggars and performers, blond and wild:

> their upright hair
> Crowned like the image of fantastic Fear;
> Or wearing, (shall we say?) in that white growth
> An ill-adjusted turban, for defence

> Or fierceness, wreathed around their sunburnt brows,
> By savage Nature? (*E*, bk. 8, lines 348–353)

Their turbans and fierceness collude with savage nature to Orientalize these children further despite their blond hair. Yet the beggars, white and at the same time distinctly other, are not limited to a specific locale, like the "Parliament of Monsters" at Bartholomew Fair, from whom Wordsworth can flee (*P*, bk. 7, line 692). Rather, the Orientalized figures in *The Excursion* "are bred, / All England through" (*E*, bk. 8, lines 369–370). Like the "modern Merlins, Wild Beasts, Puppet-shows" that Wordsworth encounters in *The Prelude* (*P*, bk. 7, line 713), the ragged offspring perform tricks for money, "an uncouth feat exhibit. . . . Heels over head, like tumblers on a stage," but they exceed the bounds set by the imperial metropole of London (*E*, bk. 8, lines 380–381). They are everywhere, just like the "Britons born and bred within the pale," and their racialized status reveals that the divide between self and other does not coincide with national borders: ragged offspring and laboring Briton, other and self, occupy the same England.

This juxtaposition I've proposed between ragged offspring and Briton, other and self, is logical, but it proves inaccurate when the Recluse completes his description of the laboring Briton. Based on his characterization of beggars who resemble nothing so much as racialized "vagrants of the gipsy tribe," we might expect the subsequent description of laboring Britons to exist in opposition, conforming to the stable vision of English England that the speakers in *The Excursion* have praised (*E*, bk. 8, line 389). And at first, the Britons do conform. They have been "early trained / To earn, by wholesome labour in the field, / The bread they eat" in contrast with the ragged offspring, who depend on tricks and begging for their sustenance (*E*, bk. 8, lines 393–395). Yet something is amiss with the young laborer whom the Recluse singles out for rhetorical attention, for the Recluse means to dispute the idealized vision of laborers produced by georgic verse. His audience may want to exclaim, "Is this the whistling plough-boy whose shrill notes / Impart new gladness to the morning air!" but the Recluse forestalls such a response, suggesting that "many [laborers], sweet to hear of in soft verse, / Are of no finer frame" (*E*, bk. 8, lines 398–402). The plough boy's whistle is a thing of poetry, not reality. His eyes, "not dim, but of healthy stare," are simultaneously "wide, sluggish, blank, and ignorant, and strange" because, as the Recluse explains, as a boy, this laborer

> never drew
> A look or motion of intelligence
> From infant-conning of the Christ-cross-row,
> Or puzzling through a primer, line by line,
> Till perfect mastery crown the pains at last. (*E*, bk. 8, lines 409–415)

In short, the young man is illiterate. In spite of his honest labor, "perfect mastery" remains elusive, and his fate seems worse than the ragged offspring's, who is at least not doomed to bear a "crust wherein his soul / Sleeps, like a caterpillar sheathed in ice" (*E*, bk. 8, lines 418–419). The Recluse fails to clarify whether the Briton's education was insufficient or whether he simply did not attend school, but the former explanation seems more likely based on the specific reference to the "Christ-cross-row" (a hornbook) and the primer. Indeed, this explanation is borne out by the Recluse's final and ardent line of questioning:

> This Boy the fields produce:
> His spade and hoe, mattock and glittering scythe,
> The carter's whip that on his shoulder rests
> In air high-towering with a boorish pomp,
> The sceptre of his sway; his country's name,
> Her equal rights, her churches and her schools—
> What have they done for him? And, let me ask,
> For tens of thousands uninformed as he?
> In brief, what liberty of *mind* is here? (*E* 8.425–433)

Line by line, this passage chips away at the gap separating ragged offspring from laboring Briton. Like the beggars, the Briton comes to have an almost primitive relationship to the earth, produced not by human parents but rather by "the fields" in which he is destined to work. His tools—spade and hoe, mattock and scythe—may be figured regally, his whip becoming a "sceptre," but as the sentence continues, they are revealed to be items on a list that terminates with "his country's name, / Her equal rights, her churches and her schools." The parallelism in this sentence, between the boy's tools of labor and his country's tools of culture, is fully pessimistic about England's boons, suggesting that the expansion of rights, the educational system, and religious institutions provide no more benefits for a Briton's mind than do his hoe and scythe. Saree Makdisi has identified in the *Lyrical Ballads* a "drive to consolidate an Occidentalized sense of self," and in some sense, that drive continues well into Wordsworth's career with the contrast that is developed in *The Excursion* between ragged offspring and laboring Briton.[77] Yet both these types (and they are rendered as types, not individuals) remain unknowable and inscrutable to the speaker who describes them. The gypsy-like children turn "a steady eye" to passers-by, but once their trick is done, "every face, that smiled / Encouragement, hath ceased to look that way" (*E*, bk. 8, lines 384–388). The eye contact and smile promise communication that never comes to fruition. Similarly, the laboring Briton's eyes are "blank, ignorant, and strange," communicating nothing beyond his own lack of knowledge, his inability to read and thus to be read. The Briton has been fully consolidated "within the pale," the ragged offspring jettisoned, and yet both are present in the English countryside, and both remain beyond the ken of subjects like the Recluse. Returning to the Wanderer's description a few pages earlier of Albion, "the blessed Isle, / Truth's consecrated residence, the seat / Impregnable of Liberty and Peace," I find it difficult to read the praise unironically. Is this blessed isle the home of illiterate Briton and beggar? Is *this* the seat impregnable of liberty and peace?

Perhaps most surprisingly, the Recluse undercuts the distinction between past and present, making it difficult to sequester a preindustrial Albion from mechanized and imperial Britain in the present. More specifically, the failure of national institutions like school and church is not attributed to the present moment and the contaminating spirit of progress and manufacturing that holds sway. The Recluse is clear throughout his diatribe that these failures have a deep history: the laboring Briton's "torpor is no pitiable work / Of modern ingenuity" (*E*, bk. 8, lines 420–421). Indeed, the Recluse opens his speech by asking

> in justice to our age,
> If there were not, before those arts appeared . . .
> If there were not, *then*, in our far-famed Isle,
> Multitudes, who from infancy had breathed
> Air imprisoned, and had lived at large;
> Yet walked beneath the sun, in human shape,
> As abject, as degraded? (*E*, bk. 8, lines 337–345)

As the Recluse insists, "our age" is not so different from back "then," before the "arts" of manufacturing developed: "multitudes" lived and continue to live in abjection. This temporal continuity between the miseries of past and the miseries of present contradicts the Wanderer's nostalgia earlier in book 8 for the wandering of his younger years. His emphatic *now* from the beginning of book 8, drawing a line in the sand between past and present, gives way to the Recluse's equally emphatic *then*, which insists that little has changed (*E*, bk. 8, lines 96, 341, emphasis in the original). It follows that "liberty," the specialty of the Wanderer's "blessed Isle," becomes an ideal that even an honest Briton cannot achieve: "What liberty of mind is here," indeed? In this book of *The Excursion*, Wordsworth has, on the one hand, fashioned an idealized version of England defined by her history, geographic isolation, and noble characteristics. Yet on the other, he has thoroughly shown this version of England to be imaginary, has divvied up this truth between speakers and scattered it throughout the book, and has constructed an alternative England, one where the past is similar to the present, where planetary currents send ships abroad and guide them inland, where the British subjects are both Occidental and Oriental, self and other.

No one answers the Recluse's question about liberty. The Vicar invites the men to his home and introduces them to his family. His wife (defined by grace, prudence, and wisdom) and his son (animated, eager, and eloquent) replace the visions of beggars and laborers, and the book comes to an end (*E*, bk. 8, lines 501–506, 572–577). Yet I have argued that the structure of book 8 undercuts such reassuring conclusions by interleaving paeans to an imaginary and isolated England with hard-nosed descriptions of a very different place—globalized Britain—where the laboring Briton is not much better off than of the racialized beggar or, as Child extrapolated, the enslaved American. Child only quotes twelve lines from *The Excursion* in her *Appeal in Favor of That Class of Americans Called Africans*. They are not, as I have demonstrated, the lines that American periodicals chose to print, but they are also not obscure: they are lines that would resonate with an American abolitionist who read the entirety of Wordsworth's poem. One way of reading Child's use of *The Excursion* might focus on the poem's imperial vision—its claim that "the world will look to Britain for leadership," its celebration of "the universal validity of parochial English values."[78] In this reading, Child's recourse to Wordsworth suggests that the imperial destiny described by the Wanderer has been achieved: two decades after *The Excursion*'s publication, some species of English morality have been successfully planted on America's shores. But when I read *The Excursion* in light of Child's epigraphs, her insistence that Wordsworth's concern for English laborers and landscapes belongs in an American antislavery tract, I am inspired to track not just the current flowing from Britain to America but also its return trip. I see in *The Excursion* not just worker bees and English culture flowing out, bound for British colonies, but also ships and goods flowing inland, "to and fro . . . with the respiration of the tides." In other words, I see the porousness of Wordsworth's England, a landscape constructed of connections to other places and other times.

Wordsworth's apprehension of these connections is often dour. The hamlet that too rapidly becomes a huge town and the new wide roads that accommodate the increase in traffic are not the emblems of Doreen Massey's Kilburn High Street, where IRA graffiti and sari shops testify to the cosmopolitan vibrancy of the place. Environmental degradation and the exploitation of workers rarely escape Wordsworth's view. (As Massey says about such global interconnection, "Some people are more in charge of it than others; some initiate flows and movement, others don't; some are more on the receiving-end of it than others; some are effectively imprisoned by it.")[79] And Wordsworth remains, at many points, conservative: his idealized England an example of how he falls back into "the forms of paternalistic sensibility," as E. P. Thompson describes him doing in *The Excursion*, the Wanderer's imperial hopes a sample of "standard post-war Tory rhetoric."[80] But that conservatism is more complex than we usually imagine: during a period when imperialism entailed rapid and large-scale changes to colonized lands, Wordsworth's conservative verse "contributes to a politics of resistance in stronger terms than his liberal and postcolonial detractors might care to admit."[81] As Katey Castellano writes, Romantic conservatism's "nascent social ecology asserts that the fate of humans and their environment are inseparable"—for Britons and non-Britons alike.[82]

Furthermore, the compelling narrative of Wordsworth's political apostasy tends to mute the details of the England he envisioned. In the end, these details make clear that he is not advocating a return to the way things were. There is beauty in globalized, industrialized Britain—the glistening ships that proceed up river, the wreaths of smoke that glitter over the crowded town. There is also degradation in Albion—the illiterate stare of the hardworking field laborer, the long history of exploitation and poverty. While it is Child's political project to recommend a specific solution, a path out of slavery and into industrialization, Wordsworth traces no path forward. She makes his poetry commensurate with a politically progressive task beyond England's shores. But while reading Wordsworth's abolitionist afterlife back into *The Excursion* may make it easier to see that poem's globalism, there is no coherent political program to be unearthed. *The Excursion* remains, in spite of its political usefulness in America, adamantly nonteleological, presenting concerns with no solutions, change with no progress, an excursion with no destination.

WORDSWORTH IN THE TROPICS

Although the conflict between Child and Wordsworth on the subject of industrialization is no more than a semblance of disagreement, such a semblance significantly reveals the nuance of Child's use of Wordsworth. His value to the American antislavery movement depends on the play between *The Excursion*'s solidly English concerns and the broadly global context it invokes. It is not that Child merely coopts the words of a famous poet in order to make her own point or that she borrows his pathos without giving much thought to its source. Rather, the disjuncture allows Child to enlist Wordsworth's verse in her political agenda without subsuming *The Excursion*'s English plight within the antislavery movement. This balancing act expands beyond the space of the epigraph to characterize Child's approach to geographic borders within the body of her *Appeal*, where she squares the transnationalism of her argument with a recognition of divisions internal to the United States.

This balance—Child's ability to make a fraught comparison without eradicating difference—distinguishes her from American writers who tried to dissociate Wordsworth from the Englishness that had come to define him. Elizabeth

Peabody, for instance, occasionally corresponded with Wordsworth beginning in 1825 and chided him once for failing to be "the poet not of the English nation but of the English language," an indictment that wishes to claim some of Wordsworth for America.[83] While Peabody's admonition was private rather than published, it reminds us that during Child's public entrance into the abolitionist movement, the desire to fashion Wordsworth as a poet of America as well as of England was strong. Twenty years later, this desire would morph into the bragging rights implicit in the swaggering assertion from the *North American Review* that "no country contains a larger number of intelligent admirers of Wordsworth's than our own."[84] Where Wordsworth's knowledge of "how to live" made him an exemplar of Englishness, in Matthew Arnold's estimation, his readership threatened to make him American. England might have produced him, but America loved him better. This literary power grab isn't surprising for an era when the fledgling United States was trying to establish a literary culture of its own. But the parameters of this American desire for Wordsworth also suggest that his Englishness stuck to him throughout. Peabody doesn't want to take him away from "the English nation"; she just wants him to belong to other Anglophone nations too. Even the *North American Review* can only claim him on the grounds of his reception—the "number of intelligent admirers" he earned in America—not his poetry. Unable to separate him from the imaginary of England, readers were forced to construct novel means of claiming the English poet for their own.

Child is not generally interested in such contests. Rather, the transnational negotiations she stages within the literary convention of the epigraph bolster the political method she advocates in her *Appeal.* From the start of her treatise she gestures beyond America, reasoning in the preface that if the book advances for "one single hour, the inevitable progress of truth and justice, [she] would not exchange the consciousness for all Rothchild's [*sic*] wealth, or Sir Walter's fame" (*A*, 5). It is not just in this avowal that the preface prefers metaphors of economy and exchange; Child also posits that her refusal to praise her country is justified by the desire to "supply what is most needed," and since "the market is so glutted with flattery," her truths will supply a demand. While the market in which she imagines herself is certainly American—her subject "admits of no encomiums on my country"—she hopes to create equal exchange between her own potential power and the riches of a French banker or the celebrity of a Scottish writer, thus suggesting that her influence as an American writer bears comparison to the prowess of continental men. In other words, Child wants the context in which she is interpreted to be of a global rather than a national scale.

More palpable than the sense of her own position, however, is the potential relationship that Child identifies between America and other slave-holding cultures in her *Appeal*, a tie that locates the possibility of emancipation not within the hypocritical trajectory established by American democracy, which betrayed its foundational values by denying freedom to so many residents, but within the examples set by other countries. Karcher claims that the *Appeal* filled an empty niche because British and French abolitionist theory was inapplicable to the United States, "where slavery was practiced not in distant colonies, but in states that formed an indissoluble part of the nation and benefited from disproportionate political representation in congress," and Child clearly recognizes this niche when she proposes to "supply what is most needed."[85] America's distinctiveness, however, does not demand a distinctly American solution. For example, in describing the American fear of educating enslaved people, she claims, "The same spirit that dictates this logic to the Arab, teaches it to the European and the American" (*A*, 11).[86] In supplying the American market with the criticism it lacked, the *Appeal* uses its transnational scope to condemn the American exceptionalism that hoarded "encomiums on [the] country" while dismissing any ameliorating influence from beyond its borders.

From Child's insistence on a comparative policy that perforates national boundaries, it does not seem to follow that difference can arise purely from geography, the influence of place: "Human nature is everywhere the same; but developed differently, by different incitements and temptations. . . . If we were educated at the South, we should no doubt vindicate slavery, and inherit as a birthright all the evils it engrafts upon the character. If they lived on our rocky soil, and under our inclement skies, their shrewdness would sometimes border upon knavery, and their frugality sometimes degenerate into parsimony. We both have our virtues, and our faults, induced by the influences under which we live, and of course, totally different in their character" (*A*, 29–30). Her environmental determinism, in which the North's "rocky soils" and "inclement skies" forge personalities heavy on knavery and parsimony, casts nature as the ruler of human virtue and vice. Yet this belief in the inescapable differences between Northerners and Southerners, however common at the time, seems incompatible with the desire to borrow policy reforms from other nations. If the North and South find it so difficult to reconcile their traits, which are "totally different" due simply to "rocky soil" and "inclement skies," why should she have faith that the Arab, European, and American share the "same spirit" of logic? When she describes emancipation in other countries, it seems clear that her desire is for emulation—They did it, so why can't we?—a desire at odds with her recognition of the intranational boundaries that separate North from South. She never quite does away with this tension. By the end of her catalog of Northern character faults, she has concluded that "*our* defects are bad enough; but they cannot, like slavery, affect the destiny and rights of millions" (*A*, 30, emphasis in the original), implying that Northern knavery and parsimony, in comparison with Southern vindication of slavery, harm relatively few and thus need not be checked. It appears then that antislavery policies imported from abroad have a lot to overcome—not just differences among nations but the even greater incompatibility of North and South. In the end, the intricacies of geographical place mean that Southerners should not be expected to exhibit the same faults as their Northern counterparts, but this desire for regional containment must be tempered by a transnational permeability that allows correspondences to thrive without leveling distinctions between the North and South or England and America. Comparison and influence do not mandate sameness.

In this context, the seemingly strange mingling of landscape with industrial noise in Child's sketch of the New England villages where "the busy hum of machinery made music with her neglected waterfalls" becomes less off-putting. Nature and politics (in the form of the social change that industrialization heralds) inhabit the same sphere for Child, as they did for generations of Americans after her. My favorite example is industrialist Henry Ford, a great and perhaps unlikely fan of Wordsworth's poetry. Like Child, Ford believed that "mechanization marked not the conquest but the realization of nature's secrets and thus the attainment of the pastoral ideal," a particularly American philosophy of nature in which industrialization springs from rather than subdues the natural world. And like Child, Ford (born in the year of the Emancipation Proclamation) saw his system of wage labor as the antidote to American chattel slavery.[87]

Ford was first exposed to canonical Anglo-American poetry via the *McGuffey Readers*, a series of primers popular in American schools through the mid-twentieth century.[88] Decades later at his rubber plantation in the Amazon, dubbed "Fordlandia," the industrialist sponsored readings, translated into Portuguese, of Emerson, Longfellow, and Wordsworth.[89] The purpose of these readings is unclear: the references to Wordsworth come from on-the-spot observers in journalistic articles who said nothing more about the program.[90] Whatever purpose they might have served likely distracted from Fordlandia's true aim: after several rubber crops failed, Ford officials brought in a consultant from the United States Department of Agriculture (USDA) who suggested that too much effort had been expended on activities other than growing rubber.[91] In more ways than one, then, Wordsworth's poetry was an odd fit for Fordlandia. The industrial context into which Ford imported Wordsworth's poetry is even more clearly odds with Wordsworth's morality than Child's advocacy of American industrialization. For example, the plight of factory workers communicating silently, using what they dubbed "fordization of the face" because talking was not permitted in Ford's factories, sounds like an outrage from book 8 of *The Excursion*.[92] (This description of "fordization of the face" is of a kind with Charles Lamb's statement in "The Superannuated Man" about his job at the East India Company: "I had grown to my desk, as it were; and the wood had entered into my soul.")[93] And Ford's agribusiness model, which demands the wholesale transformation of a region's ecology, is the end that Wordsworth fears when he complains about tree plantations in his *Guide to the Lakes*, as I discuss in chapter 4.[94] Journalists could not resist the temptation to deploy this language of agriculture in writing about Fordlandia; one colorfully claimed that Ford "has transplanted a large slice of twentieth-century civilization and methods to this land, rich in tribal and jungle lore."[95] But perhaps more subtly, the project at Fordlandia reverses the logic of Wordsworth's poetic activism, in which overt critiques of the rapidly changing English landscape are undergirded by a subtle acknowledgment of Britain's planetary environment and global networks. In Ford's philosophy, the commitment to global networks is loud, but it is underwritten by a parochialism that assumes the world to be a larger version of Dearborn, Michigan. On one hand, Henry Ford insisted on a sort of capitalistic cosmopolitanism "because a business man knows no country. He is born by chance in this or that country."[96] On the other, what mitigates national boundaries for Ford is not the recognition of moral or political contingencies between nations but rather his individual status as a man of business. And this status proved to be an unstable basis for the realities of Ford's globalism. In choosing the Amazon valley for his rubber plantation, Ford made the error that Aldous Huxley attributed to Wordsworth, if unfairly: "A few months in the jungle would have convinced [Wordsworth] that the diversity and utter strangeness of Nature are at least as real and significant as its intellectually discovered unity."[97] The litany of ticks, scorpions, hornets, ant swarms, and snakes populating the Amazon makes it clear that Ford did not base his proposition on a well-developed understanding of the landscape he chose to reform.[98] Ford understood the Amazon as an extension of America. He insisted, for instance, that American managers in Fordlandia set their watches to Michigan time, a sort of industrial Greenwich imposing temporal unity over a company of Amazonian laborers who had previously given little thought to money, let alone the measuring of time.[99] One of his managers exchanged a series of letters with a whistle manufacturer, bemoaning that no existing whistle could withstand the climate and still proclaim the time loudly enough.[100]

What the trajectory from Child to Henry Ford suggests is that Wordsworth maintained his moral capital even as the disparity between his poetry and the realities of industrial capitalism became more and more entrenched. But the content of that moral capital changed, growing more and more separable from the details of the poetry from which it grew. In Wordsworth, Child apprehended a commitment to the humanity of the laboring poor, a model for her own advocacy whose commitment to England did not prevent him from holding moral authority in

America. And through her eyes, I have argued, we apprehend a Wordsworth who understands England as but one patch of the earth—as a participant, for better or worse, in the networks of imperialism and trade that that heralded the advent of globalism during the Romantic era. In Wordsworth, Ford found a poet whose dismay at industrialization could be ignored and neutralized. Which poems by Wordsworth were translated and read to laborers in the Amazon? What would these poems have sounded like to them? While Child's use of Wordsworth seems like a new growth springing from the self-same plant, Ford's use is a graft, a cutting removed from one species and made to root onto a new one.

The years after the publication of the *Appeal* saw a proliferation of politically driven articles in which Wordsworth's avowal that "Earth is sick, / And Heaven is weary of the hollow words / Which states and kingdoms utter when they talk / Of truth and justice"—the same avowal that Child includes in the *Appeal*—is the keystone.[101] This trajectory fashions Child as an unheralded literary critic, one who recognized Wordsworth's political capital as both essential and essentially related to meditations on his work driven by philosophy and nature. Child holds nations in a similar balance, for instead of leveling the distinctions between England and America, she uses the formal qualities of her genre—from the epigraphs of the *Appeal* to the layout of the poetry column—to allow each text and each nation to exist both in solitude and in relation to the other. Unlike other American writers who "received Wordsworth upon their own terms by applying his social vision to their own circumstances," Child creates a space on the page where her "terms" and Wordsworth's coexist, where one "social vision" bolsters another without daring to speak for it.[102] Her strategic use of Wordsworth in her antislavery writing should be seen a manipulation of literary convention, and in this light, the *Appeal*'s literary status emerges as central to the transnational scope that makes the treatise remarkable.

Unlike Coetzee and Kincaid, Child was actually Wordsworth's contemporary. Her repurposing demonstrates that even during Wordsworth's life, and in particular during the years when we think of him sliding further and further into conservatism and isolationism, readers apprehended in his poetry a moral power that fortified their own diverse political commitments far beyond England's shores. To them, Wordsworth was an example not of Romantic poetry's insularity but of its expansiveness. It is not my aim to disagree with everyone who believes that *The Excursion* was an important sign of Wordsworth's decline, yet we miss Wordsworth's global engagements—the way readers repurposed him around the world and the way he recorded that world in his poetry—when we disregard it. For Wordsworth, and for readers like Child, furthering the moral progress of the nation meant reconceiving the boundaries that helped define the nation in the first place.

NOTES

1 For a more detailed account of the aftermath of Child's *Appeal*, see Carolyn L. Karcher, *The First Woman in the Republic: A Cultural Biography of Lydia Maria Child* (Durham, N.C.: Duke University Press, 1994), 173–194. Child has received much critical attention in the past twenty years, but most of this work addresses her romances, and few critics examine her *Appeal* at length. See Robert Fanuzzi, "How Mixed-Race Politics Entered the United States: Lydia Maria Child's *Appeal*," *ESQ: A Journal of the American Renaissance* 56, no. 1 (2010): 71–104; Carolyn Sorisio, *Fleshing Out America: Race, Gender, and the Politics of the Body in American Literature, 1833–1879* (Athens: University of Georgia Press, 2002), 47–78.

2 Robert Weisbuch argues, for instance, that some of Wordsworth's descriptions of London in book 7 of *The Prelude* are "seemingly inspired—the seeming is, of course, impossible—by Whitman," an example of Bloom's *apophrades*. F. O. Mathiessen had been convinced of the bond between Whitman and Wordsworth forty years earlier. Weisbuch, *Atlantic Double-Cross: American Literature and British Influence in the Age of Emerson* (Chicago: University of Chicago Press, 1986), 224; Matthiessen, *American Renaissance: Art and Expression in the Age of Emerson and Whitman* (New York: Oxford University Press, 1941), 517–625.

3 Paul Gilroy's *The Black Atlantic: Modernity and Double-Consciousness* (Cambridge, Mass.: Harvard University Press, 1993); Joseph Roach, *Cities of the Dead: Circum-Atlantic Performance* (New York: Columbia University Press, 1996).

4 Lawrence Buell, "Postcolonial Anxiety in Classic U.S. Literature," in *Postcolonial Theory and the United States: Race, Ethnicity, and Literature*, ed. Amritjit Singh and Peter Schmidt (Jackson: University Press of Mississippi, 2000), 198.

5 Elisa Tamarkin, *Anglophilia: Deference, Devotion, and Antebellum America* (Chicago: University of Chicago Press, 2008), 178–246.

6 Joel Pace and Matthew Scott's collection of essays, for instance, investigates Wordsworth's "wider social, political and artistic legacy," but this legacy does not extend to abolitionism. Pace and Scott, eds., *Wordsworth in American Literary Culture* (New York: Palgrave Macmillan, 2005), 2; Pace, "Wordsworth and America: Reception and Reform," in *The Cambridge Companion to Wordsworth*, ed. Stephen Gill (Cambridge: Cambridge University Press, 2003), 239.

7 Debbie Lee, *Slavery and the Romantic Imagination* (Philadelphia: University of Pennsylvania Press, 2002), 194; Pace, "Wordsworth and America," 239. Most studies of Romanticism and slavery are, like Lee's, interested in how the discourse of slavery influenced writers of the Romantic era rather than the other way around. See also Helen Thomas, *Romanticism and Slave Narratives: Transatlantic Testimonies* (Cambridge: Cambridge University Press, 2000).

8 "The North American Review," *Port-Folio*, August 1824, 120. The article, a wry summation of reviews recently printed in the *North American Review*, takes issue with that journal's recent praise of Wordsworth, who "does not interest, nor please his readers," according to the *Port-Folio*.

9 Sydney Smith, review of *Statistical Annals of the United States of America*, *Edinburgh Review*, January 1820, 79. This question piqued readers for a long time. The *New York Times* took on Smith in 1922 (Brander Matthews, "Answering Sidney Smith's Questions," March 26, 1922, 2), and Richard Gravil reports that Americans were answering that question with all seriousness as late as 1929, when the first article of the first issue of *American Literature* posed its own response to the then century-old inquiry. See Gravil, *Romantic Dialogues: Anglo-American Continuities, 1776–1862* (New York: St. Martin's Press, 2000), 48.

10 David Simpson, "Wordsworth in America," in *The Age of William Wordsworth: Critical Essays on the Romantic Tradition*, ed. Kenneth R. Johnston and Gene W. Ruoff (Jersey City, N.J.: Rutgers University Press, 1987), 290.

11 H. T. Tuckerman, "Wordsworth," *Southern Literary Messenger*, February 1840, 105.

12 Review of *The Poetical Works of William Wordsworth*, *Atlantic Magazine*, March 1825, 339.

13 Annabel Newton traces the trajectory further, from 1824, when Wordsworth was first widely read and "favorably received" by a culture once "inimical to [his] poetry," to the "period of full appreciation," which began with Wordsworth's death in 1850. Newton, *Wordsworth in Early American Criticism* (Chicago: University of Chicago Press, 1928), 66.

14 Pace and Scott, *Wordsworth in American Literary Culture*, 15. For more on the reception and influence of Wordsworth in America, see Gravil, *Romantic Dialogues*, 62–67, 93–101, 249–282; Lance Newman, *Our Common Dwelling: Henry Thoreau, Transcendentalism, and the Class Politics of Nature* (New York: Palgrave Macmillan, 2005), 69–95; Pace, "Wordsworth and America."

15 Leon Howard, "Wordsworth in America," *Modern Language Notes* 48, no. 6 (1933): 360. Dennie's Anglophilia is a counterpoint to the familiar narrative of anxious American literary nationalism, propounded in the earliest days of transatlantic studies by works like Weisbuch's *Atlantic Double-Cross*. For more on this counterpoint, which examines nineteenth-century writers who sought to emulate (rather than repudiate) English literary culture, see Tamarkin's *Anglophilia*; and Leonard Tennenhouse, *The Importance of Feeling English: American Literature and the British Diaspora, 1750–1850* (Princeton, N.J.: Princeton University Press, 2007).

16 "Simon Lee," *Port-Folio*, January 1801, 24.

17 "Critical Notices," *Literary Magazine and American Register*, February 1804, 336.

18 Howard, "Wordsworth in America," 360.

19 Quoted in Tamarkin, *Anglophilia*, 178.

20 Tamarkin, 179.

21 In this sense, "English English" proves quite a different designation than Olaudah Equiano's negotiations with the qualities of Englishness, such as "almost an Englishman" and "Black Christian." But Equiano, of course, lived in Britain and developed an understanding of Englishness founded on daily, lived experiences. Equiano, *The Interesting Narrative and Other Writings*, ed. Vincent Carretta (New York: Penguin, 2003), 77, 92.

22 Ian Baucom, *Out of Place: Englishness, Empire, and the Locations of Identity* (Princeton, N.J.: Princeton University Press, 1999), 5.

23 Review of *The Poetical Works of William Wordsworth*, *United States Literary Gazette*, December 1824, 246.

24 Review of *The Poetical Works of William Wordsworth*, *Atlantic Magazine*, March 1825, 340, 346.

25 Review of *Lectures on the English Poets*, *North American Review*, March 1819, 320.

26 Review of *The Poetical Works of William Wordsworth*, *United States Literary Gazette*, December 1824, 247.

27 "Lord Byron's Faults," *Southern Literary Messenger*, April 1838, 270–271.

28 Newton, *Wordsworth in Early American Criticism*, 99.

29 Review of *The Poetical Works of William Wordsworth*, *Atlantic Magazine*, April 1825, 340; review of *The Poetical Works of William Wordsworth*, *United States Literary Gazette*, December 1824, 245.

30 Review of *The Poetical Works of William Wordsworth*, *Atlantic Magazine*, April 1825, 419.

31 See "Excursion," *National Recorder*, March 1820, 156. This printing predates the 1824 publication of Wordsworth's collected works in America.

32 The unpopularity of *Lyrical Ballads* means that few Americans would have been familiar with Wordsworth's association, in 1800 at least, of aesthetic decisions and politicized subject matter, "as much pains has been taken to avoid [poetic diction] as is ordinarily taken to produce it; this has been done for the reason already alleged, to bring my language near to the language of men; and further, because the pleasure which I have proposed to myself to impart, is of a kind very different from that which is supposed by many persons to be the proper object of poetry" (*PrW*, 1:131).

33 Review of *The Miscellaneous Poems of William Wordsworth*, *North American Review*, April 1824, 365.

34 Review of *The Poetical Works of William Wordsworth*, *Literary Gazette*, January 1825, 247–248.

35 Review of *The State of Innocence and the Fall of Man*, *Analectic Magazine*, July 1815, 56.

36 "Excursion," 156; review of *The Poetical Works of William Wordsworth*, *Atlantic Magazine*, April 1825, 428.

37 Review of *The Poetical Works of William Wordsworth*, *Atlantic Magazine*, March 1825, 346.

38 Alison Hickey, *Impure Conceits: Rhetoric and Ideology in Wordsworth's Excursion* (Stanford, Calif.: Stanford University Press, 1997), 8.

39 Karcher, *First Woman*, 273. *The Liberator* had a circulation of 2,400 in 1834. C. Peter Ripley, ed., *The Black Abolitionist Papers*, vol. 3, *The United States, 1830–1846* (Chapel Hill: University of North Carolina Press, 1991), 9.

40 Quoted in Karcher, *First Woman*, 273.

41 Karcher, 273.

42 Lydia Maria Child, "Thoughts," *National Anti-Slavery Standard*, July 1840, 32, emphasis in the original.

43 *National Anti-Slavery Standard*, June 1841, 208. I have quoted the version from the *Standard*; the version in Wordsworth's *Poetical Works* is slightly different (*PW*, 4:105).

44 *National Anti-Slavery Standard*, May 20, 1841.

45 Karcher, *First Woman*, 277.

46 "Excursion," 156. Americans who had read Wordsworth's *Sonnets Dedicated to Liberty*, which were included in the 1824 American edition of his collected works, would have recognized that Wordsworth was certainly writing poetry of political advocacy. Yet the majority of periodicals printing Wordsworth after 1824 focus on *The Excursion* to the exclusion of the other three volumes of poetry included in the collection. For a rare counterexample, see "William Wordsworth," *Southern Literary Messenger*, December 1837, which notes, "The object of this sketch is to notice more particularly the '*Sonnets dedicated to Liberty*'" (705).

47 Review of *The Poetical Works of William Wordsworth*, *Atlantic Magazine*, March 1825, 348.

48 *A*, 5.

49 Karcher, *First Woman*, 158.

50 "Works of Mrs. Child," *North American Review*, July 1833, 142.

51 Zoe Trodd's recent collection includes Lydia Maria Child's writing on suffrage in its chapter on women's rights, but Child could just as easily appear in its chapters on abolition and antislavery or American Indian rights, suggesting that Child's activism was more various than she and her readers let on—and that it defined her work before and after the *Appeal.*

Trodd, *American Protest Literature* (Cambridge, Mass.: Belknap Press of Harvard University Press, 2006), 139.

52 William Lloyd Garrison's *Liberator* also argued for emancipation and not colonization during this period.

53 Karcher, *First Woman*, 192.

54 "Works of Mrs. Child," 138.

55 It clearly was not a uniquely American problem: though Britain had abolished the slave trade in 1807, slavery in the empire was not abolished until 1833, the year of Child's *Appeal*. Nevertheless, by 1833 it was consistently described as an American crisis, and for Child, as for other American abolitionists, Britain represented a paragon of social reform in comparison to America.

56 Gérard Genette, *Paratexts: Thresholds of Interpretation* (Cambridge: Cambridge University Press, 1997), 156.

57 Genette, 152.

58 Richard Macksey, foreword to *Paratexts*, by Gérard Genette (Cambridge: Cambridge University Press, 1997), xx.

59 Genette, *Paratexts*, 151.

60 See "Epilogue to 'The Padlock,'" *Gentlemen's Magazine*, October 1787, 914.

61 Julie Ellison sees this scene as an example of "industrial fancy," in which fancy, a feminized form of inspiration that Coleridge (and later, Wordsworth) juxtaposed to the more masculine powers of the imagination, is "made demonic" and has "gone berserk." Ellison, "'Nice Arts' and 'Potent Enginery': The Gendered Economy of Wordsworth's Fancy," *Centennial Review* 33, no. 4 (1989): 459.

62 A deeper investigation of the sonnet might yield the sort of critique Paul Youngquist has made recently or confirm Helen Thomas's sense of the poem as "an important example of the appropriation and concealment of abolitionist discourse contained within Romantic poetry." But this is evidently not how Child read the poem. Youngquist, "Black Romanticism: A Manifesto," *Studies in Romanticism* 56, no. 1 (2017): 8–10; Thomas, *Romanticism and Slave Narratives*, 110.

63 *HH*, 33.

64 Leah Reade Rosenberg, *Nationalism and the Formation of Caribbean Literature* (New York: Palgrave Macmillan, 2007), 106.

65 For an examination of the varying effects of industrialization in England and America, see Walter Licht, *Industrializing America* (Baltimore: Johns Hopkins University Press, 1995), 21–78; for firsthand accounts of life in the Lowell, Massachusetts, factories, see Harriet H. Robinson, *Loom and Spindle: Or, Life among the Early Mill Girls* (New York: T. Y. Crowell, 1898; rev. ed., Kailua, Hawaii: Press Pacifica, 1976).

66 Amanda Claybaugh, *The Novel of Purpose: Literature and Social Reform in the Anglo-American World* (Ithaca, N.Y.: Cornell University Press, 2007), 4.

67 See, for instance, Hickey, *Impure Conceits*, 107–112; Alan Richardson, *Literature, Education, and Romanticism: Reading as Social Practice, 1780–1832* (Cambridge: Cambridge University Press, 1994), 44–108; Tim Fulford and Peter J. Kitson, eds., *Romanticism and Colonialism: Writing and Empire, 1780–1830* (Cambridge: Cambridge University Press, 1998), 1–12; David Simpson, "Wordsworth and Empire—Just Joking," in *Land, Nation and Culture, 1740–1840*, ed. Peter de Bolla et al. (New York: Palgrave Macmillan, 2005); Samuel Baker, *Written on the Water: British Romanticism and the Maritime Empire of Culture* (Charlottesville: University of Virginia Press, 2010), 81–114.

68 Simpson, "Wordsworth and Empire," 190.

69 Review of *The Complete Poetical Works of William Wordsworth*, *North American Review*, October 1844, 341.

70 David Simpson, *Wordsworth's Historical Imagination: The Poetry of Displacement* (New York: Methuen, 1987), 195.

71 Wai Chee Dimock, "Planet and America, Set and Subset," in *Shades of the Planet: American Literature as World Literature*, ed. Wai Chee Dimock and Lawrence Buell (Princeton, N.J.: Princeton University Press, 2007), 1.

72 Gayatri Chakravorty Spivak, *Death of a Discipline* (New York: Columbia University Press, 2003), 72.

73 Gillian Beer, "The Island and the Aeroplane: The Case of Virginia Woolf," in *Nation and Narration*, ed. Homi K. Bhabha (New York: Routledge, 1990), 272.

74 Sally Bushell, *Re-reading the Excursion: Narrative, Response, and the Wordsworthian Dramatic Voice* (Aldershot: Ashgate, 2002), 91.

75 Hickey, *Impure Conceits*, 99.

76 Baker, *Written on the Water*, 91.

77 Saree Makdisi, *Making England Western: Occidentalism, Race, and Imperial Culture* (Chicago: University of Chicago Press, 2013), 88.

78 Fulford and Kitson, *Romanticism and Colonialism*, 4; Marlon B. Ross, "Romantic Quest and Conquest: Troping Masculine Power in the Crisis of Poetic Identity," in *Romanticism and Feminism*, ed. Anne K. Mellor (Bloomington: Indiana University Press, 1988), 31.

79 Doreen Massey, *Space, Place, and Gender* (Minneapolis: University of Minnesota Press, 1994), 149.

80 E. P. Thompson, *The Romantics: England in a Revolutionary Age* (New York: New Press, 1997), 67; Simpson, *Wordsworth's Historical Imagination*, 195.

81 Alan Bewell, *Natures in Translation: Romanticism and Colonial Natural History* (Baltimore: Johns Hopkins University Press, 2017), 247.

82 Katey Castellano, *The Ecology of British Romantic Conservatism, 1790–1837* (New York: Palgrave Macmillan, 2013), 7.

83 Quoted in Gravil, *Romantic Dialogues*, 64.

84 "The Life and Poetry of Wordsworth," *North American Review*, October 1851, 494.

85 Karcher, *First Woman*, 176.

86 Similarly, Child's chapter on the "Possibility of Safe Emancipation" provides a global roundup of successful emancipation stories from England and the West Indies, Chile, Brazil, Mexico, and France (*A*, 72–98).

87 Greg Grandin, *Fordlandia: The Rise and Fall of Henry Ford's Forgotten Jungle City* (New York: Picador, 2009), 257, 89.

88 Steven Watts, *The People's Tycoon* (New York: Knopf, 2005), 10–11.

89 Grandin, *Fordlandia*, 286.

90 Greg Grandin, email message to the author, October 29, 2011.

91 John Galey, "Industrialist in the Wilderness: Henry Ford's Amazon Venture," *Journal of Interamerican Studies and World Affairs* 21, no. 2 (1979): 274.

92 Grandin, *Fordlandia*, 81.

93 E. V. Lucas, ed., *The Works of Charles and Mary Lamb*, 7 vols. (London: Methuen, 1903–1905), 2:194.

94 Elizabeth Esch, "Whitened and Enlightened: The Ford Motor Company and Racial Engineering in the Brazilian Amazon," in *Company Towns in the Americas: Landscape, Power, and Working-Class Communities*, ed. Oliver J. Dinius and Angela Vergara (Athens: University of Georgia Press, 2011), 98.

95 "Life in Fordlandia!," *Iron Mountain Daily News*, May 18, 1932.

96 Quoted in Grandin, *Fordlandia*, 81–82.

97 Aldous Huxley, "Wordsworth in the Tropics," in *Collected Essays* (New York: Harper, 1971), 9.

98 Galey, "Industrialist in the Wilderness," 273–274.

99 Grandin, *Fordlandia*, 222.

100 Esch, "Whitened and Enlightened," 101.

101 See, for instance, "Pro-slavery Democracy Tamed!," *Liberator*, August 1838, 122; "To the Affiliated Unions," *Harbinger, Devoted to Social and Political Progress*, November 1847, 7; Rufus W. Clark, "What Is Patriotism?," *Advocate of Peace*, November–December 1847, 124; "State Reform School," *Rural Repository*, September 1849, 1; and "From Our Regular French Correspondent," *Independent*, July 1852, 111, all of which quote these three lines either as epigraphs or in the body text of the article and none of which predate Child's *Appeal.*

102 Pace and Scott, *Wordsworth in American Literary Culture*, 3.

4

LOCALISM UNROOTED

Jamaica Kincaid and the *Guide to the Lakes*

At last count, Jamaica Kincaid had planted 5,500 daffodils in her Vermont garden. She hoped to plant more—enough "to cover [the] entire lawn and beyond that every nook and cranny that will receive some sun"—and had chosen a variety that reminded her of "that host that danced in the breeze."[1] When Kincaid was a child in Antigua, living in an "eternal summer," daffodils and their association with spring made her long for the climate of England with equal parts curiosity and resentment. But Vermont and its seasons changed the flower: "I live in this place where there is true spring, a place where the four seasons repeat themselves one after the other in the usual order and the sight of the daffodil is a true joy." This surprising turn of events, along with Kincaid's aesthetic admiration for William Wordsworth, who "wrote beautiful things," makes it possible to see a few similarities between the two writers.[2] Like Kincaid, Wordsworth was a gardener, as the grounds of Rydal Mount remind us to this day. Like Kincaid, he was an avid plant hunter and with Dorothy would return from walks with specimens for their more permanent collection. And like Kincaid, he worried about the ethics of tending plants, particularly plants of foreign extraction commonly termed *exotics*, which both writers suspected of giving the gardener too much power.

These practices, particularly as Wordsworth outlined them in his *Guide to the District of the Lakes in the North of England* (1835), have helped define the parameters of his localism—his commitment to a beloved local setting and, moreover, the national value of this area, which Wordsworth proclaims at the end of his *Guide to the Lakes* by calling the Lake District "a sort of national property, in which every man has a right and interest who has an eye to perceive and a heart to enjoy" (*PrW*, 2:225). This statement has inspired two interrelated strands of commentary, one focusing on Wordsworth's brand of environmental thought and another trained on his construction of the nation. To critics like Scott Hess, Wordsworth's stipulation that the interest of "every man" depends on his having "an eye to perceive and a heart to enjoy" creates a kind of "Romantic gaze" in which nature becomes less ecological and more cultural, akin to an object in a museum.[3] Others have seized on Wordsworth's rhetorical shift from the Lake District to the realm of "national property," suggesting that the *Guide to the Lakes* makes the case for localism by positing the region as a synecdoche for the nation.[4] (The importance of Wordsworth's concluding edict to the nascent national parks movements in Britain and the United States is but one example of how the environmental and the national interpretations of the *Guide to the Lakes* might be intertwined.)[5] This chapter, however, draws upon the insights of postcolonial ecocriticism in order to argue that reading Wordsworth's guide environmentally means linking his localism not with his construction of the nation but rather with his awareness of Britain's colonial expansion. As Alan Bewell has recently argued, "The *Guide* is very much a colonial environmental history," and the continuities between Wordsworth and Kincaid—Antiguan transplant in Vermont, reformed hater of daffodils—reveal that while Wordsworth's localism may have bloomed into national fervor for both him and his readers, it is rooted in the imperial underpinnings of landscape and gardening mores in nineteenth-century Britain.[6]

Pertinent to this understanding of Wordsworth is the very tangible relationship to the soil that he cultivated through his labors in the gardens at Grasmere and Rydal Mount. This occupation, far more than a hobby and shared with Kincaid across centuries, is one whose material effects make these writers' localisms practical as well as theoretical. I begin this chapter with Kincaid's *My Garden (Book):* (1999), which has become an ur-text for postcolonial ecocritics thanks to its investigation of how British colonialism shaped the botanical composition of the West Indies. The essays interweave descriptions of Kincaid's own gardening practices in Vermont with forays into the history of Kew Gardens and botanical gardens in Britain's colonies as well as the travails of Carl Linnaeus and Joseph Banks, suggesting that Kincaid sees herself uncomfortably replicating colonial botanic history with her own manipulations of nature. Yet the histories that Kincaid evokes in these essays also shaped Wordsworth's natural context two centuries earlier, particularly as he represents his native landscapes in the 1835 guide, which I analyze as an impossible but germane reply to Kincaid's gardening essays. Wordsworth, like Edmund Burke in his speeches on the impeachment of Warren Hastings, saw colonialism's effects as local as well as remote. So while the *Guide to the Lakes* uses tropes of local rootedness to describe the Lake District and presents it as a national treasure, it also constructs the region more globally. The Lake District exists not as a static respite from the ceaseless movements of British imperialism but rather in direct relation to the colonial transport of people and plants to, from, and within Britain. The chapter concludes with a return to Kincaid, whose travel memoir *Among Flowers* (2005) juxtaposes a plant-hunting tour of the Himalayas with the rooted but dynamic space of Kincaid's garden, where she intends to plant the spoils from her travels. Her Vermont garden emerges as a context that is simultaneously durable and transportable, a space whose boundaries are climactic rather than physical. When read in dialogue, I argue, Kincaid and Wordsworth are not simply the antagonistic pair that they seem, with Wordsworth playing the role of hegemonic English canon in Kincaid's "empire writes back" routine.[7] Rather, they share a complicated attitude toward localism: both construe the garden as constituted by natural material that signifies local belonging, even as that local rootedness is a paradoxical manifestation of the global forces of colonial movement and botanic possession. Kincaid's role in this dialogue is to redefine localism as unrooted and movable, centered in her Vermont garden but composed of exotic plants from a colonial history she knows well. And as if in reply, Wordsworth's guide becomes a showcase less of pastoral English nationalism than of anxiety about the movement of plants, soils, and people that characterized eighteenth- and nineteenth-century colonialism.

Wordsworth's *Guide to the Lakes*, which makes clear from the title its devotion to a local setting, has frequently been analyzed through the lens of eighteenth-century landscape design, and for good reason: like Humphry Repton, the prolific landscape gardener who advocated "imitating nature so judiciously, that the interference of art shall never be detected," Wordsworth idealized landscapes that appeared "natural."[8] Even now, Wordsworth's gardens appear as such. An illustrated book on his gardens at Rydal Mount describes their rambling watercourse as "so naturalized with the surrounding terrain that it appears to have been original."[9] As John Barrell has argued, during this period the ideal garden was "no longer thought of as rigidly separated from the rest of nature"; in fact, garden and nature became so enmeshed that the gardener, "in manipulating and improving the landscape, was thus given a sanction from nature," not because he strove to imitate nature, but rather "because he saw nature as a copy of his own ideal."[10] As Barrell, Donna Landry, and Simon Pugh have shown, this idealization mandated a persistent erasure of poverty and labor in both imagination and practice.[11] Nevertheless, this sanitized "naturalness" was a hallmark of English landscape design, and as a result of the association, the ideal landscape garden became not just natural but also naturally English.

The Royal Gardens at Kew, created in 1759 and advised by Sir Joseph Banks from 1772 to 1820, are emblematic of these growing ties among landscape design, English gardening practices, and what Donal P. McCracken terms "botanic nationalism."[12] As a botanic garden, Kew broke with tradition: whereas earlier botanic gardens featured a collection of plants "overlaid upon a map of the world," Kew appears "as an English 'natural' landscape with rolling, grassy slopes, picturesque clumps of trees, and meandering water—a setting attuned to the temper of liberal, self-confident, expansionary modern science."[13] And so although the theme of a botanic garden, according to John M. Prest, "is always the same—it is that of gathering the plants together from all over the world," at Kew that theme took a different form.[14] A diverse, global collection appeared within an aesthetic frame that was coming to be recognized as both natural and distinctly English.

At Kew's helm during this period was Joseph Banks—perhaps most famous for his association with Captain James Cook's first important voyage in the Pacific on the *Bounty*—who was responsible for transforming Kew from "the summer retreat of the Royal Family" into a braggart's repository of botanic specimens.[15] But for Banks, the connection between nature and nation was not merely a one-sided relationship in which nature as represented and cultivated by Kew proved British prowess. Inversely, he also understood the nation in plant-based terms, where the healthy, functioning state resembled a tree: "Its roots are the farmers, the lower branches traders, its upper branches manufacturers, and its fruit and flowers the nobility and gentry—if its roots are not manured, the tree will droop."[16] Banks was not alone. As Simon Schama details, the oak tree served as a symbol for England's population during the eighteenth century; both were "tight-pored and tough-grained, inhospitable to pests."[17] Thus this period witnessed the simultaneous naturalization of nationalism and the layering of a uniquely English identity onto a landscape-design tradition that valued naturalness above all else.

This relationship between nation and nature does not spring from purely English soil but is rather indebted to imperial ideologies of appropriation, cultivation, and improvement. This kind of claim is of central concern to postcolonial ecocritics, who share an interest in the demands colonialism makes of not just human subjects but also natural resources. The overlap between postcolonial studies and ecocriticism has not always seemed evident. This was especially true in ecocriticism's early years, when, as Rob Nixon has said, environmental literary studies was thoroughly grounded in American studies and invested in ideas of rootedness and localism, even though "one might surely have expected environmentalism to be more, not less, transnational than other fields of literary inquiry."[18] Postcolonial criticism's necessary interest in displacement was not easy to square with this version of ecocriticism. Yet this conflict has faded as environmental criticism has jettisoned "the tendencies of some Green movements toward Western liberal universalism."[19] Like ecofeminism, founded on the belief that the domination of nature and the domination of women share a similar logic, postcolonial ecocriticism is broadly interested in how the process of "othering" occurs within the relationship of not just colonizer to colonized but also human to nonhuman nature. As Elizabeth DeLoughrey and George B. Handley have reasoned, "Since the environment stands as a nonhuman witness to the violent process of colonialism, an engagement with alterity is a constitutive aspect of postcoloniality."[20] Such an engagement with the alterity of nature is an important aspect of the history of Kew, whose gardens supported empire building as well as nation building, for "it was [in Britain's colonies] that plants that were considered to be potential sources of additional income for the British Empire could be cultivated and re-distributed."[21] In other words, Kew inspired "botanic nationalism" not simply by housing an impressive collection but also by serving as both the source of plants, seeds, and soils from Britain's colonies and the model for those colonies' own botanic gardens.[22] Similarly, phenomena such as improvement, cultivation, and conservation that are typically associated with late eighteenth-century landscape mores are rooted in not just an English tradition but also an overtly imperial one. Jill H. Casid writes, "The contested terrain of empire in the eighteenth century was constituted not just out of appropriated lands and claims of property or conquest but also out of its supposed opposite—the aesthetic, economic, and imaginative practices of 'cultivation,' or landscaping."[23] In light of these intersections, Schama's discussion of England's "Heart of Oak" takes on a different hue. The context of the English valorization of the oak tree was rampant deforestation; empire building meant ship building, and ships demanded ever more lumber.[24]

Into this matrix of landscape, nationalism, and colonial expansion comes Wordsworth's *Guide to the Lakes*, a long prose handbook for tourists that is ironically worried about tourism (which it helped generate). Originally, the guide was almost surely written for financial gain; Wordsworth began it in 1809 as a companion to the engravings in Joseph Wilkinson's *Select Views in Cumberland, Westmoreland, and Lancashire* (1810), an undertaking that he had refused a year earlier and probably only accepted because of financial hardship. But the project soon grew legs, and the appearance of expanded editions of the *Guide to the Lakes* in 1820, 1822, 1823, and 1835 suggests that Wordsworth treated (and mistreated) it as he would have any of his poems, as a perpetually unfinished document open to revision. In its desire to memorialize and preserve a proximate geographic region, the guide participates in what we might call localism, for as Ursula K. Heise reasons in her analysis of the contemporary American environmental movement, "The local as the ground for individual and communal identity and as the site of connections to nature . . . certainly fits broadly into a pattern of critique of modernity that has been repeatedly articulated in western Europe and North America for at least two centuries."[25] But the critical tendency has been to treat the guide's localism as a function of Wordsworth's nationalism—to suggest that the guide does not merely celebrate the local but also acts as an "expression of nationalism" by "encompassing the national through the local."[26] As Bewell has pointed out, during this period, the "traditional notion of local, native, or endemic natures, whose plant and animal life had always stayed put, occupying the same spots that they had been originally created to occupy, was quickly becoming a thing of the past."[27] But while Wordsworth's anxiety about exotic plants reads as "ecoxenophobia" to some, it seems important to note this anxiety is not merely about the permeability of national boundaries; it also worries the movement of people and plants *within* the United Kingdom. To focus on xenophobia and nationalism, then, is to construe Wordsworth's anxiety too narrowly: he is concerned with both the global and the intranational migration of plants.

The movement of plants inherent in colonialism shaped Wordsworth's sense of local belonging. In saying this, I am not suggesting that his anxiety about the Lake District can be read as concern for the botanic practices of British colonialism. Nevertheless, his gardens and landscape writing, centered as they are on an ideal of English localism, are also reacting to norms that stemmed from British colonialism as much as English tradition. This claim is rooted in a treatment of the garden that goes beyond its status as a metaphor or trope. Such a metaphorical status has resulted in a blind spot: what has interested critics is not that Wordsworth and Kincaid garden but that they write about it, suggesting that gardens matter not as representations in their own right but as they can be represented by other means. The garden becomes symbolically portentous but materially inert, revealing a stasis that is utterly foreign to any living garden: as Susan Stewart writes, "In making a garden one composes with living things, intervening in and contextualizing, and thus changing, their form without determining all aspects of their development or end."[28] But this claim I want to make about localism is also more specifically dependent on Kincaid, for her frequent references to Wordsworth reveal that the context of ecological imperialism is imperative to our understanding of Wordsworth's localism—as well as Kincaid's own. As much as we need Wordsworth to understand Kincaid, her repurposings help demonstrate the global scope of Wordsworth's ecological import.

BOTANICAL TRANSFERS AND THE ROYAL GARDENS AT KEW

When she refers to Wordsworth and his daffodils in an essay titled "What Joseph Banks Wrought," Kincaid pulls this English poet into the context of colonial botanic history that Banks represents. Toward the chapter's end, Kincaid delves into her botanical taste, connecting it to the practice of colonial rule in the West Indies: "There must be many ways to have someone be the way you would like them to be; I only know of two with any certainty: You can hold a gun to their head or you can clearly set out before them the thing you would like them to be, and eventually they admire it so much, without even knowing they do so, that they adopt your ways, almost to the point of sickness" (*MGB*, 141–142).[29] Kincaid moves immediately into a list of plants she likes and dislikes—"I do not really like the bougainvillea, I do not really like the hibiscus"—before landing on the plant that readers familiar with *Lucy* are waiting to hear: "I do not like daffodils, but that's a legacy of the gun-to-the-head approach, for I was forced to memorize the poem by William Wordsworth when I was a child" (*MGB*, 142). Published in 1999, her essay deviates little from the opinion of daffodils espoused by *Lucy* in 1990. It seems daffodils cannot be cleansed of their association with Wordsworth; Wordsworth cannot be cleansed of his association with colonial education.

Kincaid has reconsidered her stance since then. In 2003, she told *The Believer* she had just read *The Prelude* in its entirety and, as a result, discovered that the novel she could not finish was actually already complete.[30] (It seems appropriate to the vicissitudes of their relationship that Kincaid warms to Wordsworth by finding in his relentlessly edited and reedited epic poem the inspiration to call her own work finished.) The final nails in the coffin are the thousands of daffodils that Kincaid has planted in her garden in an effort to "vindicate" Wordsworth: "It was not [his] fault that he was implicated in colonialism."[31] Yet implicated he was, and Kincaid's newfound appreciation for Wordsworth and daffodils is commingled with the connections she draws between the dissemination of his poem and the botanical history of colonialism she details in *My Garden (Book):*. Joseph Banks advised the Royal Botanic Gardens at Kew from 1772 until his death in 1820, and during the reign of King George III (dubbed "Farmer George" for good reason), seven thousand new plants from overseas were imported into England, mostly thanks to Banks and his plant collectors.[32] In "What Joseph Banks Wrought," Kincaid addresses the aftermath of this global movement in her native Antigua, detailing the plant life now common to the island and these plants' diverse colonial provenance. But for Kincaid, as for Wordsworth, this botanic movement has implications that extend beyond the botanic garden and into the back yard. For Kincaid's own garden is neither a hortus conclusus nor a retreat, and it cannot shut out the world by opposing its rooted localism against global incursions and colonial histories: these ideologies are not opposed but rather entwined.

For Banks, Kew Gardens was evidence of Britain's superiority over other European nations. Banks guarded Kew's collection jealously, instructing his teams of plant collectors that "plants should only be exchanged [between Kew and other nations' botanic gardens] . . . when there was an advantage to be obtained."[33] Any exchange was to "ensure that it detracted as little as possible from Kew's superiority." This attitude resulted in a variety of undermining behaviors, such as leaving labels off packages and trading only seeds of the "least curious & least beautiful Plants."

The Imperial Gardens at Vienna represented the main threat to Kew's superiority and thus probably received many unlabeled packages full of mundane plant life, but Banks didn't want any advantage going to the Royal Gardens at Paris either. Plant collectors were reminded in their contracts that if any of the plants they found for Kew appeared "in any circuitous manner whatever" at another garden, "[their] having parted with it will be deemed a breach of the fidelity [they] unquestionably owe to [their] employers."[34]

The swaggering trickery of Kew and other gardens may serve as evidence of "botanic nationalism," but the source of this nationalism was global: Kew, like its counterparts in Vienna and Paris, was not known for its collection of national flora but for its colonial exotics. Thus the pride that Kew inspired was self-consciously indebted to Britain's colonial holdings—which is to say that the term *botanic nationalism* only captures half the story, for during this period, the study of botany was not separable from the colonial project that gave it fodder to study. (Indeed, this trend had begun significantly earlier, as Sir Hans Sloane's natural history of Jamaica, published in 1707, suggests.)[35] Such an emphasis on botany makes Kew Gardens sound like an academic endeavor; indeed, art historian James Elkins categorizes Kew as a garden of "historical condensation," "a garden that is a text, replete with cultural and historical information."[36] This is certainly the case. Banks was also president of the Royal Society, which "offered prize awards and gold medals for anyone who could improve the plant economy in the West Indies by importing consumable items."[37] But Kew's role was also economic because it could cultivate valuable plants for global use and distribution.[38] As a "clearing house" for the import, cultivation, and export of economically important plants, Kew's role in the maintenance of British colonies is difficult to overstate.[39] The history of the cinchona tree (whose bark provided much-needed quinine to British colonies) is just one example: though Jesuits had been using the remedy for centuries, when British plant collectors stole the tree from South America and resuscitated it at Kew after a long transatlantic journey, the remedy could be finally transported to India, where it was most needed.[40] As the example of quinine suggests, the economic importance of Kew was not rooted solely in plants' status as food; other venues for plants were purely commercial. Bewell writes that gardening had become "a fashionable leisure activity among all social ranks" by the 1760s, "with the result that the demand for new and fashionable plants reached new heights."[41] Scientific inquiry, colonial expansion, and commerce during the late eighteenth century were thus deeply intertwined—and with Kew acting as centralized hub, England became the source for economically valuable exotics and, paradoxically, their new native home. As Banks bragged, Kew Gardens "is the nursing mother of all the rest, who draw from England the greater part of the exotics they cultivate in their Botanic

Gardens," a boast that blurs the distinction between the Royal Botanic Garden and the nation that housed it.[42]

This metaphor, in which England becomes "nursing mother" of colonial exotics, lessens the distance between the discourses of natural landscape and human behavior. The intersection is a familiar one during a period of English history obsessed with the latest fashion in landscape design; as Alistair M. Duckworth has pointed out, one sign of Fanny Price's good character in *Mansfield Park* is her horror at the plans to "improve" the estate at Sotherton.[43] If that novel dramatizes how "improvements" might refer both to landscapes and to characters like Fanny, whose tenure at Mansfield Park changes her into a person who can recognize the slovenly impropriety of her childhood home, other terms are equally capable of making the leap. Neither *exotic*, *native*, *cultivation*, nor *hybrid* is limited in their usage to the realm of flora.[44] This slippage seems to be on Kincaid's mind when she muses that typically English "contrasting lawns and massed ornamental beds are signs of something . . . someone has been humbled, someone is on his knees wondering what happened, someone will have an eternal love of concrete" (*MGB*, 140). To her eyes, a tidily managed landscape demonstrates the gardener's control not just of nature but of other humans as well.

What Banks's image of England as "nursing mother" also achieves is the effacement of any more original mother, casting England as the unlikely natal source of economically important exotics.[45] This effacement implies that exotics cultivated at Kew were imaginatively naturalized, or understood as living "naturally" in a place where they were not actually native. The plants retained the value of their exotic status—many of them could only survive in a hothouse—at the same time that they grew to be the adopted products of a new British mother. Reborn in England, these plants were then exported for use in the colonies or traded for new plants in deals with other nations' botanic gardens.[46] But they also went to Britain's colonial botanic gardens, which had sprung up all over the empire: as Richard Drayton explains, "In Asia, the Caribbean, the Southern Indian and Atlantic Oceans, and the Pacific world, a cluster of botanic gardens arose in correspondence, via Sir Joseph Banks, with the Royal Garden at Kew."[47] Modeled on Kew, these far-flung gardens replicated Kew's collection, one renowned for its biological diversity. Thus at the same time that Kew was metonymically scaling down the British Empire into a highly controlled collection of specimens, it was reproducing itself across the world, creating a codified canon of "exotics"—still exotic enough to qualify as such but leveled by the cultivation they shared at the English nursery.

The tension between botanic diversity and global reproduction is further heightened by Kew's layout, which borrowed heavily from eighteenth-century English landscape practices in its naturalized geography. Like Milton's paradise, Kew is unmistakably English. Putting aside its pagoda, it was designed as (and still looks like) a natural English landscape, a process begun during the 1760s, when the garden's buildings were razed by Lancelot "Capability" Brown, who redesigned the grounds to fit his penchant for "undulating lawns" and man-made water features.[48] This Englishness means that Kew's reproducibility included more than the diverse collection of exotics that it replicated in botanic gardens across the empire. As the model garden, Kew also offered up a stable picture of "natural" English beauty for the colonial gardens to follow. Such a dynamic serves as a specific example of what Casid terms "colonial intermixing and imperial picturesque": "Plants were introduced [to the colonies] from all over the globe and yet arranged to seem like a mythic England in its much vaunted picturesque diversity and variety."[49] However, what makes the example of Kew and its imperial subsidiaries especially pertinent is the scope of this diversity. Kew promised more than *picturesque* diversity—that is, aesthetic diversity unified by an overarching plan. It also provided a botanic diversity that could be marketed as a distinctly English product despite the distant and varied sources of the collection. By turning it into a reproducible and transferable product, Kew paradoxically transformed colonial diversity into a national export, replacing material nativity with the imaginary but potently English nursing mother. And so to say, as Casid does, that the colony was "a place at once radically transformed and yet conserved in its 'difference'" is almost but not quite right, because that "difference" is even more removed from reality than its scare quotes already imply. The botanic diversity that British colonialism imposed on its holdings was stripped of its nativity.[50] Far from being composed of plants "from all over the globe," the botanic diversity exported to the colonies had been repackaged as, somehow, native to Kew.

This is the history Kincaid calls up by discussing Banks in *My Garden (Book):*. Like Wordsworth's *Guide to the Lakes*, which bridges the gap between aesthetic treatise and guidebook, Kincaid's collection of essays is generically hybrid. Some postcolonial critics interested in Kincaid's blunt treatment of Columbus, Linnaeus, and Banks find the parts about seed catalogs "self-indulgently tedious"; some gardeners who come for the description of seed catalogs may wonder at essays on the violence of colonial history.[51] Moreover, Kincaid's childhood visits to the St. John's Botanical Garden in Antigua affirm the narrative of botanic diversity and prowess inherent in the development of Britain's botanic gardens. Devoting a whole chapter to the St. John's garden, she describes it containing "plants from various parts of the then British Empire, places that had the same climate as my own; but as I remember, none of the plants were native to Antigua" (*MGB*, 120). Here is the repackaged exotic diversity that characterized the relationship between colonial botanic gardens and the hub at Kew more than a century earlier: the plants Kincaid saw as a child were from nowhere more particular than the "British Empire," their variety leveled by a shared conqueror. In this formulation, the plants become a microcosm for Britain's colonial holdings, distinct locations made uniform by their status as part of the British Empire.

This safe amalgam of diversity and sameness is not restricted by the walls of the St. John's Botanical Garden, however: it spreads outward, overwhelming any knowledge of what once counted as Antiguan nativity. A botany enthusiast in school, Kincaid studied "the botany of the British Empire in Africa and Asia, some of the very same plants that are now widely cultivated in Antigua and must seem to most Antiguans (if they ever think about it) as typical of their native landscape" (*MGB*, 138–139). As it progresses, the description of her studies condenses the wide expanse of the British Empire and its continental holdings to the "typical"—to what exemplifies the "native landscape" of a relatively small island. This condensation is in line with the homogenizing process that Ian Gregory Strachan critiques in his examination of Caribbean tourism by using pointedly reductive references to "the islands" and identifying the "paradise discourse" that clings to them as a whole.[52] What Kincaid's memory of her studies traces is the process by which Antigua's role as one of "the islands," one of the former British colonies, helped erase the category of botanic nativity. It follows then that the power inherent in the movement of plants and the redefinition of a native landscape is as clear to Kincaid as it was to Joseph Banks. She knew this even as a child: "The botanical garden reinforced for me how powerful were the people who had conquered me; they could bring to me the botany of the world they owned" (*MGB*, 120). Kincaid here aligns two vectors of hegemony: the empire disseminated and systematized botany; by extension, it "conquered [her]." Banks might have preferred to hear this statement from the director of the Imperial Gardens at Vienna, but its content stands as an avowal of "the stories the powerful people want to tell with trees," of botany's ability to prove national power.[53]

Comparing a botanic garden with one in the back yard is a difficult task given the differences in scale, labor, composition, and aim. But such a comparison becomes apropos given the visibility of exotics in even the most informal of gardens and, more significantly, these plants' dependence on the colonizing mission of Kew and other national botanic gardens. In this light, it is not surprising to see how quickly Kincaid moves from her discussion of the colonial botanic garden to a critical examination of her own backyard garden: in her view, the aims and inspirations that might seem to distinguish one genre of garden from another are not very different. In general, Kincaid associates botanic gardens with objectification and subjection, with certain prospects making her think, "Oh, this is the back yard of someone else, someone far away, someone's landscape the botanical garden can make an object" (*MGB*, 148). The botanic garden succeeds in objectifying people as well as plants, in part because of the labor that the garden both perpetually demands and fastidiously hides and because the garden acts as a "shrine of Possession" that can turn a visitor into "an object, a mere thing, within it" (*MGB*, 148). If these observations seem limited in their scope, Kincaid would disagree: all gardening is suspect. She insists quite broadly that "there is a relationship between gardening and prosperity" (*MGB*, 138) and realizes with "bitterness" that she planned her own garden only out of desire and "knew the name, proper and common, of each thing growing in it" (*MGB*, 121). Such prosperity and knowledge are reminders of Kincaid's own status as conqueror: "Just now the leaves in the shade bed are all complementary (but not in a predictable way—in a way I had not expected, a thrilling way). And I thought how I had crossed a line; but at whose expense? I cannot begin to look, because what if it is someone I know? I have joined the conquering class: who else could afford this garden—a garden in which I grow things that it would be much cheaper to buy at the store?" (*MGB*, 122–123). However keenly Kincaid recognizes her status as upper-middle-class conqueror (the chapter originally appeared in the *New Yorker*), that status is in no way well defined by the previous passage. On one level, the passage coherently documents the movement from thrill to guilt, both of them wrapped up in Kincaid's recognition that even a backyard garden in Vermont depends on—and is thus complicit with—the history of colonial movement. Her emphasis on knowledge and taxonomy—"the name, proper and common, of each thing growing" in the garden—makes this connection clear and draws Kincaid into the realm of binomial nomenclature and scientific inquiry. (One thinks back to Wordsworth's classification "Poems on the naming of places.") However, Kincaid's sense that she has "crossed a line" springs strangely from her admiration of her plants' unpredictable growth and coloration: it is not her self-aware manipulation of nature but rather her lack of power in the face of her capricious plant life that inspires her guilt. Kincaid never makes the mistake of thinking herself in perfect control of her garden. As Susie O'Brien argues, to garden is "actively to recognize the extent to which culture is shaped by nature and vice versa, but also—and this point is crucial for Kincaid—to resist the urge to make them analogous."[54] But what Kincaid's guilt makes clear is that colonialism's botanic violence affects people as well as plants. As she says in a pointed non sequitur, Nina Simone's autobiography is "an essential companion to any work of Vita Sackville-West's. There is no mention of the garden in Nina Simone's account of her life, as there is no mention of the sad weight of the world in Sackville-West's account of her gardening" (*MGB*, 83). As gardener designer, laborer, and writer, Kincaid is limited in her ability to reproduce the dynamic between subjugator and subjugated. But when she wonders "at whose expense" she admires her shade bed, she brings "the sad weight of the world" into that local realm, suggesting that the benefits of the local garden belong not to localism but to affluence: she admires the complementary leaves at the expense of those who cannot afford to grow plants for leisure.

As her anxiety makes clear, Kincaid theorizes that the garden is, in O'Brien's words, "as troubling to economic as it is to ecological models of environmental interaction" because its products supply no particular demand.[55] By opting out of a larger and more exacting system of exchange, her labor becomes a privilege, a reminder that she belongs to a class whose garden beds, however toil filled, reveal that they needn't have labored in the first place. The economic realities of gardening lead Kincaid to wonder, "Who else could afford this garden—a garden in which I grow things that it would be much cheaper to buy at the store?" Though Kincaid posits buying "things" at the store as a less expensive alternative to growing things in the garden, one assumes that much of her garden already originated at a store in some form—opting out of capitalistic exchange is not an option.[56] And so there seems no way out of wondering "at whose expense," for the botanic movement that the garden demands is not a historical phenomenon unique to colonial rule. Even outside the bounds of colonialism, this transportability is inherently a thrilling and guilt-inspiring quality to those gardeners who exploit it in their back yards.

EXOTICS IN THE LAKE DISTRICT

Naturalization is not a word Wordsworth uses in his *Guide to the Lakes*—or almost anywhere else, for that matter. Yet like many gardeners, he was invested in what it means to make something natural, to emulate nature, to meld it with art. These aims, and terms like *native* and *natural* that cluster around them, help explicate the incursion of colonialism into his highly local guidebook. In the horticultural world, naturalization is the process by which a plant becomes "established so that it lives wild in a place where it is not native."[57] According to this logic, the gulf between the exotic and the natural can be bridged once the plant is seen accepting its new climate. This interplay of nativity, foreignness, and movement raises the question of what counts as local, what consequences spring from "composing with living things," in Stewart's words, when those living things have come from far away. In Wordsworth's *Guide to the Lakes*, the answer to these questions depends on the internal consequences that he sees colonialism as effecting on England itself.

The terms of this discussion are loaded. Raymond Williams has entries on *native* and *nature* in his *Keywords* (both derive from the past participle of the Latin *nascor*, "to be born"), and although "to naturalize" suffers from no dearth of precise definitions, its most basic meaning is its most troubling: "to make natural." Williams gets at the problem of negotiating artful fabrication with the innate and preexisting implications of the "natural" by tracing the development of *nature* through the eighteenth century, when it becomes associated with the countryside: "Nature is what man has not made, though if he made it long enough ago—a hedgerow or a desert—it will usually be included as natural."[58] Williams can be nothing but upfront about the trickiness of *nature*, "the most complex word in the language," acknowledging that although he can divide its meanings into three general categories, "precise meanings are variable and at times even opposed."[59] *Nature* is that which is not man-made—except when it's not. *Nature* provides the antidote for "an 'artificial' or 'mechanical' society," except when it is itself made.[60] Wordsworth plunges headlong into this set of hazy indistinctions in his *Guide to the Lakes*, most notably when he issues his gardening imperative: "Work, where you can, in the spirit of nature, with an invisible hand of art" (*PrW*, 2:211–212). The alliance he sees between nature and art is palpable but far from absolute. In the last century, Alexander Pope had recommended that the gardener "let Nature never be forgot" and "consult the genius of the place in all," imbuing that genius with artistic abilities: it "paints as you plant, and, as you work, designs."[61] In contrast, Wordsworth's edict separates art from nature, situating art in the realm of human effort. The two remain closely linked—the gardener must use this "invisible hand of art" in order to work "in the spirit of nature"—but the teams have been picked, and nature is on its own.

Like *exotic*, the term *native*, particularly when used as a substantive, refers to "the inferior inhabitants of a place subjected to alien political power or conquest," and was commonly employed "as a term for 'non-Europeans' in the period of colonialism and imperialism," though such usage has clearly fallen out of favor.[62] Throughout the period of this use, though, *native* also carried a nonpejorative meaning and was "a very positive word when applied to one's own place or person." The vacillation between laudatory and derogatory, local and colonial, subject and subjugated reveals the deictic nature of the term: its meaning depends on where you stand and where you're pointing. For Wordsworth, *native* almost always hews to this positive denotation.[63] Yet his recommendations in the *Guide to the Lakes* partake in the tension between the "good" native and the "bad": the guide is devoted to the native species of the Lake District, yet the book's audience is primarily the inferior natives of other counties who have recently come to admire the lake's "native attractions" and have "erected their habitations in it" (*PrW*, 2:218). This intersection is the source of what Wordsworth critiques as the primary error of Lake District landscaping practices, an error committed primarily by natives of other counties concerning the use of nonnative plants. New residents, whether they be damnable plantation owners or well-meaning lovers of "native beauty," must realize that "after the feeling has been gratified that prompts us to gather round our dwelling a few flowers and shrubs, which from the circumstance of their not being native, may, by their very looks, remind us that they owe their existence to our hands, and their prosperity to our care; they will see that, after this natural desire has been provided for, the course of all beyond has been predetermined by the spirit of the place" (*PrW*, 2:218). Channeling Pope, Wordsworth insists upon the decisive power of "the spirit of the place," suggesting that the planting of exotics cannot matter very much. In the end, the genius of the place will determine the ultimate course. Yet there is a repetitive opposition structuring his claim that "they owe *their* existence to *our* hands, and *their* prosperity to *our* care," one that emphasizes the boundary between those pronouns over all else. The possessive *their* is consistently trumped by the dominant *our* nipping at its heels, a structural reminder that exotics have no "existence" (let alone "prosperity") if they are not under "our care." To Wordsworth, there is something beguiling about this heightened boundary between the gardener and the plant. The plant's nonnative status, legible in its "very looks," reminds the gardener of the plant's dependence, and Wordsworth recognizes a "natural desire" in the cultivation of this dependence. But by turning immediately to "the spirit of place," Wordsworth seems to leave something unsaid. The desire to plant nonnative species may be "natural," but I would hazard that Wordsworth sees the desire as morally suspect nevertheless—and not merely because "the spirit of the place" is in charge.

A few lines later, he clarifies that "the introduction of a few exotic plants" may be justified, "provided they be confined almost to the doors of the house" (*PrW*, 2:218–219). This is a strangely specific recommendation, perhaps, but in it lies the heart of Wordsworth's objection to nonnative plants. It is not simply that planting exotics is relatively pointless given the limited power of the gardener in the face of nature. More significantly, Wordsworth's recommendation suggests that planting and caring for nonnative species has the potential to send the gardener on a sort of botanical power trip. Restricting such plants to a defined perimeter does more than limit their numbers. It keeps these plants near the house, where they may not be mistaken for native specimens. The gardener, feeding on his "natural desire" to tend to plants that visibly "owe their existence to [his] care," shall not be tricked into thinking this dynamic representative of his relationship with nature at large. Exotics remain near the house, becoming almost a feature of the built rather than the natural environment.[64]

At moments like this one, the rulebook connects the terms of local belonging with the influence of colonial expansion on gardening practices. So at a time when it was possible—easy, even—for an amateur gardener to acquire and plant species from all over the world, Wordsworth advised caution: being a responsible local resident meant treating both native and exotic plant species with deliberation and care. This inverse relationship between local belonging and global botanical exchange is not purely Wordsworth's creation, however. Terms like *native* and *natural* reached the height of their definitional instability during the Romantic era. This is likely not a coincidence; the escalation of the British Empire between 1790 and 1830 certainly intensified the vacillation of these words.[65] In their shifts and contradictions, the terms begin to illuminate the mutual interdependence of the local and the colonial. In both these geopolitical realms, however vaguely defined they may be, the art of gardening depends on the ability to fabricate the natural and the native, and these are categories that, as we have seen, rely on a renounced "out there" for their meaning. This dependence is perhaps not surprising; it is an integral part of Edward Said's argument that what defines "European culture" is a "comparison with all the non-European peoples and cultures" or Homi K. Bhabha's insistence that Englishness only has meaning belatedly, in reference to "colonial difference."[66] Yet these theorizations are quite broad: Said's "European culture" (or, in the case of Bhabha, the "English book") produces usefully sweeping binaries that oppose Europe to the Orient, or Britain to India. The case of the local and the colonial operates on a different scale, absent the category of nation. It's not just that Englishness, for example, is defined in opposition to the colonized other (though this is true) but rather that defining the local depends on the colonial. Praising the local "native" means rejecting the colonial "native."[67] For this reason, I want to resist interpreting Wordsworth's focus on the local as a microcosm for the nationalistic fervor, as Wordsworth himself would seem to do when he concludes his *Guide to the Lakes* with a reference to "persons of pure taste throughout the whole island" who recognize the Lake District as "a sort of national property." While the Lake District may exemplify the best England has to offer in Wordsworth's eyes, to substitute the region for the nation risks ignoring the local on its own terms. As a governmental employee from 1813 onward—his position as the distributor of stamps for Westmoreland made his family financially secure for the first time—Wordsworth had an understanding of the British state that went beyond the pastoral beauty of the Lake District. Focusing on Wordsworth's implied construction of the nation, to the exclusion of his actual representation of the local, means ignoring the realm in which he saw the effects of colonialism most clearly.

In the *Guide to the Lakes*, Wordsworth's primary concern centers on preservation, specifically the preservation of the Lake District's native appearance. This appearance has a surprisingly specific birthdate. Throughout, the guide distinguishes sharply between present England and the England of sixty years ago.[68] It is not until the third section, however, that Wordsworth reveals what exactly happened sixty years ago: "A practice, denominated Ornamental Gardening, was at that time becoming prevalent over England" (*PrW*, 2:207). As a result, "a relish for select parts of natural scenery" developed, spurring travelers "to wander over the island in search of sequestered spots," such as those hidden in the Lake District. In other words, Capability Brown and his picturesque landscapes have created a booming class of tourists who are newly capable of appreciating the Lake District. This shift sixty years since is precisely the impetus for Wordsworth's *Guide to the Lakes,* and he finds himself in the strange position of writing a tome that could benefit him financially (for once) while also bemoaning the effects of very shift on which that financial success depends. A peculiar trait of the guide is thus the overwhelming attention Wordsworth pays to the appearance of buildings in the Lake District and the strict recommendations he outlines for them. After all, this was a self-proclaimed guide for tourists, not an advisory pamphlet for residents. His rationale becomes clear, though, toward the end of the main text, where Wordsworth explains that his aim has been "to preserve the native beauty of this delightful place, because still further changes in its appearance must inevitably follow, from the change of inhabitants and owners which is rapidly taking place" (*PrW*, 2:223). In other words, this is as much a guide for house hunters as it is for tourists, a guide that in spite of its backward glances is "neither defensive nor elegiac."[69] Ideally, it seems, Wordsworth's conservation should follow a straightforward path: he writes and publishes recommendations that are read by new inhabitants who take his suggestions to heart and act in concert with the district's "native beauty." But Kincaid's discussion of memory in the garden suggests another path: "Memory is a gardener's real palette; memory as it summons up the past, memory as it shapes the present, memory as it dictates the future" (*MGB*, 218–219). In this context, Wordsworth's desire "to preserve" might have no material outcome beyond the textual product in which he inscribed that desire. He memorializes a version of the Lake District that predates his birth.[70]

For Wordsworth, the process of naturalizing exotics is not limited to the plant world. Like J. C. Loudon's *Suburban Gardener* (1838), which is as much about houses as it is about gardens, Wordsworth's *Guide to the Lakes* was significantly concerned with how man-made structures might complement the landscape so completely as to transcend their artificial origins:

> As these houses have been, from father to son, inhabited by persons engaged in the same occupations, yet necessarily with changes in their circumstances, they have received without incongruity additions and accommodations adapted to the needs of each successive occupant, who, being for the most part proprietor, was at liberty to follow his own fancy: so that these humble dwellings remind the contemplative spectator of a production of nature, and may (using a strong expression) rather be said to have grown than to have been erected;—to have risen, by an instinct of their

> own, out of the native rock—so little is there in them of formality, such is their wildness and beauty. (*PrW*, 2:202)

The ideal structure, in his eyes, was a cottage passed down "from father to son" and "inhabited by persons engaged in the same occupations," a place with aesthetic as well as political significance insofar as "the strong instincts of self-interest (family and property) are combined into a sympathetic community" capable of cultivating "traditional republican virtues" (*PrW*, 2:202).[71] White-washed infrequently and expanded "without incongruity," the structures become to a spectator like Wordsworth "a production of nature" and seem "to have risen, by an instinct of their own, out of the native rock." To describe humble cottages as hardy plants that spring from the earth is to give them lives of their own, lives directed not by the practical concerns of the fathers and sons who built them but rather by their own natural "instincts." It is also to suggest that the process of naturalization is so long in duration that it exceeds the realm of conceivable time. The rock from which these cottages seem to spring is, as Wordsworth explains earlier, a product of "Nature's first great dealings with the superficies of the earth," a designation he uses in reference to the sublime and one that gives the aesthetic category the temporal edge of geologic time (*PrW*, 2:181). Noting his consistent efforts to include more geologic history in the *Guide to the Lakes* and "the importance he consistently attached to geologic principles," Theresa M. Kelley argues that for Wordsworth, the sublime is "down, hidden, and primitive"—in need of excavation.[72] Sublime landscapes are sublimely old, sublimely deep. These temporal indications make the actual construction of a house almost inconceivable: its nativity is so stalwart in Wordsworth's account that it seems to have built itself out of ancient Cumbrian rock.

In effect, Wordsworth suggests that such cottages are as native as the English oak. This nativity has two sources: the cottages' seeming age and their removal from human effort. In an echo of certain eighteenth-century landscaping practices, laboring father and son slowly fade from the scene as the sentence progresses. The grammatical dominance of the cottages, subject of both halves of Wordsworth's long and complex sentence, act like the hills and drifts of trees that landscape designers like Capability Brown often constructed in order to obscure any view of the adjacent property where farm laborers might otherwise be visible.[73] On the next page, the humble cottages don "a vegetable garb," and in this costume they "appear to be received into the bosom of the living principle of things, as it acts and exists among the woods and fields; and, by their colour and their shape, affectingly direct the thoughts to that tranquil course of nature and simplicity, along which the humble-minded inhabitants have, through so many generations, been led" (*PrW*, 2:203). The interpolation of cottages into the realm of flora continues here, with houses becoming a part of "the living principle of things." Moreover, their influence waxes as the agency of "humble-minded inhabitants" wanes. In a reversal of what must, logically speaking, be the order of operations—inhabitants build cottages that appear natural—the cottages "direct the thoughts," leading the inhabitants down a "course of nature and simplicity" that guides their actions. This process is cyclical and unending, a trend of "so many generations" instigated not by human effort but by the instinctual and plantlike agency of the built environment. The passive voice crops up again when Wordsworth dubs the scene "the representative idea of a mountain-cottage in this country so beautifully formed in itself, so richly adorned by the hand of nature." While such a designation recognizes the cottage as fundamentally unreal, a "representative idea," it also construes it as a hermetic structure, receptive only to "the hand of nature." The cagey passivity of *formed* denies any specific agent of production; in fact, insofar as the cottage was formed "in itself," it seems almost self-propagating, as if its gestation occurred within its already existing walls. Paired with the implication that the ideal local cottage exists out of time, this self-sufficiency makes the cottage seem even more native than the inhabitants who built it, a part of the natural rather than the built environment.

Houses here are subject to naturalization: in spite of their manufacture, they may be materially and imaginatively included as a natural aspect of the landscape. It follows, then, that houses, like plants, can also be exotics. After detailing his aversion to white houses—"white destroys the *gradations* of distance"—Wordsworth reveals his preference to be highly local (*PrW*, 2:215–516, emphasis in the original). White houses are fine elsewhere, along the Danube. But the Lakes demand a different palate, "something between a cream and a dust-colour, commonly called stone colour" (*PrW*, 2:217). In a section of the *Guide to the Lakes* called "Changes, and rules of taste for preventing their bad effects," such detailed fussiness seems almost de rigueur. But more surprising is Wordsworth's identification of inappropriately sized and colored houses in the Lake District as "exotics in architecture." Because Wordsworth was a practicing gardener with strong convictions about exotic plants, I think we must understand him as using this term deliberately.

The use of *exotic* in reference to plant life is common in writings about landscapes and in this context often appears as a substantive rather than an adjective: *exotics* for "exotic plants."[74] When Wordsworth refers to houses as exotics, then, he is using figuratively a term reserved for foreign plants. Houses that are too big or too white are like larches or rhododendrons, appropriate in other climes but incongruous with the particular features of the Lake District. In this light, what is unique about Wordsworth's use of *exotics* is how he articulates its boundaries. A few pages earlier, he laments the influx of outsiders: "Persons, who in Leicestershire or Northamptonshire would probably have built a modest dwelling like those of their sensible neighbours, have been turned out of their course; and, acting a part, no wonder if, having had little experience, they act it ill. The craving for prospect, also, which is immoderate, particularly in new settlers, has rendered it impossible that buildings, whatever might have been their architecture, should in most instances be ornamental to the landscape; rising as they do from the summits of naked hills in staring contrast to the snugness and privacy of the ancient houses" (*PrW*, 2:211). In two sentences, Wordsworth effectively redefines what it means to be an exotic: it means quite specifically to be not from the Lake District. Although the botanical definition of *exotic* is broad and highly contextual, encompassing plants of any foreign extraction, the term when used in Northern England clearly does not signify plants (or buildings) from Leicestershire or Northamptonshire, a few counties from the Lake District. In figuring the houses that midlanders build in the Lake District as exotics, then, Wordsworth reduces the distance between local and foreign to about two hundred miles.[75] Adding to his exoticization of the Midlands is his creation of a settler class—not merely a group of Englishmen from Leicestershire who have decided to relocate to another county but rather a division of colonists infiltrating a place that, in this figuration at least, becomes the colony of the Lake District.

It is certainly possible to attach too much meaning to Wordsworth's diction here. Elsewhere in the *Guide to the Lakes*, he uses *settler* generically, referring twice to the area's "first settlers," for instance (*PrW*, 2:189, 194). These newcomers are of a different class, located in the past and notable for having been almost instantaneously naturalized to the area, such that "the plough of the first settlers . . . followed naturally the veins of richer, dryer, or less stony soil" to create "an intermixture of wood and lawn, with a grace and wildness which it would have been impossible for the hand of studied art to produce" (*PrW*, 2:189). These are the settlers who became the Lake District's stalwart inhabitants, passing their modest homes down "from father to son," allowing the structures to grow "by an instinct of their own, out of the native rock." Contrast them with the "new settlers," whose "craving for prospect . . . has rendered it impossible that buildings, whatever might have been their architecture, should in most instances be ornamental to the landscape"; who "erect new mansions out of the ruins of the ancient cottages, whose little enclosures, with all the wild graces that grew out of them, disappear" (*PrW*, 2:211, 224). These settlers are the nouveaux riches, and their association with "exotics in architecture" reveals their particular threat, in Wordsworth's estimation. By utilizing the diction of imperialism—calling them settlers and their homes exotics, Wordsworth insinuates that they mimic, on a smaller scale, the process of colonization.

These midlanders are not innately colonialists. Had they stayed in Leicestershire, they might have taken a cue from their "sensible neighbours" and constructed a "modest dwelling." Rather, it is their wealth and their intranational movement that characterizes them as "new settlers." Although Wordsworth attributes the settlers' bad taste to the knowledge that their houses might be "looked at and commented upon" because the district is "an object of general admiration," suggesting that bad taste springs from social anxiety rather than from their sheer status as settlers, the fact remains that his diction involves him far more in the discourse of colonialism than national belonging. Thus when Wordsworth uses "exotics in architecture" to describe the houses these settlers build in the Lake District, he creates a world in which the local is so implicated in colonization that settlers are infiltrating from ever closer—England is being colonized by itself. In other words, this is a scheme in which Britain poses a threat not just to the lands and people it colonizes but also to its very heart.

In the final sentence of his *Guide to the Lakes*, Wordsworth zooms out and becomes inclusive, concluding with a now familiar statement: "In this wish the author will be joined by persons of pure taste throughout the whole island, who, by their visits (often repeated) to the Lakes in the North of England, testify that they deem the district a sort of national property, in which every man has a right and interest who has an eye to perceive and a heart to enjoy" (*PrW*, 2:225).

Though the "pure taste" stipulation must leave some new settlers by the wayside, the rhetorical shift from district to country movingly connects the local to the national, giving every Briton "a right and interest" in this new "national property." In this formulation, the Lake District acts as a portal to national pride, a microcosm of what makes England England. But consider the sentence that immediately precedes Wordsworth's magnanimous conclusion: "It is then much to be wished, that a better taste should prevail among these new proprietors; and, as they cannot be expected to leave things to themselves, that skill and knowledge should prevent unnecessary deviations from that path of simplicity and beauty along which, without design and unconsciously, their humble predecessors have moved." When Wordsworth calls the Lake District "a sort of national property," he has only just ceased haranguing about "strangers" and "wealthy purchasers" and "new settlers." It is they who inspire the wish for "better taste" that leads Wordsworth toward his conclusion. On the outskirts of his rousing statement about national property lurk the Midland interlopers and their exotic architecture, suggesting that the transition from local to national is not as smooth as Wordsworth makes it sound. Cumbria, Northamptonshire, and Leicestershire are not coequals, counties that together partially constitute the nation, or even counties that individually serve as microcosms of it. Rather, the Lake District becomes so intensely local that the imaginative distance between it and its surrounding counties appears vast; as the foreground sharpens, the middle ground recedes. Northamptonshire and Leicestershire are not a few counties away but half a world. Or perhaps it is rather the reverse: half a world away has drawn ever closer and is now settled in the Midlands.

Like a locavore who vows only to eat food from within a one-hundred-mile radius, Wordsworth has two categories, near and far, and thus emphasizes the chasm between the local and everything else over the gradations that make the Lake District an intelligible part of the nation. As Nicola Trott argues, even for the Wordsworth of the *Lyrical Ballads*, "imperialist expansion appears as a contamination, not of the colonized, but of the colonizer and the old country."[76] Trott's observation supports the work that James K. Chandler and David Bromwich have done on Wordsworth and Burke, who understood as early as the 1780s that colonial expansion was, as Uday Singh Mehta puts it, "doubly implicating": "The oppression of India rebounds with similar effects on Britain; the British delinquents of India will become the commons of Great Britain."[77] Wordsworth never seemed particularly concerned with India, yet the figurative language he uses in the *Guide to the Lakes* suggests another moment when he "saw a Burke looking forward, as it were, toward him," as Chandler writes.[78] In his speeches on the impeachment of Warren Hastings, Burke locates the consequences of the trial in the future:

> It is according to the judgement [on this case] that you shall pronounce upon the past transactions of India, connected with those principles, that the whole rule, tenure, tendency and character, of our future government in India is to be finally decided. My lords, it will take its course and work its whole impression from the business of this hour. My lords, it is not only the interest of a great empire which is concerned, which is now a most considerable part of the British Empire, but, my lords, the credit and honour of the British nation will themselves be decided by this decision.[79]

Perhaps not surprisingly, Burke here emphasizes a temporal through line, delineating the connections between the "*past* transactions of India" and "the whole rule, tenure, tendency and character, of our *future* government in India." The innovation, in Burke's understanding of the case, is to suggest that British actions in India (the British Empire) will have effects in Britain proper (the British nation). The emphatically reflexive *themselves* similarly draws attention to imperiled British "credit and honour." But the future tense—Britain's honor "will be decided"—casts Burke's argument as prophecy rather than testimony. In the *Guide to the Lakes*, Wordsworth testifies. Unlike *The Excursion*, the guide has little to say about Britain's imperial project: no "industrious bees" set off to address the "appointed needs / Of Britain" in new locales, "on every shore" (*E*, bk. 9, lines 370–380). In the guide, imperialism only appears linguistically, and in this mode, it figures movement within the nation rather than between center and periphery. The practices that bind metropole and colony become a language capable of describing the tenuous bond between Leicestershire and Cumbria. Here, then, is one way in which Burke's fear about the doubly implicating nature of colonial expansion comes to fruition. In Wordsworth's view, the large-scale movement of people and plants that colonialism entails has altered what it means to move people and plants at all, even within Britain.

At some point, it seems important to part ways with Wordsworth and acknowledge that there are clear distinctions to be made between British colonialism as it was practiced in the early nineteenth century and the influx of nouveaux riches Britons to the Lake District during the same period. Even internally, his figuration is inconsistent: the arrival of "new settlers" casts the Lake District as a colony, while the arrival of "exotics in architecture" casts it as the imperial metropole, natural home to native rather than exotic specimens. This figuration, however muddled, continues as Wordsworth unveils his guide's antagonist, the larch tree, native to northern climates but not England, and the "plantations" on which it is cultivated (*PrW*, 2:217). Wordsworth's use of the term *plantations* here is highly specific. Only planted tracts of trees earn the moniker; in fact, only tracts of larches and the occasional fir qualify. In contrast, Wordsworth saves the more pastoral *farm* for enclosures of land that he can call by name: the farm of Tarn Hows, the farm of Blowick. The lack of overlap between these two terms is significant at a time when, as Casid argues, "the idea of colony as plantation and the plantation as farm mythicized empire as anticonquest by making empire as rooted and natural as rural England was supposed to be."[80] In other words, the imaginative transformation of colony into plantation into farm made colonial rule seem "natural," securing the innocence of colonists "from imperial assertions while at the same time enacting European hegemony," as Mary Louise Pratt explains.[81] Wordsworth resists this slippage. Farms are farms and tracts of larches are plantations. By distinguishing between farm and plantation, using the latter only to describe the unnatural "vegetable manufactory" that "thrusts every other tree out of the way," Wordsworth suggests that the plantations he sees are not simply cultivated tracts of plant life (*PrW*, 2:217). Rather, the emphasis in *vegetable manufactory* on mechanized production and monoculture aligns his use of the term more with the sugar, cotton, and tobacco plantations associated with colonial agriculture.

As Richard Grove has explained, by the end of the eighteenth century, it became clear that while timber resources were limited, demand for lumber, particularly from the navy, was unlikely to slow.[82] This disparity between supply and demand was not particularly specialized knowledge. During the years when Wordsworth was first composing his *Guide to the Lakes*, the bishop of Llandaff—Richard Watson, a resident of Cumbria—did the math, concluding that if the navy used oak trees, "500 acres would supply the annual consumption, and fifty thousand acres would supply the demand for ever, if trees of one hundred years' growth are large enough for navy timber."[83] But if the navy switched to larch trees, which grow more quickly than oaks, that number could be greatly reduced. For this reason, Watson was a staunch advocate of larch plantations in the Lake District: "I know of no means more honourable, more certain, or more advantageous, of increasing a man's property, and promoting at the same time the public good, than by planting larches on mountainous districts."[84] As his association of larches with honor suggests, Watson's devotion to the tree had an almost moral foundation. After building a home in Winandermere in 1789, he reported spending his years there "principally . . . in planting larches, and in planting in the hearts of my children principles of piety, of benevolence, and of self-government."[85] The chiasmus here—planting trees, planting virtues—was not merely clever. Watson believed larches were key to British self-government and economic independence, as they could grow on the "barrenest" mountains and produce "pitch, tar, rosin, turpentine" locally, preventing "expensive *continental alliances*."[86] But his relationship to the larch was also startlingly personal, as he revealed in a letter about the composition of his *Anecdotes*. Suspecting that "the court" will be "ashamed" to read his *Anecdotes* and realize its "neglect of him," Watson comforts himself: "My larches thrive beyond my hopes; and the prospect of their rendering my family as independent in fortune as their father has always been in spirit, lifts me far above any repining at the loss of such honours and emoluments as are in the power of courts to bestow."[87] The larches here do not act as mere metaphors for the growth of greatness; they themselves ensure the financial success of Watson and his family.

The depth of Watson's advocacy begins to explain the vitriol of Wordsworth's condemnation. No tree but the larch earns mention in the *Guide to the Lakes*'s table of contents, and it appears in the body of the text more frequently than any other tree (even the oak, a tree Wordsworth actually liked). Unlike Watson, Wordsworth's judgment rests on aesthetic rather than moral or economic grounds. He cannot but acknowledge the area's "want . . . of timber trees" (*PrW*, 2:189), but he also cannot forgive the ugliness of the larch—a "spiky tree" whose branches have "little dignity," a tree that in summer "neither affords shade nor shelter" and in winter "appears absolutely dead" (*PrW*, 2:221). Most troubling, however, is its behavior en masse. In a plantation, placed amid forests of native trees, the larch never blends into its surroundings. As planted specimens, the trees "must generally start all at the same time," and they thus achieve a blocky uniformity antithetical to the varied appearance of a "native woods" (*PrW*, 2:220, 222). No matter how many are gathered, "the appearance is still the same—a collection of separate individual trees, obstinately presenting themselves as such" (*PrW*, 2:221). This aesthetic individuality—evidence of the larches' "obstinacy" and seeming agency—offends Wordsworth because it prevents a collection of trees from looking vast and unending and sublime in the sense that Burke evokes by associating sublimity with "eternity" and "infinity," with "a croud of great and confused images; which affect because they are crouded and confused."[88] The "separate individual" larches stand in opposition to the sublimely confused crowd.

But like the midlanders who would not be tasteless settlers if they only stayed in Leicestershire, the larches are not innately deficient. When limited to its native habitat, the larch "may sweep from valley to valley, and from hill to hill" and thus produce "a sublime image": "For sublimity will never be wanting, where the sense of innumerable multitude is lost in, and alternates with, that of intense unity; and to the ready perception of this effect, similarity and almost identity of individual form and monotony of colour contribute. But this feeling is confined to the native immeasurable forest; no artificial plantation can give it" (*PrW*, 2:222). The association here is not between sublimity and any particular forest composition but rather between sublimity and nativity. Only as a native can the larch achieve sublimity; only in a native forest can larches become immeasurable, obscure, crowded. Like a house well suited to the moors that stands out as too white in the Lake District, the larch might be sublime in Siberia but is only spiky in Cumbria. By contrasting the "native immeasurable forest" and the "artificial plantation" of larches, Wordsworth presents an approach to landscape aesthetics that diverged decisively from that of Kew Gardens, where contemporary English landscape design was constituted through the botanical spoils of British imperialism. Plants from around the world were arranged in a recognizably English landscape. This approach, reproduced in colonial botanical gardens around the world, effectively effaced the nativity of exotics, creating a class of plants that, to return to Kincaid's example, "are now widely cultivated in Antigua and must seem to most Antiguans (if they ever think about it) as typical of their native landscape." Native to colder northern climes like the Lake District, the larch tree could become naturalized there; it could, in time, strike residents as "typical of their native landscape." Indeed, larch trees now cover 5.5 percent of the district's forest areas; the larch is the namesake of numerous Lake District tourist lodgings.[89] Yet by depicting their tracts as plantations, Wordsworth insists upon their otherness in part for practical reasons—regimented rows of similarly sized trees do not make a forest—and in part, I suspect, for ideological ones. As I argued in the previous chapter, *The Excursion* shows Wordsworth to have understood and represented England's participation in global networks forged by capitalism and imperialism. Plantations in the Lake District juxtaposed the botanical effects of global movement against the features of the local landscapes that made the Lake District aesthetically distinct rather than endeavoring to commingle the two harmoniously, as Kew Gardens did.

By placing settlers, exotics, and plantations in the Lake District, Wordsworth insists that the practices of colonialism have local as well as remote effects. In this sense, Wordsworth's concerns echo again those of Burke's in his speeches on Warren Hastings. In order to clarify Hastings's particular abuses, Burke recapitulates the history of the East India Company, insisting that when it accepted the *diwani*, or the right to collect revenue, in 1765, "Great Britain made a virtual act of union with [India], by which they bound themselves as securities for their subjects, to preserve the people in all the rights, laws and liberties, which their natural, original Sovereign was bound to enforce."[90] By dubbing the charter "a virtual act of union," Burke implicitly compares Britain's role in India to its role in Scotland, made part of the United Kingdom by the Act of Union in 1707. Whereas colonial rule became, in Sara Suleri's words, "sequentially dependent on enactments of successive usurpation, with each usurping moment implying a singular and unprecedented logic," Burke attempts to situate India within Britain's historical trajectory.[91] The relationship with India is not singular; the Act of Union with Scotland serves as its precedent. The effect of his comparison between India and Scotland is that India suddenly seems improbably proximate—a Celtic periphery rather than a far-off holding—perhaps no better integrated into the United Kingdom than Scotland (and, a few years hence, Ireland) but far closer, with parliamentary representation to boot.

The Act of Union that Burke proposes leaves the cultural order of India intact, but in evoking the case of Scotland, Burke also lessens India's separation from England. A century later, the historian J. R. Seeley would take Burke's recommendation to its apogee. In his history of the British Empire, *The Expansion of England* (1883), Seeley argued for an empire ruled by "the family bond" rather than the "gun-to-the-head approach" that Kincaid articulates.[92] Reasoning that it didn't make sense to question the profits and losses of the colonies because they should be "regarded as simply an extension of the nation," Seeley wondered, "Who ever thought of inquiring whether Cornwall or Kent rendered any sufficient return for the money which we lay out upon them, whether those counties were worth keeping?" The pronouns in this rhetorical question are peculiar: who are *we* if not Cornwall and Kent? Seeley's point is that Britain should treat its colonies not as possessions but as extensions; Canada and Australia are no different from Cornwall and Kent. Yet his question also posits the reverse, importing a Manichean logic of us versus them into the nation itself. In this way, his defense of imperialism replicates Wordsworth's concerns for the Lake District; both writers use the language of colonialism to describe the constitution of England proper. But Seeley's argument also represents the reverse of Wordsworth's concerns for the Lake District. While Wordsworth saw counties turning into colonies, Seeley argues colonies should be treated as counties. What Wordsworth's fears suggest is that by the time Seeley writes his imperial history, there will be no "local" counties on which to model Britain's relationship to its colonies. The familial bond that ties Cornwall to England, Leicestershire to Cumbria will have already become colonial in its logic. The success of the British Empire, in Seeley's view, depends on an understanding of England that Wordsworth hoped would never become prevalent.

Wordsworth was not in danger of living in a place where the nativity of plant life might be entirely forgotten or rewritten; the Lake District was not about to become colonial Antigua. Yet no place is immune to the botanic erasures that Kincaid describes, and the recommendations in Wordsworth's *Guide to the Lakes* align him with Kincaid, particularly with her belief that even a garden, in its artifice and local rootedness, cannot wall out the histories that moved plants and people across the globe. For Wordsworth, colonialism was not merely a set of practices that happened beyond England's shores. In providing an apt language for the rapidly changing English countryside, colonialism became for him a highly local concern.

UNROOTING THE GARDEN

When it came to their actual gardens, William and Dorothy Wordsworth grew mostly native plants. But for Kincaid, the relationship between the local garden and the exotic plant is not theoretical. Kincaid, for whom set definitions are anathema, comes as close as she can to a static designation in her travel memoir *Among Flowers*: "In particular a gardener is a person who at least once in the gardening year feels the urge to possess completely at least one plant" (*AF*, 32). Although this definition is phrased as potential rather than actual possession—the gardener "feels the urge" but does not actually "possess completely" any plant—its repetitive understatements, *at least once*, *at least one*, signal the potentially unbounded nature of this desire for possession. Kincaid gives an example:

> You can hear this form of possession in the voice of someone who will utter a sentence like this: "I saw some *Codonopsis* growing up there, couldn't tell which one it was but I took seeds anyway." That is no ordinary sentence said in an ordinary voice. The person who says such a sentence is in a complicated state of craving, for they are aware that they haven't invented *Codonopsis*, but having found it in its natural growing area, a place where most people who grow *Codonopsis* as an ornament would shun living, they feel godlike, as if they had invented *Codonopsis*, as if without them no one growing *Codonopsis* as an ornament would do so. (*AF*, 32–33)

Plumbing the depths of her botanic desire, Kincaid articulates the similarities between plant hunters like herself and predecessors like Banks and Carl Linnaeus, originator of the system of binomial nomenclature, whom she might prefer to hold at an arm's length but cannot. Possession turns into invention, the "godlike" ability to make a plant from Nepal appear in little gardens around the world. Kincaid clearly finds humor in this reasoning—the feeling of invention chafes against the awareness of not actually having "invented" a plant—yet that prideful possession is not so different from Banks's efforts to keep his best specimens for England and trade nothing valuable with other nations' botanic gardens. In spite of her humor, Kincaid has already detailed the ramifications of the gardener's desire for possession in *My Garden (Book):*, where she describes the garden as a "shrine of Possession" that renders plant and human alike "an object, a mere thing, within it" (*MGB*, 148). Like Wordsworth, for whom exotic plants become particularly objectified in the garden, where they "remind us that they owe their existence to our hands, and their prosperity to our care," Kincaid cannot ignore the possessive dynamic between gardener and exotic. But both writers also acknowledge the "thrill," what Wordsworth calls the "natural desire," implicit in their joyful manipulations of plant life (*PrW*, 2:281). Similarly, Kincaid takes great joy in the importation of exotics: indeed, the premise of *Among Flowers* is a plant-hunting expedition she undertook with other gardeners in the Himalayas. Botanic exploration is at the heart of the localism so important to Kincaid and her Vermont garden, an exploration that manages to narrow the boundary of what counts as local while making those boundaries harder and harder to discern.

Kincaid's memoir came into being because she was asked to write "about any place in the world I wished and doing something in that place I liked doing" (*AF*, 1). She chose plant hunting: "I answered immediately that I would like to go hunting in southwestern China for seeds, which would eventually become flower-bearing shrubs and trees and herbaceous perennials in my garden."[93] This is one way in which Kincaid's gardening practices differed from Wordsworth's, and not simply because of the ease of twenty-first-century travel. Kincaid does not shun exotic plants in her garden. Although William—and Dorothy, in particular—enjoyed plant hunting, their expeditions stayed close to home. Dorothy's Grasmere journals are peppered with reports of gathering plants, always within walking distance.[94] Since their gardens at Grasmere, and eventually at Rydal Mount, were materially constituted by local plants, the relationship between the local and the global was usually figurative for William Wordsworth, as I have detailed. In contrast, from the first page of Kincaid's travel narrative, the local depends on the vastly far away for its material constitution—the trip's value is located in what exotic specimens it can provide for Kincaid's own garden in Vermont. Seeds from the Himalayas "would eventually become" plants in her garden.

It is difficult to tell if this interdependency heightens or minimizes the distinction between the local and the global, between Kincaid's backyard garden and everywhere else. On the one hand, plant hunting emphasizes geographic similarities: there is no point in collecting seeds that cannot be cultivated at home, so such a hunt attaches great importance to finding climatic intersections rather than disparities (larches that thrive in Northern England as much as in their native Siberia, for instance). Kincaid is most invested in the journey when she and her botanist companions reach an altitude where they can find "beautiful plants native to the Himalaya but that will grow happily in Vermont or somewhere like that" (*AF*, 112). This botanic transferability is a specific incarnation of her expectation that there would "be no border between myself and what I was seeing before me" during these travels (*AF*, 20). The profound lack of boundaries in these moments should remind us, perhaps uncomfortably, of how colonial botanic gardens replicated the sanitized collection of colonial exotics curated from around the empire—a collection of plants whose native boundaries had been erased, plants that would grow happily in some place or another, "or somewhere like that."

On the other hand, Kincaid can feign little interest in plants that she cannot grow in her own garden, suggesting that the power of plant hunting to level the geographic playing field is limited. A familiar refrain throughout *Among Flowers* is Kincaid's indifference to most of the plants they encounter. She recalls habitually considering whatever plant was in front of her, "wondering if I was seeing something new, and always wondering if I could grow it—and when I realized I could not, I had no interest in the thing before me whatsoever" (*AF*, 95); a few pages later, she says, "I was not so very interested because almost none of it would thrive in my garden" (*AF*, 106). In the end, Kincaid's lack of interest in plants that cannot grow in her climate overpowers the memoir's early embrace of permeability because it suggests that some borders she expected not to find do in fact persist—these plants are interesting, those are not; this climate is too warm, that one is not—and, moreover, that these borders delineate her botanic desire.

In other words, Kincaid's travels do not threaten to collapse the boundaries of localism. Her local garden is a context, however rooted, that she carries with her—one that conditions whatever she sees. During her hike, defamiliarization is constant. Once removed from her Vermont garden, Kincaid cannot recognize even familiar plants because "when seeing it in a place that was new to me, I found it mysterious and foreign," an experience she finds "most annoying" (*AF*, 114). Rhododendrons, a very common though exotic shrub in New England, grow natively in the Himalayas, "with a trunk as thick as a pine and thirty feet tall, and with leaves almost as long as my lower arm," and seem "as magical as seeing the mountain Makalu from a distance" (*AF*, 122). Vermont may stay right where it is, but as a context, its ability to alter Kincaid's perception of flora, familiar or not, is unshakeable. What Kincaid's experiences suggest, then, is that while the local is not in danger of collapsing into the global, it is a highly transportable and clingy context. This complicated dynamic is also at play in Kincaid's use of United States Department of Agriculture (USDA) hardiness zones to mark the stages of her travel in *Among Flowers*. Adopted by the USDA in 1960, the hardiness zone map currently divides the United States into eleven regions primarily on the basis of temperature. Although the system does not take other climate factors into account, many gardeners and nursery catalogs still use these zones to predict which plants will grow where (see figure 4.1). In some ways, then, it makes good sense for Kincaid to remark, as she and her companions hike higher into the mountains, "Now we were on our way to collecting things I most definitely would be able to grow in my garden zone of USDA 5" (*AF*, 112). The hardiness zones provide a codified and empirical method for recognizing climatic similarities.

On the other hand, the zones are set by the USDA, so Kincaid is using a decidedly bounded and national rubric in order to describe the moment at which her travels transcend the boundary between Vermont and Nepal. Although a USDA map from 1990 included southern Canada and Mexico, the 2012 update left out these neighbors and instead "focused on creating the highest-quality PHZM [plant hardiness zone map] for the United States and Puerto Rico" and was considered "improved" by some because the removal made the map "easier to read."[95] Using temperature data, it's easy enough to speculate about the correspondence of zones in other countries, as Kincaid does in *Among Flowers*. Canada and Europe have done this, producing their own maps using the same scale as the USDA. But Australia, for instance, uses a different one, and even the West Coast of the United States cannot abide by the USDA zones, relying instead on a more fine-grained map established forty years ago by *Sunset* magazine.

Part of the hardiness zone map's appeal, especially for the layperson, is its novelty: it provides a radically different method of mapping the country. Instead of seeing the nation divided into familiar states, we see it divided into striations of wavy, colorful bands. Parts of northern New Mexico suddenly become affiliated with northern Nebraska and Iowa; Cape Cod and Long Island share the same zone as much of Virginia and North Carolina. Carrying the zones into Nepal extends this novelty—without Kincaid, we might never know the climatic similarities between Vermont and the Himalayas—but in doing so, Kincaid also treats the localism described by hardiness zones as a transportable context. This is especially true in her formulation, where zone 5 is "my garden zone of USDA 5," a phrase that overwhelms the broad, sweeping swaths of the zone map with the possessive locality of *my garden*. At the same time that she enters what she suspects to be a climate comparable to zone 5, she narrows the term to designate not the shared climate of Vermont, Illinois, and Colorado but rather the climate of her garden. In other words,

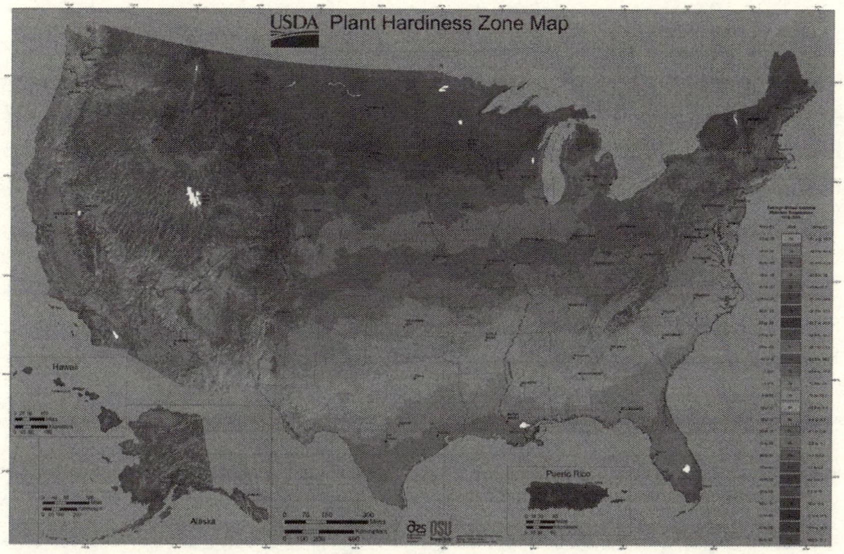

FIGURE 4.1. USDA hardiness zone map, 2012. Courtesy of the United States National Arboretum.

the zone is most rooted in its specific locale, southern Vermont, at the moment of its broadest use, in the Himalayas. *Among Flowers*, like Wordsworth's daffodils, suggests that the local, another trickily deictic term, possesses both a material foundation and a contextual movability, qualities that for Kincaid are not necessarily at odds.

The garden, in the end, is a fantasy of nature whose literal rootedness makes the exotic look local, whose construction makes hard labor look like easy instinct. If these appearances strike us as slightly treacherous, there is good reason. I have aimed to show that Wordsworth and Kincaid—whom critics often assume to be at opposite ends of some ideological spectrum—both recognized this treachery and understood how the landscapes that signified their local belonging were in fact defined against and through colonialism's botanic incursions. The danger in my argument is that by attending to the garden's dark side, we miss the joy that both writers found in their landscapes and in representing these landscapes, and this is a serious risk. Without joy, it is easy to interpret the colonial movement of plants and seeds solely as an exercise in bolstering nationalism, an erasure of previous forms of knowledge, a danger to the stability of ecosystems where plants are thoughtlessly introduced. For it was all these things. But Wordsworth's "natural desire" for exotics and Kincaid's "urge to possess," her seed-collecting expedition to the Himalayas and his and Dorothy's plant-hunting hikes across the Lake District, demand that we bring more hermeneutic breadth to the table in order to account for the joy each found in the movement of plants—a movement whose dangers they knew intimately. For me, this means interpreting the relationship between the colonial and the local in a manner consistent with the concomitant pleasure and trepidation each writer felt in moving and shaping nature. It means recognizing that colonialism's botanic movement creates a localism whose ability to produce joy stems from that localism's astonishing transportability as much as from its literal and figurative rootedness.

In one of the first books about Wordsworth's afterlives, *Wordsworth and the Victorians* (1998), Stephen Gill discusses an early meeting of the Wordsworth Society in 1883 where members discussed the possibility of a "Permanent Lake District Defense Society." As Gill reports, "Members had just listened to a paper on Wordsworth's *Guide to the Lakes* . . . a cue for [Wordsworth fan Reverend Hardwicke Drummond] Rawnsley to remind them of its contemporary relevance."[96] Since its publication, the guide has been convincing readers that the Lake District is especially deserving of admiration and protection and simultaneously associating Wordsworth with this most worthy district. The success of the guide even helped ensure that Wordsworth became one of the tourist sites in the region he had described for the benefit of tourists. Seen from the vantage point of this afterlife, Wordsworth's Lake District looks something like Thomas Hardy's Wessex: it is based on a real place but so deeply associated with one author's vision that the region becomes, in part, imaginary. Yet as David Simpson reminds us, in Wordsworth's verse, "the local is always permeated by the figures of those who have themselves been the servants or followers of empire and foreign wars, figures who have been abroad and come home," and so the version of Wordsworth handed down by the tourist industry is a simulacrum, one so committed to associating the poet with Lake District localism that the complexities of that localism fall to the wayside.[97] For years the polished front page of the Wordsworth Trust website featured an image of daffodils in its rotating flip book of poems, paintings, and stock photographs. It's gone for now, but it will probably return: nothing says Wordsworth quite like daffodils. But the unlikely bond between Kincaid and Wordsworth suggests that "I wandered lonely as a cloud" is more than iconic, a poem that encapsulates "Wordsworth." The daffodils belong to a neglected but far-reaching body of work in which Wordsworth reckoned with what it meant to be native, literally and figuratively; what it meant to move—and be moved by—plants.

NOTES

1 Jamaica Kincaid, "Garden: Dances with Daffodils," *Architectural Digest*, March 31, 2007, http://www.architecturaldigest.com/story/gardens-article (accessed January 20, 2016).

2 Kathleen M. Balutansky, "On Gardening: An Interview with Jamaica Kincaid," *Callaloo* 25, no. 3 (2002): 799.

3 Scott Hess, *William Wordsworth and the Ecology of Authorship: The Roots of Environmentalism in Nineteenth-Century Culture* (Charlottesville: University of Virginia Press, 2012), 68–115. Lisa Ottum and Seth T. Reno's recent collection also clarifies the terms of Wordsworth's environmentalism by linking it to the affect evoked by phrases like "a heart to enjoy." Ottum and Reno, *Wordsworth and the Green Romantics: Affect and Ecology in the Nineteenth Century* (Durham: University of New Hampshire Press, 2016).

4 James M. Garrett, *Wordsworth and the Writing of the Nation* (Aldershot: Ashgate, 2008), 149–176. See also Andrew Hazucha, "Neither Deep nor Shallow but National: Eco-nationalism in Wordsworth's *Guide to the Lakes*," *ISLE (Interdisciplinary Studies in Literature and Environment)* 9, no. 2 (2002): 61–73; Benjamin Kim, "Generating a National Sublime: Wordsworth's *The River Duddon* and *The Guide to the Lakes*," *Studies in Romanticism* 45, no. 1 (2006): 49–75.

5 See the electronic edition of Nicholas Mason et al., eds., *A Guide through the District of the Lakes in the North of England, with a Description of the Scenery, &c. for the Use of Tourists and Residents*, 5th ed., Romantic Circles, April 2015, par. 93n1, https://www.rc.umd.edu/editions/guide_lakes/editions.2015.guide_lakes.1835.html (accessed January 21, 2016).

6 Alan Bewell, *Natures in Translation: Romanticism and Colonial Natural History* (Baltimore: Johns Hopkins University Press, 2017), 255.

7 Kincaid's long-standing hatred of daffodils has been difficult to ignore—both *Lucy* and *My Garden (Book):* are insistent on this point. As a result, postcolonial criticism has tended to posit Wordsworth as the "preeminent cultural icon"—the "canonical English author," a "manifestation of cultural imperialism" against whom Kincaid chafes. Such readings accurately capture colonial readers' resentment but reduce Wordsworth to his imperial function, thus muting the nuance in Kincaid's canny readings of Wordsworth's polyvalent texts. Moira Ferguson, "*Lucy* and the Mark of the Colonizer," *Modern Fiction Studies* 39, no. 2 (1993): 242; Ian Smith, "Misusing Canonical Intertexts: Jamaica Kincaid, Wordsworth and Colonialism's 'Absent Things,'" *Callaloo* 25, no. 3 (2002): 816; Jocelyn Stitt, "Producing the Colonial Subject: Romantic Pedagogy and Mimicry in Jamaica Kincaid's Writing," *ARIEL* 37, nos. 2–3 (2006): 142.

8 Quoted in David C. Streatfield, "Art and Nature in the English Landscape Garden: Design Theory and Practice, 1700–1818," in *Landscape in the Gardens and the Literature of Eighteenth-Century England*, ed. David C. Streatfield and Alistair M. Duckworth (Los Angeles: William Andrews Clark Memorial Library, 1981), 68–69.

9 Carole Buchanan and Richard Buchanan, *Wordsworth's Gardens* (Lubbock: Texas Tech University Press, 2001), 154.

10 John Barrell, *The Idea of Landscape and the Sense of Place, 1730–1840* (Cambridge: Cambridge University Press, 1972), 46, 47.

11 For instance, drifts of trees were often placed so that they obscured any view of the adjacent property where farm laborers might otherwise be visible. Donna Landry's work on the countryside suggests compellingly that "not production, but consumption and pleasure, recreation and retreat, were the goods associated with the countryside." Similarly, Simon Pugh describes the garden's ability to hide the complicated means of its own production: "The ideological separation of rural exploitation (the nameless thousands who laboured to make the great gardens of England) and the money markets that have always sustained such grandiose schemes are subsumed into a 'landscape,' value-free." In the realm of artistic representation, John Barrel identifies "the constraints which governed how the labouring,

the vagrant, and the mendicant poor could be portrayed so as to be an acceptable part of the décor of the drawing rooms of the polite." The imaginative proximity of *garden*, *landscape*, and *nature* during this period has resulted in some slippage between the terms. Landry, *The Invention of the Countryside: Hunting, Walking and Ecology in English Literature, 1671–1831* (New York: Palgrave, 2001), 2; Pugh, *Garden, Nature, Language* (Manchester: Manchester University Press, 1988), 1; Barrell, *The Dark Side of the Landscape: The Rural Poor in English Painting, 1730–1840* (Cambridge: Cambridge University Press, 1980), 5.

12 Donal P. McCracken, *Gardens of Empire: Botanical Institutions of the Victorian British Empire* (London: Leicester University Press, 1997), 3.

13 Charles Willard Moore et al., *The Poetics of Gardens* (Cambridge, Mass.: MIT Press, 1988), 111, 113.

14 John M. Prest, *The Garden of Eden: The Botanic Garden and the Recreation of Paradise* (New Haven, Conn.: Yale University Press, 1981), 44.

15 Ray Desmond, *The History of the Royal Botanic Gardens Kew* (London: Kew, 2007), 65.

16 The political implications of spreading manure onto the tree's "roots," its agrarian laborers, and associating the nobility with the short-lived flowers a tree produces once a year are notable. Quoted in Richard Drayton, *Nature's Government: Science, Imperial Britain, and the "Improvement" of the World* (New Haven, Conn.: Yale University Press, 2000), 98.

17 Simon Schama, *Landscape and Memory* (New York: A. A. Knopf, 1995), 172.

18 Rob Nixon, "Environmentalism and Postcolonialism," in *Postcolonial Studies and Beyond*, ed. Ania Loomba et al. (Durham, N.C.: Duke University Press, 2005), 234.

19 Graham Huggan, "'Greening' Postcolonialism: Ecocritical Perspectives," *Modern Fiction Studies* 50, no. 3 (2004): 702.

20 Elizabeth DeLoughrey and George B. Handley, *Postcolonial Ecologies: Literatures of the Environment* (New York: Oxford University Press, 2011), 8. Ramachandra Guha's critique of deep ecology is a classic investigation of this mismatch between postcolonial theory and ecocriticism, which was especially potent in ecocriticism's early years. But as Huggan points out, the conflict between postcolonial and ecocritical studies is not an inevitable one. Postcolonial studies has "renewed, rather than belatedly discovered, its commitment to the environment," and environmental criticism has jettisoned "the tendencies of some Green movements toward Western liberal universalism." Guha, "Radical American Environmentalism and Wilderness Preservation: A Third World Critique," *Environmental Ethics* 11 (1989): 234; Huggan, "'Greening' Postcolonialism," 702.

21 John Gascoigne, *Science in the Service of Empire: Joseph Banks, the British State and the Uses of Science in the Age of Revolution* (Cambridge: Cambridge University Press, 1998), 130; Lucile Brockway, *Science and Colonial Expansion: The Role of the British Royal Botanic Gardens* (New York: Academic Press, 1979), 10.

22 When Queen Victoria ascended the throne, Britain had more colonial botanic gardens (either existing or established) than any other rival imperial power. McCracken, *Gardens of Empire*, 2–3.

23 Jill H. Casid, *Sowing Empire: Landscape and Colonization* (Minneapolis: University of Minnesota Press, 2005). In *Nature's Government*, Drayton explains how the language and practice of "improvements" also applied in British colonies and explores not just the aesthetic but also the moral and religious dimensions of such improvements. Richard Grove's point about the development of conservation is especially important to a discussion of Wordsworth, whose writing is often read as protoenvironmental: as Grove says, "The seeds of modern conservation developed as an integral part of the European encounter with the tropics." Drayton, *Nature's Government*, 89; Grove, *Green Imperialism: Colonial Expansion, Tropical Island Edens,*

and the Origins of Environmentalism, 1600–1860 (Cambridge: Cambridge University Press, 1995), 3.

24 Schama, *Landscape and Memory*, 153.

25 Ursula K. Heise, *Sense of Place and Sense of Planet: The Environmental Imagination of the Global* (Oxford: Oxford University Press, 2008), 9.

26 Kim, "Generating a National Sublime," 50. Similarly, Hazucha's ecological approach suggests that in the rationale of the *Guide to the Lakes*, "foreigners who bring non-native flora into northern England . . . are contributing to the ruination of an ecosystem and, because of their ignorance of the way that ecosystem works, the ruination of a culture that in its previously insular condition has been for centuries a kind of Eden." Hazucha, "Neither Deep nor Shallow," 69–70.

27 Bewell, *Natures in Translation*, 78.

28 Susan Stewart, "Garden Agon," *Representations* 62 (1998): 111.

29 Kincaid's distinction is similar to the contrast that Edward Said, drawing on Antonio Gramsci, draws between domination and hegemony, which operates through consent rather than force. Said, *Orientalism* (New York: Vintage, 1994), 7.

30 Robert Birnbaum, "Interview with Jamaica Kincaid," *Believer* 1, no. 4 (2003), http://www.believermag.com/issues/200307/?read=interview_kincaid (accessed January 20, 2016).

31 Colleen Smith, "Garden Path Leads to Surprising Places," *Denver Post*, February 10, 2008, http://www.denverpost.com/ci_8200836 (accessed January 20, 2016).

32 W. B. Turrill, *The Royal Botanic Gardens at Kew* (London: H. Jenkins, 1959), 23–24.

33 Gascoigne, *Science in the Service*, 163.

34 Desmond, *Royal Botanic Gardens*, 114.

35 Hans Sloane, *A Voyage to the Islands Madera, Barbados, Nieves, S. Christophers, and Jamaica*, vol. 1 (London: B. M., 1707).

36 James Elkins, "On the Conceptual Analysis of Gardens," *Journal of Garden History* 13, no. 4 (1993): 190.

37 Elizabeth DeLoughrey, "Globalizing the Routes of Breadfruit and Other Bounties," *Journal of Colonialism and Colonial History* 8, no. 3 (2007): par. 23, http://muse.jhu.edu./article/230160.

38 Gascoigne, *Science in the Service*, 130.

39 Toby Musgrave and Will Musgrave, *An Empire of Plants: People and Plants That Changed the World* (London: Cassell, 2000), 147.

40 Kavita Philip, *Civilizing Natures: Race, Resources, and Modernity in Colonial South India* (New Brunswick, N.J.: Rutgers University Press, 2004), 183.

41 Bewell, *Natures in Translation*, 59.

42 Gascoigne, *Science in the Service*, 134.

43 Alistair M. Duckworth, *The Improvement of the Estate: A Study of Jane Austen's Novels* (Baltimore: Johns Hopkins University Press, 1971), 35–80.

44 Drayton has argued that the moral exigencies Britain felt toward its empire apply to plants as well as colonized subjects: "Both the varieties of the human conscience and the expanse of Creation were estates which those at the vanguard of reason had both a duty and a right to 'improve.'" Drayton, *Nature's Government*, 89.

45 Henry Jones's poem "Kew Gardens" (1763) uses similar language to describe the collection of foreign orphan plants cared for by an English nurse. See Bewell, *Natures in Translation*, 74.

46 Desmond, *Royal Botanic Gardens*, 115.

47 Drayton, *Nature's Government*, 121.

48 Desmond, *Royal Botanic Gardens*, 66.

49 Casid, *Sowing Empire*, 14.

50 Casid, 14.

51 Lizabeth Paravisini-Gebert, *Jamaica Kincaid: A Critical Companion* (Westport, Conn.: Greenwood Press, 1999), 40.

52 Ian Gregory Strachan, *Paradise and Plantation: Tourism and Culture in the Anglophone Caribbean* (Charlottesville: University of Virginia Press, 2002), 1.

53 Garth Myers, *Urban Environments in Africa: A Critical Analysis of Environmental Politics* (Bristol: Policy Press, 2016), 80.

54 Susie O'Brien, "The Garden and the World: Jamaica Kincaid and the Cultural Borders of Ecocriticism," *Mosaic* 35, no. 2 (2002): 177.

55 O'Brien, 175.

56 The plants that Kincaid describes here are astilbe, hosta, and ranunculus, none of which are grown from seed (*MGB*, 122). Though gardeners often trade plants, it seems just as likely that Kincaid purchased these plants at the store and planted them into her garden.

57 *OED Online*, s.v. "naturalize," http://www.oed.com/view/Entry/125343 (accessed January 13, 2016).

58 Raymond Williams, *Keywords: A Vocabulary of Culture and Society*, rev. ed. (New York: Oxford University Press, 1983), 223.

59 Williams, 219.

60 Williams, 223.

61 Alexander Pope, *The Poems of Alexander Pope*, ed. John Butt (London: Methuen, 1963), 590.

62 Williams, *Keywords*, 215.

63 Lane Cooper, ed., *A Concordance to the Poems of William Wordsworth* (London: Smith, Elder, 1911), 643.

64 This seems a distinction worth making even though Wordsworth's participation in such discourses is inconsistent. For instance, the distinction between gardening and landscape design is not one that he made with any reliability. What we might consider to be an issue of landscape—for example, Wordsworth's recommendation of "having our houses belong to the country"—is one that he proposes as a revision to "the modern system of gardening." William Wordsworth and Dorothy Wordsworth, *The Early Letters of William and Dorothy Wordsworth (1787–1805)*, ed. Ernest de Selincourt (Oxford: Clarendon Press, 1935), 524.

65 More than 150 million people were brought under the rule of the British Empire during the Romantic era. Saree Makdisi, *Romantic Imperialism: Universal Empire and the Culture of Modernity* (Cambridge: Cambridge University Press, 1998), xi.

66 Said, *Orientalism*, 7; Homi K. Bhabha, *The Location of Culture*, 2nd ed. (New York: Routledge, 2004), 153.

67 The flip side of this dependence is seen in Casid's point about "tropical" plants: "Those species of flora most symbolically associated with the 'tropics' were precisely those plants by which the British grafted one idea of island paradise onto another." Delineating the local in the colonies meant actually importing plants that could then be defined as local. Casid, *Sowing Empire*, 7.

68 His edits in 1820 and 1833 reveal how emphatic he was about the date of this shift: the 1810 guide places it forty years ago; the 1820 guide fifty; the 1833 guide sixty (*PrW*, 2:206n1665).

69 Stephen Gill, *Wordsworth and the Victorians* (Oxford: Oxford University Press, 1998), 248.

70 The Wordsworth industry that has sprung up in the Lake District underlines Kincaid's point. Wordsworth's memories of the district have shaped its current form more than he could have imagined.

71 David Simpson, *Wordsworth's Historical Imagination: The Poetry of Displacement* (New York: Methuen, 1987), 70.

72 Theresa M. Kelley, *Wordsworth's Revisionary Aesthetics* (Cambridge: Cambridge University Press, 1988), 20.

73 Or else the "ha-ha" (a sunken fence delineating property lines) that was invisible from the distance and made the property seem infinite. John Barrell has more generally demonstrated how landscape art can hide the complicated means of production, arguing that in the eighteenth and early nineteenth centuries, "the art of rural life offers us the image of a stable, unified, almost egalitarian society" despite the reality of social conflict between the rich and poor. Barrell focuses his attention on "the constraints which governed how the labouring, the vagrant, and the mendicant poor could be portrayed so as to be an acceptable part of the *décor* of the drawing rooms of the polite." Barrell, *Dark Side of the Landscape*, 5.

74 *OED Online*, s.v. "exotic," http://www.oed.com/view/Entry/66403 (accessed January 4, 2016).

75 This "colonization" is the final stage in this colonial history that Bewell sees Wordsworth tracing in the *Guide to the Lakes*, beginning with the Celts and ending with these English "settlers." Bewell, *Natures in Translation*, 255–256.

76 Nicola Trott, "Wordsworth's Loves of the Plants," in *1800: The New Lyrical Ballads*, ed. Nicola Trott and Seamus Perry (New York: Palgrave, 2001), 155. David Simpson has similarly argued that Wordsworth "renders imperialism a local, domestic issue requiring moral vigilance even in the most apparently sequestered places." Simpson, *Wordsworth, Commodification and Social Concern: The Poetics of Modernity* (Cambridge: Cambridge University Press, 2009), 96–97.

77 Uday Singh Mehta, *Liberalism and Empire: A Study in Nineteenth-Century British Liberal Thought* (Chicago: University of Chicago Press, 1999), 170–171.

78 James K. Chandler, *Wordsworth's Second Nature: A Study of the Poetry and Politics* (Chicago: University of Chicago Press, 1984), 29. Importantly, though, Chandler (as well as David Bromwich) situates the similarities between Burke and Wordsworth in an earlier era as well. Bromwich argues that "Wordsworth was a Burkean thinker already by the late 1790s," as Trott's argument about the *Lyrical Ballads* implies. Bromwich, *A Choice of Inheritance: Self and Community from Edmund Burke to Robert Frost* (Cambridge, Mass.: Harvard University Press, 1989), 63.

79 Edmund Burke, *The Writings and Speeches of Edmund Burke*, 9 vols., ed. Paul Langford (Oxford: Clarendon Press, 1981), 6:271.

80 Casid, *Sowing Empire*, 8.

81 Mary Louise Pratt, *Imperial Eyes: Travel Writing and Transculturation*, 2nd ed. (London: Routledge, 2008), 9.

82 Grove, *Green Imperialism*, 309.

83 Richard Watson, *Anecdotes of the Life of Richard Watson, Bishop of Llandaff* (London: T. Cadell and W. Davies, 1817), 364.

84 Watson, 436. The recent online edition of the *Guide to the Lakes* by Romantic Circles speculates that Wordsworth latched onto the larch tree in particular in order to counter Watson's advocacy and not to echo Uvedale Price's condemnation of the tree, as readers have often assumed. Mason et al., *Guide through the District*, par. 86.

85 Watson, *Anecdotes*, 240.

86 Watson, 338, emphasis in the original.

87 Watson, 505–506.

88 Burke, *Writings and Speeches*, 1:234.

89 "Ramorum Disease of Larch Trees in Cumbria," *Forestry Commission England*, http://www.forestry.gov.uk/forestry/infd-9cyg8x (accessed January 8, 2016).

90 Burke, *Writings and Speeches*, 6:282.

91 Sara Suleri Goodyear, *The Rhetoric of English India* (Chicago: University of Chicago Press, 1992), 47.

92 John Robert Seeley, *The Expansion of England* (Boston: Roberts Brothers, 1883), 63.

93 As Shelley Saguaro notes, "There is something more than a little ironic in Kincaid's undertaking which echoes aspects she has often critiqued." Saguaro, *Garden Plots: The Politics and Poetics of Gardens* (Aldershot: Ashgate, 2006), 227.

94 See, for instance, May 16, 1800, "I carried a basket for mosses, and gathered some wild plants"; or June 7, 1800, "We went up the hill, to gather sods and plants." Judith Page and Elise Smith situate this gardening practice within the context of botanic imperialism: "Since Dorothy was especially interested in cultivating local transplants from the wild, her garden was a kind of reverse colony in which native plants found a home." Dorothy Wordsworth, *Journals of Dorothy Wordsworth*, 2 vols., ed. E. de Selincourt (New York: Macmillan, 1941), 1:38, 45; Page and Smith, *Women, Literature, and the Domesticated Landscape: England's Disciples of Flora, 1780–1870* (Cambridge: Cambridge University Press, 2011), 154.

95 "What's New," USDA Agricultural Research Service, http://planthardiness.ars.usda.gov/PHZMWeb/AboutWhatsNew.aspx (accessed January 13, 2016); David J. Ellis, "The USDA Plant Hardiness Map 2003 Edition," *American Gardener* 82, no. 3 (May/June 2003): 30.

96 Gill, *Wordsworth and the Victorians*, 257.

97 David Simpson, "Wordsworth and Empire—Just Joking," in *Land, Nation and Culture, 1740–1840*, ed. Peter de Bolla et al. (New York: Palgrave Macmillan, 2005), 192.

CONCLUSION

LET US LEAVE THE ROOTEDNESS of the daffodil for the airiness of William Wordsworth's lonely cloud. In a 2002 article about Wordsworth's daffodils in the *Atlantic*, Phyllis Rose articulated her dislike for the poem by reaching for a surprising tool: the n+7 exercise, developed by the Ouvroir de Littérature Potentielle (Workshop of Potential Literature; OULIPO). An affiliation of mostly French writers and mathematicians, OULIPO encourages writing under extreme formal constraints—a eulogy that uses only the letters needed to spell the name of the dead, for example, or a novel that eschews the letter *E*. In the n+7 exercise, every noun in an existing text is replaced with the seventh noun that appears after it in a dictionary; if the existing text is a poem, then meter and rhyme may be respected, in which case it is usually necessary to shuffle through more than seven nouns to find a suitable substitute. (The choice of dictionary makes a difference in the resulting text: an expansive dictionary like the *Oxford English* won't alter the text as much as a concise dictionary will.) In order to reveal the faults of "I wandered lonely as a cloud," Rose quotes an example of the n+7 technique in action, Harry Mathews's "The Imbeciles," a poem that is somewhat like a cross between William Wordsworth and Gertrude Stein:

> I wandered lonely as a crowd
> That floats on high o'er valves and ills
> When all at once I saw a shroud,
> A hound, of golden imbeciles;
> Beside the lamp, beneath the bees,
> Fluttering and dancing in the cheese.[1]

Rose's point is that the n+7 substitutions afford an opportunity to focus on syntax and "residual vocabulary"—to escape from the famous flowers and witness how the poem is still rife with "falseness, banality, poeticism, and sentimentality" even without the daffodils.[2] Yet there are things to admire about "The Imbeciles" as a poem in its own right:

I like the dark assonance of "a shroud, / A hound" and its contrast with the "golden" hue of the poem's subject. Perhaps best of all, the poem's opening simile becomes the contradictory but suggestive "I wandered lonely as a crowd," a line that moves the original poem's *crowd* up two lines so that it no longer refers to the cheerful host of daffodils but rather acts as the vehicle for the speaker's simile. Mathews may find Wordsworth "nauseatingly bourgeois," but the line is strangely appropriate; Wordsworth *would* find a crowd lonely.[3] Moreover, the line draws attention to the simile itself, the incongruity of *lonely* and *crowd* revealing the churning gears of figurative language.

Wordsworth's poem about daffodils was often anthologized under a title that Wordsworth never gave it: "The Daffodils." But if we go by his original title, which is merely the poem's first line, the cloud begins to rise in importance. After all, it is the cloud that gives the poem's speaker his elevated point of view, that facilitates his solitude, that enables the transition from loneliness to community. And if generations of readers objected to the daffodil, there is perhaps also reason to query the cloud, as Laura Mullen has done in *Dark Archive* (2011), a section of which, titled "Cloud Cover," explicitly and repeatedly repurposes Wordsworth's "I wandered lonely as a cloud." Mullen quotes and riffs on many of the poem's famous lines—"inward eye," "jocund company"—but returns again and again to the clouds. For the speakers of her poems, clouds recur because their range of signification is vast, and as a result, they reveal the coercive and duplicitous potential of figurative language.

The opening line of "The Imbeciles" revels in the strain that can underpin figurative language: lonely as a *crowd*? The reasonable simile becomes a conceit, its objects "yoked by violence together," as Samuel Johnson said about metaphysical poetry. Mullen's critique is broader and centers on Wordsworth's opener, "I wandered lonely as a cloud." In one line of poetry, she writes, "I wandered like 'like,'" and the repetition of simile's key word in scare quotes stops the speaker's nascent simile in its tracks (*DA*, 5). The critique takes firmer shape in "By and by," where the subject becomes the ethics of writing similes:

> The necessity or so it seems of forcing
> A shape on these of saying *like*
> Of saying see what I see see
> What I ask you to see
>
> Seeing
>   How far you'll go
>   with or on what
>   grounds we
>
> Already that shape is dissolving

> Already that shape
> Already another
> *very like a wail* (*DA*, 13, emphasis in the original)

In this final line, Mullen refers to the conversation between Hamlet and Polonius about clouds ("Do you see yonder cloud that's almost in shape of a camel? . . . Methinks it is like a weasel. . . . Or like a whale. Very like a whale"). This scene occurs at the height of Hamlet's madness routine, and in alluding to it, Mullen gives an example of the problem she has just described: "See what I see," see a camel or a whale in that cloud. But by replacing Hamlet's *whale* with the mournful homophone *wail*, Mullen backs herself into a corner. She becomes her object of critique by saying, in effect, "See / What I ask you to see" or rather "Hear what I ask you to hear," this pun on whale and wail. The reference to *Hamlet* also makes it clear that the intervening lines, "Already that shape is dissolving / Already that shape / Already another," which seem at first quite abstract, have also been about clouds, the repetition seeming to speed the clouds' shiftiness. The speaker of this poem suggests that writing a simile, "forcing / A shape" and "saying *like*," is as arbitrary as deciding which animal a cloud resembles. The cloud shaped like a whale quickly dissolves into a cloud shaped like a wail—or so we are told.

Mullen's objection to figurative language is both contradictory and capacious, punctuated by her many revisions of Wordsworth's opening line: "I Wandered Networks like a Cloud," "I Wandered (Phony) As," "I Wandered Her Voice," "Cloud as Lonely," "Wandered lonely in the voice of another who had no voice," "Wandered lonely as / White box to be dissolved" (*DA*, 9, 12, 16, 37, 5, 25). But her objection more particularly stems from the many meanings of clouds. A professor at Louisiana State University, Mullen wrote *Dark Archive* in the aftermath of Hurricane Katrina, and several poems describe a devastated post-Katrina landscape: "Here a tent of azure plastic / there someone's roof on the ground / someone's boat on a roof and mashed / car piled on car crushed torn split ruined" (*DA*, 15). In this setting, it might seem almost careless to use a cloud as a metaphor for solitude, for not all clouds are lonely and therefore unthreatening. In contrast to Wordsworth's singular cloud, *Dark Archive* contains multitudes, some of them figurative, some literal. One poem mentions an "altocumulus"; another is titled "Stratocumulus" (*DA*, 16, 21). In one poem, clouds are energetically threatening; they "scud by / seemingly / flashing dark and / bright" (*DA*, 3). In another, the clouds' compatriots are gusts and squalls: "Wind-rippled clouds / by the field where the storm-tossed / barge crushed the houses" (*DA*, 15). But clouds also lead Mullen out of landscape description and into the realm of fanciful association. One poem mentions "a cloud in all its vagueness"; another poem begins climatically and becomes figurative: "Composed of minute water droplets / And cancelled checks the 'page / Left blank intentionally'" (*DA*, 47, 32). "Stratocumulus" reverses the trajectory, its final line, "Sad cloud / Oh no . . . that's *science*," shifting between levels of signification as the cloud breaks free of the pathetic fallacy to become meteorological (*DA*, 22). These poems do not deny that clouds have symbolic power, but they also have physical power, and Wordsworth's simile stands in contrast to the sometimes destructive variety that Mullen knows clouds to possess.

The cloud has one final signification evoked by *Dark Archive*—cloud storage—and in concluding, I want to carry this newfangled meaning back to Wordsworth. Throughout her collection, Mullen is wary of how technology enables us to consume rather than engage the world around us. In "I Wandered Networks like a Cloud," Mullen's most sustained rewriting of Wordsworth's poem, daffodils that flash on the inward eye are replaced with refugees that flash on the television screen: "Ten thousand saw I at a glance, / Hurrying nowhere, like worried ants" (*DA*, 9). The speaker's solitude and remoteness is an apt concern for a collection of poems named after an inaccessible archive. A "dark" archive preserves material, but its aim is not to make that material available to the public; it serves as a failsafe, a backup of a "light" archive in the event of disaster or catastrophic loss. There are many disasters and losses in *Dark Archive*—the hurricane, most obviously, but also death and heartbreak. But what makes an archive dark is not its connection to disaster but rather its inaccessibility. The dark archive provides no routine access to the data it stores. In an essay that concludes her collection, Mullen criticizes Wordsworth because he "used his sister's record of the outing in his writing" and then "decided not to include his sister in the experience he recounts," implicitly suggesting that Dorothy Wordsworth represents the dark archive of her brother's visible achievements (*DA*, 129). In this reading, Dorothy was William's failsafe, his data storage: she wrote about daffodils in her journal, he turned her words into a poem, and her record remained inaccessible for generations.

But the dark archive also provides some insight into "I wandered lonely as a cloud" itself, and not just its vexed composition history. Today, creators of a dark archive might choose to use the cloud for large-scale data preservation. The logic of cloud-based storage solutions like iCloud or Dropbox is that by storing files remotely rather than locally, those files become more readily accessible. Files saved at home can be opened later at work. Images taken on a phone can be passively stored for later consumption in a medium and setting yet to be determined. Or, to transpose the process back two centuries, an image of daffodils captured by the lake can be accessed later on the couch. By gazing—and gazing—at the flowers, the speaker of Wordsworth's poem imprints them on his memory, after which the flowers may then "flash upon that inward eye" wherever a vacant or pensive mood strikes. The comparison of "the cloud" to the speaker's mind is akin to what Richard Menke has said about "I wandered lonely as a cloud"—namely, that the poem is uninterested in the medium of writing and instead "treats memory as a medium for virtual perception and for experience liberated from the constraints of time and place."[4] The speaker's memory here is not an inaccessible archive but rather serves as a kind of cloud storage, a medium capable of preserving experiences for other times and other places.

Cloud storage is one of the latest advances in globalization's time-space compression. The transfer of data is almost instantaneous, regardless of the distance traversed. You take a picture with your phone; seconds later, it shows up on your computer, wherever your computer happens to be. The dark archive implicitly asks what can and should be retrievable and by whom, while the cloud would make us wonder what is worth saving in the first place—if only we had a moment to consider the question. There are echoes between this denotation of the cloud and Wordsworth's poem, specifically in the transfer of images via memory, but there is also a key difference: the importance, for Wordsworth, of time passing. An unspecified but significant temporal gap separates the experience of seeing the daffodils from that of remembering them; in the preface to *Lyrical Ballads*, the "overflow of powerful feeling" only becomes capable of inspiring poetry once enough time has passed for it to be recollected elsewhere, "in tranquillity" (*PrW*, 1.148). So the cloud's compression of time and space would not have suited Wordsworth's poetic theory any more than the imperial circulation of people and plants suited his vision of the Lake District, a place he aimed to preserve even as his representations of it made clear that the entanglement of the local and global spheres was, in his mind, a fait accompli. Such efforts, in the *Guide to the Lakes* and *The Excursion*, are recognizably conservative in their desire to preserve a place as it used to be; like Scott's *Waverley*, Wordsworth's guide consistently refers back to a time "sixty years since." Yet if such strains are conservative, the political register of other sentiments is harder to plot. Wordsworth's barely expressed desire in the *Guide to the Lakes* to tend an exotic plant and know that it owed its life to his care; his sense, in *The Excursion*, that Britons were "as abject, as degraded" in picturesque Albion as in modern Britain—such sentiments do not posit the past as retrievable, or necessarily worthy of recovery. As Andrew Bennett explains, writing was, for Wordsworth, "an assertion of that which will remain in the future."[5] As assertions of that which would remain in the future, Wordsworth's later works do not envision the perseverance of an isolated and self-sufficient England, preserver of truth and liberty and peace. They envision a Britain who sends forth worker bees to her colonies and a nation colonized from within; vistas graced by trading ships and prospects marred by larch plantations supplying lumber for boat building; a working populace exploited in factories; and fast-growing towns delicately wreathed in glittering smoke. These scenes represent the scope of Wordsworth's global thinking, which did not extend to imagine his own dissemination around the world. But the writing that remains, that defines Wordsworth's posterity, *has* traveled the globe, and the interpretation of his writing is, in turn, indelibly shaped by technologies whose compression of the Anglophone world aided in his poetry's dissemination.

NOTES

1 Harry Mathews and Alastair Brotchie, *Oulipo Compendium* (London: Atlas, 1998), 199.

2 Phyllis Rose, "Dances with Daffodils," *Atlantic*, April 2002, http://www.theatlantic.com/past/docs/issues/2002/04/rose.htm (accessed November 14, 2016).

3 Rose. For more on the relationship between *cloud* and *crowd*, see Arden Reed: "The crowd is the urban version of a cloud, likewise a shifting a temporary ensemble, more or less disordered, with an indefinite number of elements and no clear boundaries." Reed, *Romantic Weather: The Climates of Coleridge and Baudelaire* (Providence, R.I.: Brown University Press, 1983), 16.

4 Richard Menke, "The Wordsworths' Daffodils: On the Page, upon the Inward Eye, in Their Media Ecology," in *Media, Technology, and Literature in the Nineteenth Century: Image, Sound, Touch*, ed. Colette Colligan and Margaret Linley (Farnham: Ashgate, 2011), 23.

5 Andrew Bennett, *Romantic Poets and the Culture of Posterity* (Cambridge: Cambridge University Press, 1999), 96.

ACKNOWLEDGMENTS

THIS WOULD HAVE BEEN A very different book without the support of Saree Makdisi, who convinced me it was worthwhile to write about Wordsworth, and Jonathan Grossman, whose belief in the project's scope kept me from backing down. Barbara Packer started me on this path, and I have missed her erudition and no-nonsense advice. Liz DeLoughrey's influence made this a far richer book. I hope Alison Hickey glimpses her impact on this book, because I am grateful for it. Thanks to Glenn Brewer, Joe Bristow, Will Clark, Noah Comet, Jon Mee, Ian Newman, Sina Rahmani, and Jenny Sharpe for leads, conversation, and advice. A crew of Romanticists—Thora Brylowe, Julia Carlson, Evan Gottlieb, Nick Mason, Mike Nicholson, Stephanie Weiner, and various interlocutors at NASSR—gave conversation, feedback, and mentorship.

My colleagues at Trinity College have been generous with their knowledge, encouragement, and critiques: Barbara Benedict, Sarah Bilston, Sheila Fisher, Chris Hager, Joan Hedrick, Paul Lauter, Tennyson O'Donnell, Jennifer Regan-Lefebvre, Gary Reger, Milla Riggio, Chloe Wheatley, and Hilary Wyss. David Rosen deserves extra thanks for reading the whole manuscript, much of it twice, and generously helping me discover a structure for the book. In the English department, Christina Bolio and Margaret Grasso make everything possible, and I am thankful for their help.

At Bucknell, Greg Clingham and Kate Parker have shepherded this book with kindness and insight. I am especially grateful to the press's anonymous reader, whose suggestions were so sharp and correct that I adopted pretty much all of them. Portions of chapters 3 and 4 were first published in, respectively, *Modern Philology* 111, no. 1 (2013) and *ISLE: Interdisciplinary Studies in Literature and Environment* 22, no. 2 (2015). Thanks also to Sam Brawand for copyediting the manuscript and doing the index.

Family and friends didn't have to read the work in progress to help its progress immeasurably (though some of them did read it). Caitlin Elsaesser, Shane

Ewegan, Megan Greenwell, Dan Mrozowski, Ethan Rutherford, Kari Theurer, and the Scarborough family helped ease the burden and celebrate the milestones. I would be adrift without the advice and love of Katherine Isokawa and Justine Pizzo. The Eichenlaub family—Michele, Herb, Ryan, and Lindsay—have shared so much cheer and support. (And I don't know how I would have proofread the book without Michele's help.) Ann Bergren's wise counsel helped me navigate the many stages of learning and writing. This book is dedicated to my parents, Jim Bergren and Nancy Vander Pyl, who taught me how to learn, promoted my education above all else, and helped me when I struggled. And I am grateful every day for the joyfulness and support of Justin Eichenlaub.

BIBLIOGRAPHY

Abrams, M. H. *Natural Supernaturalism: Tradition and Revolution in Romantic Literature*. New York: W. W. Norton, 1971.

Abrams, M. H., and Stephen Greenblatt, eds. *The Norton Anthology of English Literature*. 7th ed. New York: W. W. Norton, 2000.

Appadurai, Arjun. *Modernity at Large: Cultural Dimensions of Globalization*. Minneapolis: University of Minnesota Press, 1996.

Arac, Jonathan. "Anglo-Globalism?" *New Left Review* 16 (2002): 35–45.

Aravamudan, Srinivas. *Tropicopolitans: Colonialism and Agency, 1688–1804*. Durham, N.C.: Duke University Press, 1999.

Arnold, Matthew. *The Complete Prose Works of Matthew Arnold*. 11 vols. Edited by R. H. Super. Ann Arbor: University of Michigan Press, 1960–1977.

Ashcroft, Bill, Gareth Griffiths, and Helen Tiffin. *The Empire Writes Back: Theory and Practice in Post-colonial Literatures*. 2nd ed. London: Routledge, 2003.

Attwell, David. "Introduction." *Current Writing: Text and Reception in Southern Africa* 5, no. 2 (1993): 1–6.

Atwood, Margaret. *Survival: A Thematic Guide to Canadian Literature*. Toronto: House of Anansi, 1972.

Baker, Geoffrey. "The Limits of Sympathy: J. M. Coetzee's Evolving Ethics of Engagement." *ARIEL* 36, nos. 1–2 (2005): 27–49.

Baker, Samuel. "Sailing Blind: Climate, Intention, and Local and Global Orientation in Wordsworth and Byron." In *Global Romanticism: Origins, Orientations, and Entanglements, 1760–1820*, edited by Evan Gottlieb, 95–107. Lewisburg, Pa.: Bucknell University Press, 2015.

———. *Written on the Water: British Romanticism and the Maritime Empire of Culture*. Charlottesville: University of Virginia Press, 2010.

Baldick, Chris. *The Social Mission of English Criticism, 1848–1932*. Oxford: Clarendon Press, 1983.

Balutansky, Kathleen M. "On Gardening: An Interview with Jamaica Kincaid." *Callaloo* 25, no. 3 (2002): 790–800.

Barbauld, Anna Laetitia. *Lessons for Children of Two to Three Years Old*. London: J. Johnson, 1778.

Barnard, Rita. "Coetzee in/and Afrikaans." *Journal of Literary Studies* 25, no. 4 (2009): 84–105.

———. "J. M. Coetzee's *Disgrace* and the South African Pastoral." *Contemporary Literature* 44, no. 2 (2003): 199–224.

Barrell, John. *The Dark Side of the Landscape: The Rural Poor in English Painting, 1730–1840*. Cambridge: Cambridge University Press, 1980.

———. *The Idea of Landscape and the Sense of Place, 1730–1840*. Cambridge: Cambridge University Press, 1972.

Barrow, C. M. *The Poetical Selections Prescribed for the Matriculation Examination of the University of Madras*. Mangalore: C. Stolz, 1871.

Bate, Jonathan. *Romantic Ecology: Wordsworth and the Environmental Tradition*. New York: Routledge, 2013.

Baucom, Ian. *Out of Place: Englishness, Empire, and the Locations of Identity*. Princeton, N.J.: Princeton University Press, 1999.

Beer, Gillian. "The Island and the Aeroplane: The Case of Virginia Woolf." In *Nation and Narration*, edited by Homi K. Bhabha, 265–290. New York: Routledge, 1990.

Behr, Abraham Leslie. *New Perspectives in South African Education: A Review of Education in South Africa, 1652–1984*. Durban: Butterworths, 1984.

Bennett, Andrew. *Romantic Poets and the Culture of Posterity*. Cambridge: Cambridge University Press, 1999.

Bethlehem, Louise. "In the Between: Time, Space, Text in Recent South African Literary Theory." *English in Africa* 27, no. 1 (2000): 140–158.

Bewell, Alan. *Natures in Translation: Romanticism and Colonial Natural History*. Baltimore: Johns Hopkins University Press, 2017.

Bhabha, Homi K. *The Location of Culture*. 2nd ed. New York: Routledge, 2004.

Binder, Wolfgang. "An Interview with Lorna Goodison." *Commonwealth* 13, no. 2 (1991): 49–59.

Bloom, Harold. *The Anxiety of Influence*. New York: Oxford University Press, 1973.

———. *The Visionary Company: A Reading of English Romantic Poetry*. Ithaca, N.Y.: Cornell University Press, 1971.

Braziel, Jana Evans. "Daffodils, Rhizomes, Migrations: Narrative Coming of Age in the Diasporic Writings of Edwidge Danticat and Jamaica Kincaid." *Meridians* 3, no. 2 (2003): 110–131.

Brockway, Lucile. *Science and Colonial Expansion: The Role of the British Royal Botanic Gardens*. New York: Academic Press, 1979.

Broglio, Ron. "Mapping British Earth and Sky." *Wordsworth Circle* 33, no. 2 (2002): 70–76.

Bromwich, David. *A Choice of Inheritance: Self and Community from Edmund Burke to Robert Frost*. Cambridge, Mass.: Harvard University Press, 1989.

———. *Disowned by Memory: Wordsworth's Poetry of the 1790s*. Chicago: University of Chicago Press, 1998.

Bryant, William Cullen. *The Poetical Works*. New York: D. Appleton, 1903.

Buchanan, Carole, and Richard Buchanan. *Wordsworth's Gardens*. Lubbock: Texas Tech University Press, 2001.

Buell, Lawrence. "Ecoglobalist Affects: The Emergence of U.S. Environmental Imagination on a Planetary Scale." In *Shades of the Planet: American Literature as World Literature*, edited by Wai Chee Dimock and Lawrence Buell, 227–248. Princeton, N.J.: Princeton University Press, 2007.

———. "Postcolonial Anxiety in Classic U.S. Literature." In *Postcolonial Theory and the United States: Race, Ethnicity, and Literature*, edited by Amritjit Singh and Peter Schmidt, 196–219. Jackson: University Press of Mississippi, 2000.

Burke, Edmund. *The Writings and Speeches of Edmund Burke*. 9 vols. Edited by Paul Langford. Oxford: Clarendon Press, 1981.

Burton, Mary E. *The One Wordsworth*. 2nd ed. Hamden, Conn.: Archon, 1972.

Bushell, Sally. *Re-reading the Excursion: Narrative, Response, and the Wordsworthian Dramatic Voice*. Aldershot: Ashgate, 2002.

Byron, George Gordon (Lord Byron). *The Major Works*. Edited by Jerome J. McGann. Oxford: Oxford University Press, 2000.

Cambridge University. *Cambridge School Certificate Examination Book of Question Papers Set in December 1931*. Cambridge: Cambridge University Press, 1932.

Carlson, Julia Sandstrom. "The Map at the Limits of His Paper: A Cartographic Reading of *The Prelude*, Book 6: 'Cambridge and the Alps.'" *Studies in Romanticism* 49, no. 3 (2010): 375–404.

Carroll, Siobhan. *An Empire of Air and Water: Uncolonizable Space in the British Imagination, 1750–1850*. Philadelphia: University of Pennsylvania Press, 2015.

Carusi, Annamaria. "Post, Post and Post: Or, Where Is South African Literature in All This?" *ARIEL* 20, no. 4 (1989): 79–95.

Casid, Jill H. *Sowing Empire: Landscape and Colonization*. Minneapolis: University of Minnesota Press, 2005.

Castellano, Katey. *The Ecology of British Romantic Conservatism, 1790–1837*. New York: Palgrave Macmillan, 2013.

Chander, Manu Samriti. *Brown Romantics: Poetry and Nationalism in the Global Nineteenth Century*. Lewisburg, Pa.: Bucknell University Press, 2017.

Chandler, James K. *Wordsworth's Second Nature: A Study of the Poetry and Politics*. Chicago: University of Chicago Press, 1984.

Cheah, Pheng. *What Is a World? On Postcolonial Literature as World Literature*. Durham, N.C.: Duke University Press, 2016.

Chew, Shirley. "Wordsworth's *Prelude*: A Prospect in the Mind." In *Discharging the Canon: Cross-Cultural Readings in Literature*, edited by Peter Hyland, 133–146. Singapore: Singapore University Press, 1986.

Child, Lydia Maria. *An Appeal in Favor of That Class of Americans Called Africans*. Amherst: University of Massachusetts Press, 1996.

Chrisman, Laura. "The Imperial Unconscious? Representations of Imperial Discourse." *Critical Quarterly* 32, no. 3 (1990): 38–58.

Christensen, Jerome. *Romanticism at the End of History*. Baltimore: Johns Hopkins University Press, 2000.

Christopher, A. J. *The Atlas of Changing South Africa*. 2nd ed. London: Routledge, 2001.

Claybaugh, Amanda. *The Novel of Purpose: Literature and Social Reform in the Anglo-American World*. Ithaca, N.Y.: Cornell University Press, 2007.

Cliff, Michelle. *Abeng*. New York: Plume, 1995.

Coetzee, J. M. *Boyhood: Scenes from Provincial Life*. New York: Viking, 1997.

———. *Disgrace*. New York: Penguin, 1999.

———. *Doubling the Point: Essays and Interviews*. Edited by David Attwell. Cambridge, Mass.: Harvard University Press, 1992.

———. *White Writing: On the Culture of Letters in South Africa*. New Haven, Conn.: Yale University Press, 1988.

———. *Youth: Scenes from Provincial Life II*. New York: Penguin, 2002.

Cooper, Lane, ed. *A Concordance to the Poems of William Wordsworth*. London: Smith, Elder, 1911.

Cooper, Pamela. "Metamorphosis and Sexuality: Reading the Strange Passions of *Disgrace*." *Research in African Literatures* 36, no. 4 (2005): 22–39.

Cooppan, Vilashini. "World Literature and Global Theory: Comparative Literature for the New Millennium." *symploke* 9, nos. 1–2 (2001): 15–43.

Coovadia, Imraan. "Coetzee in and out of Cape Town." *Kritika Kultura* 18 (2012): 103–115.

Damrosch, David. *How to Read World Literature*. Chichester: Wiley-Blackwell, 2008.

Danticat, Edwidge. *Breath, Eyes, Memory*. New York: Vintage, 1994.

Dean, Elizabeth, Paul Hartmann, and May Katzen. *History in Black and White: An Analysis of South African School History Textbooks*. Paris: Unesco, 1983.

de Graef, Ortwin. "Suffering, Sympathy, Circulation: Smith, Wordsworth, Coetzee." *European Journal of English Studies* 7, no. 3 (2003): 311–331.

de Kock, Leon. "South Africa in the Global Imaginary: An Introduction." *Poetics Today* 22, no. 2 (2001): 263–298.

DeLoughrey, Elizabeth. "Globalizing the Routes of Breadfruit and Other Bounties." *Journal of Colonialism and Colonial History* 8, no. 3 (2007). http://muse.jhu.edu./article/230160.

DeLoughrey, Elizabeth, and George B. Handley. *Postcolonial Ecologies: Literatures of the Environment*. New York: Oxford University Press, 2011.

de Man, Paul. *Blindness and Insight: Essays in the Rhetoric of Contemporary Criticism*. 2nd ed. Minneapolis: University of Minnesota Press, 1983.

———. "Time and History in Wordsworth." *Diacritics* 17, no. 4 (1987): 4–17.

Demaus, Robert. *English Literature and Composition: A Guide to Candidates in Those Departments in the Indian Civil Service*. London: Longmans, Green, 1866.

Desai, Kiran. *The Inheritance of Loss*. New York: Grove Press, 2006.

Desmond, Ray. *The History of the Royal Botanic Gardens Kew*. London: Kew, 2007.

Dimock, Wai Chee. "Planet and America, Set and Subset." In *Shades of the Planet: American Literature as World Literature*, edited by Wai Chee Dimock and Lawrence Buell, 1–16. Princeton, N.J.: Princeton University Press, 2007.

———. *Through Other Continents: American Literature across Deep Time*. Princeton, N.J.: Princeton University Press, 2006.

Drayton, Richard. *Nature's Government: Science, Imperial Britain, and the "Improvement" of the World*. New Haven, Conn.: Yale University Press, 2000.

Duckworth, Alistair M. *The Improvement of the Estate: A Study of Jane Austen's Novels*. Baltimore: Johns Hopkins University Press, 1971.

Eastley, Aaron. "Naipaul's Children: Representations of Humor and Ruin in 'Miguel Street.'" *Journal of Caribbean Literatures* 5, no. 2 (2008): 47–59.

Elder, John. *Imagining the Earth: Poetry and the Vision of Nature*. Urbana: University of Illinois Press, 1985.

Eliot, T. S. *Selected Essays*. New York: Harcourt, Brace, 1950.

———. *The Use of Poetry and the Use of Criticism*. Cambridge, Mass.: Harvard University Press, 1933.

Elkins, James. "On the Conceptual Analysis of Gardens." *Journal of Garden History* 13, no. 4 (1993): 189–198.

Ellison, Julie. "'Nice Arts' and 'Potent Enginery': The Gendered Economy of Wordsworth's Fancy." *Centennial Review* 33, no. 4 (1989): 441–467.

Equiano, Olaudah. *The Interesting Narrative and Other Writings*. Edited by Vincent Carretta. New York: Penguin, 2003.

Esch, Elizabeth. "Whitened and Enlightened: The Ford Motor Company and Racial Engineering in the Brazilian Amazon." In *Company Towns in the Americas: Landscape, Power, and Working-Class Communities*, edited by Oliver J. Dinius and Angela Vergara, 91–110. Athens: University of Georgia Press, 2011.

Fanuzzi, Robert. "How Mixed-Race Politics Entered the United States: Lydia Maria Child's *Appeal*." *ESQ: A Journal of the American Renaissance* 56, no. 1 (2010): 71–104.

Ferguson, Frances. *Wordsworth: Language as Counter-spirit*. New Haven, Conn.: Yale University Press, 1977.

Ferguson, Moira. "*Lucy* and the Mark of the Colonizer." *Modern Fiction Studies* 39, no. 2 (1993): 237–259.

Field, Barron, ed. *Geographical Memoirs on New South Wales*. London: John Murray, 1825.

Foucault, Michel. *The Order of Things: An Archaeology of the Human Sciences*. New York: Vintage, 1994.

Fulford, Tim. *The Late Poetry of the Lake Poets: Romanticism Revised*. Cambridge: Cambridge University Press, 2013.

Fulford, Tim, and Peter J. Kitson, eds. *Romanticism and Colonialism: Writing and Empire, 1780–1830*. Cambridge: Cambridge University Press, 1998.

Galey, John. "Industrialist in the Wilderness: Henry Ford's Amazon Venture." *Journal of Interamerican Studies and World Affairs* 21, no. 2 (1979): 261–289.

Galperin, William H. *Revision and Authority in Wordsworth: The Interpretation of a Career*. Philadelphia: University of Pennsylvania Press, 1989.

Garrett, James M. *Wordsworth and the Writing of the Nation*. Aldershot: Ashgate, 2008.

Gascoigne, John. *Science in the Service of Empire: Joseph Banks, the British State and the Uses of Science in the Age of Revolution*. Cambridge: Cambridge University Press, 1998.

Genette, Gérard. *Paratexts: Thresholds of Interpretation*. Cambridge: Cambridge University Press, 1997.

Gething, Mrs. *Selections from Modern Authors*. Darlington: J. Wilson, 1838.

Gibson, Mary Ellis, ed. *Anglophone Poetry in Colonial India, 1780–1913: A Critical Anthology*. Athens: Ohio University Press, 2011.

Gidal, Eric. *Ossianic Unconformities: Bardic Poetry in the Industrial Age*. Charlottesville: University of Virginia Press, 2015.

Gilbert, Sandra M., and Susan Gubar. *The Madwoman in the Attic*. 2nd ed. New Haven, Conn.: Yale University Press, 2000.

Gill, Stephen. *Wordsworth and the Victorians*. Oxford: Oxford University Press, 1998.

———. *Wordsworth's Revisitings*. New York: Oxford University Press, 2011.

Gilroy, Paul. *The Black Atlantic: Modernity and Double-Consciousness*. Cambridge, Mass.: Harvard University Press, 1993.

Goodison, Lorna. *Turn Thanks*. Urbana: University of Illinois Press, 1999.

Goodyear, Sara Suleri. *The Rhetoric of English India*. Chicago: University of Chicago Press, 1992.

Gottlieb, Evan, ed. *Global Romanticism: Origins, Orientations, and Entanglements, 1760–1820*. Lewisburg, Pa.: Bucknell University Press, 2015.

Grandin, Greg. *Fordlandia: The Rise and Fall of Henry Ford's Forgotten Jungle City*. New York: Picador, 2009.

Gravil, Richard. *Romantic Dialogues: Anglo-American Continuities, 1776–1862*. New York: St. Martin's Press, 2000.

Groombridge, Richard. *A Guide to the Matriculation Examination*. Groombridge's Guides to the Examinations of the University of London. London: Groombridge, 1878.

Grove, Richard. *Green Imperialism: Colonial Expansion, Tropical Island Edens, and the Origins of Environmentalism, 1600–1860*. Cambridge: Cambridge University Press, 1995.

Guha, Ramachandra. "Radical American Environmentalism and Wilderness Preservation: A Third World Critique." *Environmental Ethics* 11 (1989): 71–83.

Guillory, John. *Cultural Capital: The Problem of Literary Canon Formation*. Chicago: University of Chicago Press, 1993.

Hall, Stuart. "The Local and the Global: Globalization and Ethnicity." In *Dangerous Liaisons: Gender, Nation, and Postcolonial Perspectives*, edited by Anne McClintock, Aamir Mufti, and Ella Shohat, 173–187. Minneapolis: University of Minnesota Press, 1997.

Hammond, S. A. "Education in the British West Indies." *Journal of Negro Education* 15, no. 3 (1946): 427–449.

Hanley, Keith. "Crossings Out: The Problem of Textual Passage in *The Prelude*." In *Romantic Revisions*, edited by Robert Brinkley and Keith Hanley, 103–135. Cambridge: Cambridge University Press, 1992.

Hartman, Geoffrey H. *Criticism in the Wilderness: The Study of Literature Today*. 2nd ed. New Haven, Conn.: Yale University Press, 2007.

———. *Wordsworth's Poetry 1787–1814*. 1964. Reprint, Cambridge, Mass.: Harvard University Press, 1987.

Hayot, Eric. *On Literary Worlds*. New York: Oxford University Press, 2012.

Hazucha, Andrew. "Neither Deep nor Shallow but National: Eco-nationalism in Wordsworth's *Guide to the Lakes*." *ISLE (Interdisciplinary Studies in Literature and Environment)* 9, no. 2 (2002): 61–73.

Heise, Ursula K. *Sense of Place and Sense of Planet: The Environmental Imagination of the Global*. Oxford: Oxford University Press, 2008.

Hess, Scott. *William Wordsworth and the Ecology of Authorship: The Roots of Environmentalism in Nineteenth-Century Culture*. Charlottesville: University of Virginia Press, 2012.

Hickey, Alison. "Dark Characters, Native Ground: Wordsworth's Imagination of Imperialism." In *Romanticism, Race, and Imperial Culture, 1780–1834*, edited by Alan Richardson and Sonia Hofkosh, 283–307. Bloomington: Indiana University Press, 1996.

———. *Impure Conceits: Rhetoric and Ideology in Wordsworth's Excursion*. Stanford, Calif.: Stanford University Press, 1997.

Hine, Joseph. *Selections from the Poems of William Wordsworth, Esq*. London: Edward Moxon, 1831.

Hofmeyr, Isabel. "Building a Nation from Words: Afrikaans Language, Literature and Ethnic Identity, 1902–1924." In *The Politics of Race, Class and Nationalism in Twentieth Century South Africa*, edited by Shula Marks and Stanley Trapido, 95–123. New York: Longman, 1987.

Howard, Leon. "Wordsworth in America." *Modern Language Notes* 48, no. 6 (1933): 359–365.

Huggan, Graham. "'Greening' Postcolonialism: Ecocritical Perspectives." *Modern Fiction Studies* 50, no. 3 (2004): 701–733.

Huxley, Aldous. "Wordsworth in the Tropics." In *Collected Essays*, 1–10. New York: Harper, 1971.

Iser, Wolfgang. *The Implied Reader: Patterns in Communication in Prose Fiction from Bunyan to Beckett*. Baltimore: Johns Hopkins University Press, 1974.

Jacobus, Mary. *Romanticism, Writing and Sexual Difference: Essays on the Prelude*. Oxford: Oxford University Press, 1989.

James, Cynthia. "'You'll Soon Get Used to Our Language': Language, Parody and West Indian Identity in Andrea Levy's *Small Island*." *Journal of West Indian Literature* 18, no. 2 (2010): 45–64.

James, Louis. *Caribbean Literature in English*. London: Routledge, 1999.

James Smith & Son. *Classical Selections in Verse*. Liverpool: James Smith, 1808.

Jameson, Fredric. "Notes on Globalization as a Philosophical Issue." In *The Cultures of Globalization*, edited by Fredric Jameson and Masao Miyoshi, 54–80. Durham, N.C.: Duke University Press, 1998.

Jansen, Jonathan D. *Knowledge in the Blood: Confronting Race and the Apartheid Past*. Stanford, Calif.: Stanford University Press, 2009.

Jarvis, Robin. *Romantic Writing and Pedestrian Travel*. London: Macmillan, 1997.

Jauss, Hans Robert. *Toward an Aesthetic of Reception*. Minneapolis: University of Minnesota Press, 1982.

Jay, Paul L. *Global Matters: The Transnational Turn in Literary Studies*. Ithaca, N.Y.: Cornell University Press, 2010.

Jeffrey, Francis. *Contributions to the Edinburgh Review by Francis Jeffrey*. London: Longman, Brown, Green, and Longmans, 1855.

Johnston, Kenneth. *Wordsworth and "The Recluse."* New Haven, Conn.: Yale University Press, 1984.

Jolly, Rosemary. "Rehearsals of Liberation: Contemporary Postcolonial Discourse and the New South Africa." *PMLA* 110, no. 1 (1995): 17–29.

Jones, Mark. *The "Lucy Poems": A Case Study in Literary Knowledge*. Toronto: University of Toronto Press, 1995.

Juta. *Matriculation Examination Questions, English*. Cape Town: Juta, 1948.

———. *Matriculation Examination Questions, English, February 1932–December 1941*. 4th ed. Cape Town: Juta, 1948.

———. *Matriculation Examination Questions Set in the English Papers 1905–1922*. Cape Town: Juta, 1922.

Kamada, Roy Osamu. *Postcolonial Romanticisms: Landscape and the Possibilities of Inheritance*. New York: Peter Lang, 2010.

Kandel, I. L., et al. *Report of the Committee Appointed to Enquire into the System of Secondary Education in Jamaica*. Kingston: Government Printer, 1943.

Karcher, Carolyn L. *The First Woman in the Republic: A Cultural Biography of Lydia Maria Child*. Durham, N.C.: Duke University Press, 1994.

Kelley, Theresa M. *Wordsworth's Revisionary Aesthetics*. Cambridge: Cambridge University Press, 1988.

Kiely, Robert. *Reverse Tradition: Postmodern Fictions and the Nineteenth Century Novel*. Cambridge, Mass.: Harvard University Press, 1993.

Kim, Benjamin. "Generating a National Sublime: Wordsworth's *The River Duddon* and *The Guide to the Lakes*." *Studies in Romanticism* 45, no. 1 (2006): 49–75.

Kincaid, Jamaica. *Among Flowers: A Walk in the Himalaya*. Washington, D.C.: National Geographic, 2005.

———. *Lucy*. New York: Farrar, Straus and Giroux, 1990.

———. *My Garden (Book):*. New York: Farrar, Straus and Giroux, 1999.

Kingston Government Printer. *A Plan for Post-primary Education in Jamaica; Being the Report of the Secondary Education Continuation Committee*. Kingston: Government Printer, 1945.

Labbe, Jacqueline M. *Romantic Visualities: Landscape, Gender and Romanticism*. New York: St. Martin's Press, 1998.

Lahiri, Jhumpa. *The Namesake*. Boston: Houghton Mifflin, 2003.

Landry, Donna. *The Invention of the Countryside: Hunting, Walking and Ecology in English Literature, 1671–1831*. New York: Palgrave, 2001.

Lee, Debbie. *Slavery and the Romantic Imagination*. Philadelphia: University of Pennsylvania Press, 2002.

Levin, Susan M. *Dorothy Wordsworth and Romanticism*. New Brunswick, N.J.: Rutgers University Press, 1987.

Levinson, Marjorie. "Of Being Numerous." *Studies in Romanticism* 49, no. 4 (2010): 633–657.

———. *Wordsworth's Great Period Poems: Four Essays*. Cambridge: Cambridge University Press, 1986.

Levy, Andrea. *Small Island*. New York: Picador, 2004.

Licht, Walter. *Industrializing America*. Baltimore: Johns Hopkins University Press, 1995.

Lim, Shirley. "The Dispossessing Eye: Reading Wordsworth on the Equatorial Line." In *Discharging the Canon: Cross-Cultural Readings in Literature*, edited by Peter Hyland, 126–132. Singapore: Singapore University Press, 1986.

Liu, Alan. *Local Transcendence: Essays on Postmodern Historicism and the Database*. Chicago: University of Chicago Press, 2008.

———. *Wordsworth: The Sense of History*. Stanford, Calif.: Stanford University Press, 1989.

Loudon, J. C. *The Suburban Gardener*. New York: Garland, 1982.

Lowe, Edward C., ed. *The Young Englishman's First Poetry Book*. London: James Parker, 1868.

Lucas, E. V., ed. *The Works of Charles and Mary Lamb*. 7 vols. London: Methuen, 1903–1905.

Macaulay, Thomas Babington. *Prose and Poetry*. 2nd ed. Edited by G. M. Young. Cambridge, Mass.: Harvard University Press, 1967.

Macksey, Richard. Foreword to *Paratexts: Thresholds of Interpretation*, by Gérard Genette. Cambridge: Cambridge University Press, 1997.

Makdisi, Jean Said. *Beirut Fragments: A War Memoir*. New York: Persea Books, 1990.

Makdisi, Saree. *Making England Western: Occidentalism, Race, and Imperial Culture*. Chicago: University of Chicago Press, 2013.

———. *Romantic Imperialism: Universal Empire and the Culture of Modernity*. Cambridge: Cambridge University Press, 1998.

Manning, Peter J. *Reading Romantics: Text and Context*. New York: Oxford University Press, 1990.

Marais, Mike. "J. M. Coetzee's *Disgrace* and the Task of the Imagination." *Journal of Modern Literature* 29, no. 2 (2006): 75–93.

Marks, Shula, and Stanley Trapido. *The Politics of Race, Class, and Nationalism in Twentieth-Century South Africa*. New York: Longman, 1987.

Marriott, G. R. L. *Papers Given in the London University Matriculation Examination*. London: Hirst Smyth, 1881.

Martin, William. *The Moral and Intellectual School Book*. London: Darton and Clark, 1838.

Massey, Doreen. *Space, Place, and Gender*. Minneapolis: University of Minnesota Press, 1994.

Mathews, Harry, and Alastair Brotchie. *Oulipo Compendium*. London: Atlas, 1998.

Matthiessen, F. O. *American Renaissance: Art and Expression in the Age of Emerson and Whitman.* New York: Oxford University Press, 1941.

McCracken, Donal P. *Gardens of Empire: Botanical Institutions of the Victorian British Empire.* London: Leicester University Press, 1997.

McDonald, William E., ed. *Encountering Disgrace: Reading and Teaching Coetzee's Novel.* Rochester, N.Y.: Camden House, 2009.

McDunnah, Michael G. "'We Are Not Asked to Condemn': Sympathy, Subjectivity, and the Narration of *Disgrace*." In *Encountering Disgrace: Reading and Teaching Coetzee's Novel*, edited by William E. McDonald, 15–47. Rochester, N.Y.: Camden House, 2009.

McGann, Jerome J. "Is Romanticism Finished?" In *The Cambridge History of English Romantic Literature*, edited by James Chandler, 648–664. Cambridge: Cambridge University Press, 2009.

———. *The Romantic Ideology: A Critical Investigation.* Chicago: University of Chicago Press, 1983.

McInturff, Kate. "Rex Oedipus: The Ethics of Sympathy in Recent Work by J. M. Coetzee." *Postcolonial Text* 3, no. 4 (2007): 1–20.

McKay, Claude. *Complete Poems.* Edited by William J. Maxwell. Urbana: University of Illinois Press, 2008.

———. *Home to Harlem.* Boston: Northeastern University Press, 1987.

Mehta, Uday Singh. *Liberalism and Empire: A Study in Nineteenth-Century British Liberal Thought.* Chicago: University of Chicago Press, 1999.

Menely, Tobias, and Jesse Oak Taylor. "Introduction." In *Anthropocene Reading: Literary History in Geologic Times*, edited by Tobias Menely and Jesse Oak Taylor, 1–24. University Park: Pennsylvania State University Press, 2017.

Menke, Richard. "The Wordsworths' Daffodils: On the Page, upon the Inward Eye, in Their Media Ecology." In *Media, Technology, and Literature in the Nineteenth Century: Image, Sound, Touch*, edited by Colette Colligan and Margaret Linley, 23–41. Farnham: Ashgate, 2011.

Michael, Ian. *The Teaching of English: From the Sixteenth Century to 1870.* Cambridge: Cambridge University Press, 1987.

Moja, Teboho, and Fred M. Hayward. "Higher Education Policy Development in Contemporary South Africa." In *Implementing Education Policies: The South African Experience*, edited by Yusuf Sayed and Jonathan D. Jansen, 112–123. Cape Town: University of Cape Town Press, 2001.

Moore, Charles Willard, William J. Mitchell, and William Turnbull. *The Poetics of Gardens.* Cambridge, Mass.: MIT Press, 1988.

Morton, Timothy. *The Ecological Thought.* Cambridge, Mass.: Harvard University Press, 2012.

Mukherjee, Ankhi. *What Is a Classic? Postcolonial Rewriting and Invention of the Canon.* Stanford, Calif.: Stanford University Press, 2013.

Mullen, Laura. *Dark Archive.* Berkeley: University of California Press, 2011.

Musgrave, Toby, and Will Musgrave. *An Empire of Plants: People and Plants That Changed the World.* London: Cassell, 2000.

Myers, Garth. *Urban Environments in Africa: A Critical Analysis of Environmental Politics.* Bristol: Policy Press, 2016.

Naipaul, V. S. *Miguel Street.* New York: Vintage, 2002.

———. *The Overcrowded Barracoon.* Harmondsworth: Penguin, 1984.

Newman, Lance. *Our Common Dwelling: Henry Thoreau, Transcendentalism, and the Class Politics of Nature.* New York: Palgrave Macmillan, 2005.

Newton, Annabel. *Wordsworth in Early American Criticism*. Chicago: University of Chicago Press, 1928.

Nichols, Ashton. *Beyond Romantic Ecocriticism: Toward Urbanatural Roosting*. New York: Palgrave Macmillan, 2011.

Nixon, Rob. "Environmentalism and Postcolonialism." In *Postcolonial Studies and Beyond*, edited by Ania Loomba, Suvir Kaul, Matti Bunzl, Antoinette Burton, and Jed Esty, 233–251. Durham, N.C.: Duke University Press, 2005.

Noyes, Russell, Kenkichi Kamijima, Mine Okachi, and Koicki Senbokuya. "Wordsworth in Japan." *Wordsworth Circle* 1 (1970): 5–13.

Nussbaum, Felicity A., ed. *The Global Eighteenth Century*. Baltimore: Johns Hopkins University Press, 2003.

O'Brien, Susie. "The Garden and the World: Jamaica Kincaid and the Cultural Borders of Ecocriticism." *Mosaic* 35, no. 2 (2002): 167–184.

Ottum, Lisa, and Seth T. Reno, eds. *Wordsworth and the Green Romantics: Affect and Ecology in the Nineteenth Century*. Durham: University of New Hampshire Press, 2016.

Pace, Joel. "Wordsworth and America: Reception and Reform." In *The Cambridge Companion to Wordsworth*, edited by Stephen Gill, 230–245. Cambridge: Cambridge University Press, 2003.

Pace, Joel, and Matthew Scott, eds. *Wordsworth in American Literary Culture*. New York: Palgrave Macmillan, 2005.

Page, Judith W., and Elise L. Smith. *Women, Literature, and the Domesticated Landscape: England's Disciples of Flora, 1780–1870*. Cambridge: Cambridge University Press, 2011.

Palmer, D. J. *The Rise of English Studies: An Account of the Study of English Language and Literature from Its Origin to the Making of the Oxford English School*. London: Oxford University Press, 1965.

Paravisini-Gebert, Lizabeth. *Jamaica Kincaid: A Critical Companion*. Westport, Conn.: Greenwood Press, 1999.

Parker, John W. *Readings in Poetry: A Selection from the Best English Poets*. 7th ed. London: John W. Parker, 1843.

Parry, Benita. "Problems in Current Theories of Colonial Discourse." *Oxford Literary Review* 9, nos. 1–2 (1987): 27–58.

———. "Speech and Silence in the Fictions of J. M. Coetzee." In *Writing South Africa: Literature, Apartheid, and Democracy, 1970–1996*, edited by Derek Attridge and Rosemary Jolly, 149–165. Cambridge: Cambridge University Press, 1998.

Payne, Joseph. *Studies in English Poetry*. 3rd ed. London: Arthur Hall, Virtue, 1856.

Philip, Kavita. *Civilizing Natures: Race, Resources, and Modernity in Colonial South India*. New Brunswick, N.J.: Rutgers University Press, 2004.

Pope, Alexander. *The Poems of Alexander Pope*. Edited by John Butt. London: Methuen, 1963.

Poyner, Jane. *J. M. Coetzee and the Paradox of Postcolonial Authorship*. Burlington, Vt.: Ashgate, 2009.

Pratt, Mary Louise. *Imperial Eyes: Travel Writing and Transculturation*. 2nd ed. London: Routledge, 2008.

Prest, John M. *The Garden of Eden: The Botanic Garden and the Recreation of Paradise*. New Haven, Conn.: Yale University Press, 1981.

Pugh, Simon. *Garden, Nature, Language*. Manchester: Manchester University Press, 1988.

Ram Dayal Agarwala. *The Allahabad University Matriculation Exam Papers from 1908 to 1909*. Allahabad: Ram Dayal Agarwala, 1911.

Reed, Arden. *Romantic Weather: The Climates of Coleridge and Baudelaire*. Providence, R.I.: Brown University Press, 1983.

Reed, Mark. "The Speaker of 'The Prelude.'" In *Bicentenary Wordsworth Studies in Memory of John Alban Finch*, edited by Jonathan Wordsworth, 276–293. Ithaca, N.Y.: Cornell University Press, 1970.

Reid, Ian. *Wordsworth and the Formation of English Studies*. Aldershot: Ashgate, 2004.

Rhys, Jean. "The Day They Burned the Books." In *Tigers Are Better-Looking*, 40–46. London: Andre Deutsch, 1976.

Richardson, Alan. *Literature, Education, and Romanticism: Reading as Social Practice, 1780–1832*. Cambridge: Cambridge University Press, 1994.

Ripley, C. Peter, ed. *The Black Abolitionist Papers*. Vol. 3, *The United States, 1830–1846*. Chapel Hill: University of North Carolina Press, 1991.

Roach, Joseph. *Cities of the Dead: Circum-Atlantic Performance*. New York: Columbia University Press, 1996.

Robbins, Bruce. "Comparative Cosmopolitanisms." In *Cosmopolitics: Thinking and Feeling beyond the Nation*, edited by Pheng Cheah and Bruce Robbins, 246–264. Minneapolis: University of Minnesota Press, 1998.

Robinson, Harriet H. *Loom and Spindle: Or, Life among the Early Mill Girls*. New York: T. Y. Crowell, 1898. Rev. ed., Kailua, Hawaii: Press Pacifica, 1976.

Robson, Catherine. *Heart Beats: Everyday Life and the Memorized Poem*. Princeton, N.J.: Princeton University Press, 2012.

Rohrbach, Emily. *Modernity's Mist: British Romanticism and the Poetics of Anticipation*. New York: Fordham University Press, 2016.

Rose, Brian, and Raymond Tunmer, eds. *Documents in South African Education*. Johannesburg: Donker, 1975.

Rosen, David. *Power, Plain English, and the Rise of Modern Poetry*. New Haven, Conn.: Yale University Press, 2006.

Rosenberg, Leah Reade. *Nationalism and the Formation of Caribbean Literature*. New York: Palgrave Macmillan, 2007.

Ross, Marlon B. "Romantic Quest and Conquest: Troping Masculine Power in the Crisis of Poetic Identity." In *Romanticism and Feminism*, edited by Anne K. Mellor, 26–51. Bloomington: Indiana University Press, 1988.

Rubin, Joan Shelley. *Songs of Ourselves: The Uses of Poetry in America*. Cambridge, Mass.: Belknap Press of Harvard University Press, 2007.

Russell, Richard. "The Yeatsian Intertexts of Coetzee's *Disgrace*." *Journal of Commonwealth and Postcolonial Studies* 2, no. 2 (2014): 3–18.

Saguaro, Shelley. *Garden Plots: The Politics and Poetics of Gardens*. Aldershot: Ashgate, 2006.

Said, Edward. *Orientalism*. New York: Vintage, 1994.

Satthianadhan, S. *Four Years in an English University*. 2nd ed. Madras: Srinivasa, Varadachari, 1893.

Schama, Simon. *Landscape and Memory*. New York: A. A. Knopf, 1995.

Schneider, Ben Ross, Jr. *Wordsworth's Cambridge Education*. Cambridge: Cambridge University Press, 1957.

Schreiner, Olive. *Story of an African Farm*. 1883. Reprint, Oxford: Oxford University Press, 1992.

Seeley, John Robert. *The Expansion of England*. Boston: Roberts Brothers, 1883.

Segall, Kimberly Wedeven. "Pursuing Ghosts: The Traumatic Sublime in J. M. Coetzee's *Disgrace*." *Research in African Literatures* 36, no. 4 (2005): 40–54.

Senior, Olive. *Talking of Trees*. Kingston: Calabash, 1985.

Shankman, Lillian F. "Review of *Barron Field's 'Memoirs of Wordsworth*.'" *Wordsworth Circle* 9, no. 3 (1978): 240–241.

Shorter, Thomas, ed. *Poetry for School and Home*. London: T. J. Allman, 1861.

Simpson, David. "Wordsworth and Empire—Just Joking." In *Land, Nation and Culture, 1740–1840*, edited by Peter de Bolla, Nigel Leask, and David Simpson, 188–201. New York: Palgrave Macmillan, 2005.

———. *Wordsworth, Commodification and Social Concern: The Poetics of Modernity*. Cambridge: Cambridge University Press, 2009.

———. "Wordsworth in America." In *The Age of William Wordsworth: Critical Essays on the Romantic Tradition*, edited by Kenneth R. Johnston and Gene W. Ruoff, 276–290. Jersey City, N.J.: Rutgers University Press, 1987.

———. *Wordsworth's Historical Imagination: The Poetry of Displacement*. New York: Methuen, 1987.

Sloane, Hans. *A Voyage to the Islands Madera, Barbados, Nieves, S. Christophers, and Jamaica*. 2 vols. London: B. M., 1707–1725.

Smith, Ian. "Misusing Canonical Intertexts: Jamaica Kincaid, Wordsworth and Colonialism's 'Absent Things.'" *Callaloo* 25, no. 3 (2002): 801–820.

Sole, Kelwyn. "South Africa Passes the Posts." *Alternation (Durban)* 4, no. 1 (1997): 116–151.

Sorisio, Carolyn. *Fleshing Out America: Race, Gender, and the Politics of the Body in American Literature, 1833–1879*. Athens: University of Georgia Press, 2002.

Spivak, Gayatri Chakravorty. *Death of a Discipline*. New York: Columbia University Press, 2003.

———. "Ethics and Politics in Tagore, Coetzee, and Certain Scenes of Teaching." *Diacritics* 32, nos. 3–4 (2002): 17–31.

Stewart, Susan. "Garden Agon." *Representations* 62 (1998): 111–143.

Stitt, Jocelyn. "Producing the Colonial Subject: Romantic Pedagogy and Mimicry in Jamaica Kincaid's Writing." *ARIEL* 37, nos. 2–3 (2006): 137–167.

Strachan, Ian Gregory. *Paradise and Plantation: Tourism and Culture in the Anglophone Caribbean*. Charlottesville: University of Virginia Press, 2002.

Streatfield, David C. "Art and Nature in the English Landscape Garden: Design Theory and Practice, 1700–1818." In *Landscape in the Gardens and the Literature of Eighteenth-Century England*, edited by David C. Streatfield and Alistair M. Duckworth, 3–87. Los Angeles: William Andrews Clark Memorial Library, 1981.

Tamarkin, Elisa. *Anglophilia: Deference, Devotion, and Antebellum America*. Chicago: University of Chicago Press, 2008.

Tennenhouse, Leonard. *The Importance of Feeling English: American Literature and the British Diaspora, 1750–1850*. Princeton, N.J.: Princeton University Press, 2007.

Thom, Alexander. *Selections from the British Poets*. 2 vols. Dublin: Alexander Thom, 1855.

Thomas, Helen. *Romanticism and Slave Narratives: Transatlantic Testimonies*. Cambridge: Cambridge University Press, 2000.

Thompson, E. P. *The Romantics: England in a Revolutionary Age*. New York: New Press, 1997.

Tiffin, Helen. "Cold Hearts and (Foreign) Tongues: Recitation and the Reclamation of the Female Body in the Works of Erna Brodber and Jamaica Kincaid." *Callaloo* 16, no. 4 (1993): 909–921.

Trodd, Zoe. *American Protest Literature*. Cambridge, Mass.: Belknap Press of Harvard University Press, 2006.

Trott, Nicola. "Wordsworth's Loves of the Plants." In *1800: The New Lyrical Ballads*, edited by Nicola Trott and Seamus Perry, 141–168. New York: Palgrave, 2001.

Turrill, W. B. *The Royal Botanic Gardens at Kew*. London: H. Jenkins, 1959.

University Examination Postal Institution. *Guide to the Cambridge Higher Local Examination*. London: University Examination Postal Institution, 1899.

Vermeulen, Pieter. "Wordsworth and the Recollection of South Africa." In *J. M. Coetzee in Context and Theory*, edited by Elleke Boehmer, Robert Eaglestone, and Katy Iddiols, 47–59. London: Continuum, 2009.

Viljoen, Louise. "Postcolonialism and Recent Women's Writing in Afrikaans." *World Literature Today* 70, no. 1 (1996): 63–72.

Visser, Nicholas. "Postcoloniality of a Special Type: Theory and Its Appropriations in South Africa." *Yearbook of English Studies* 27 (1997): 79–94.

Viswanathan, Gauri. *Masks of Conquest: Literary Study and British Rule in India*. New York: Columbia University Press, 1989.

Wallerstein, Immanuel. *The Modern World System I: Capitalist Agriculture and the Origins of the European World Economy in the Sixteenth Century*. Berkeley: University of California Press, 2011.

Ward, John Powell. "'Will No One Tell Me What She Sings?' Women and Gender in the Poetry of William Wordsworth." *Studies in Romanticism* 36, no. 4 (1997): 611–633.

Watson, Richard. *Anecdotes of the Life of Richard Watson, Bishop of Llandaff*. London: T. Cadell and W. Davies, 1817.

Watts, Steven. *The People's Tycoon*. New York: Knopf, 2005.

Weisbuch, Robert. *Atlantic Double-Cross: American Literature and British Influence in the Age of Emerson*. Chicago: University of Chicago Press, 1986.

Weiskel, Thomas. *The Romantic Sublime: Studies in the Structure and Psychology of Transcendence*. Baltimore: Johns Hopkins University Press, 1976.

Wenzel, Jennifer. "The Pastoral Promise and the Political Imperative: The *Plaasroman* Tradition in an Era of Land Reform." *Modern Fiction Studies* 46, no. 1 (2000): 90–113.

Wicomb, Zoë. "Translations in the Yard of Africa." *Journal of Literary Studies* 18, nos. 3–4 (2002): 209–223.

Wildi, Max. "Wordsworth and the Simplon Pass II." *English Studies* 43, no. 5 (1962): 359–377.

Williams, Raymond. *Keywords: A Vocabulary of Culture and Society*. Rev. ed. New York: Oxford University Press, 1983.

Winokur, Scott. "The Unsparing Vision of V. S. Naipaul." In *Conversations with V. S. Naipaul*, edited by Feroza F. Jussawalla, 114–129. Jackson: University Press of Mississippi, 1997.

Wolfson, Susan J. "Individual in Community: Dorothy Wordsworth in Conversation with William." In *Romanticism and Feminism*, edited by Anne K. Mellor, 139–166. Bloomington: Indiana University Press, 1988.

Woof, Pamela. "The 'Lucy' Poems: Poetry of Mourning." *Wordsworth Circle* 30, no. 1 (1999): 28–36.

Wordsworth, Dorothy. *Journals of Dorothy Wordsworth*. 2 vols. Edited by E. de Selincourt. New York: Macmillan, 1941.

Wordsworth, William. *The Borderers*. Edited by Robert Osborn. Ithaca, N.Y.: Cornell University Press, 1982.

———. *Poems (1815)*. 2 vols. Edited by Jonathan Wordsworth. Oxford: Woodstock Books, 1989.

———. *The Poetical Works of William Wordsworth*. 5 vols. Edited by E. de Selincourt. Oxford: Clarendon Press, 1940–1949.

———. *The Prelude, 1799, 1805, 1850*. Edited by Jonathan Wordsworth, M. H. Abrams, and Stephen Gill. New York: Norton, 1979.

———. *The Prose Works of William Wordsworth*. 3 vols. Edited by W. J. B. Owen and Jane Worthington Smyser. Oxford: Clarendon Press, 1974.

Wordsworth, William, and Dorothy Wordsworth. *The Early Letters of William and Dorothy Wordsworth (1787–1805)*. Edited by Ernest de Selincourt. Oxford: Clarendon Press, 1935.

Workman, Walter P. *The Questions Set at the Matriculation Examination of the London University, June 1880*. London: Joseph Hughes, 1880.

Youngquist, Paul. "Black Romanticism: A Manifesto." *Studies in Romanticism* 56, no. 1 (2017): 3–14.

INDEX

Page numbers in *italics* refer to figures.

ABOUT THE AUTHOR

KATHERINE BERGREN is an assistant professor of English at Trinity College.